This Baffling World

This Baffling World

John Godwin

PICTURE RESEARCH
MARION GEISINGER

HART PUBLISHING COMPANY, INC.
NEW YORK CITY

Contents

LIST OF ILLUSTRATIONS

THE JINX SHIP

THE ABC OF ESP

ACKNOWLEDGMENTS

AMERICAN AIRLINES INC.   633 3rd Avenue, New York, N.Y.
   103

ANSBACH MUSEUM   8800 Ansbach, Ansbach, West Germany
   335, 336, 337, 343, 347, 348, 352 (3), 353 (2), 354-355, 356 (2), 357,
   358-359, 360, 363, 366

ATLANTIC COMPANIES, THE   Atlantic Building, 45 Wall Street, New York,
   N.Y.
   178, 185

BARBADOS MUSEUM AND HISTORICAL SOCIETY, THE
       St. Ann's Garrison, Barbados, West Indies
   229, 230, 231, 232, 233

BARBADOS PUBLIC LIBRARY   Barbados, West Indies
   218

BETTMANN ARCHIVE INC., THE   136 East 57th Street, New York, N.Y.
   266

BRITISH MUSEUM, THE   Great Russell Street, London WC1, England
   290, 292

BROWN BROTHERS   220 West 42nd Street, New York, N.Y.
   378, 386

CULVER PICTURES INC.   660 First Avenue, New York, N.Y.
   126, 139, 140, 148, 269, 271, 280, 309, 374-375, 376-377, 380, 381, 383,
   384, 398-399

EUROPEAN PICTURES SERVICE   39 West 32nd Street, New York, N.Y.
   276, 372

FARRAR, STRAUS & GIROUX, INC.   19 Union Square West, New York, N.Y.
       (Pictures from "Thoughts Through Space" by Sir Hubert Wilkins
       and Harold M. Sherman)
   210, 211, 212, 213

GERMANISCHES NATIONALMUSEUM   85 Nürnberg 1, Nürnberg, Germany
   338, 344-345, 350, 364-365

GRANGER COLLECTION, THE   37 West 39th Street, New York, N.Y.
   131, 142, 287

HARRISON FORMAN WORLD TRAVEL, INC.   500 Fifth Avenue,
       New York, N.Y.
   163

13

HISTORICAL PICTURES SERVICE   2753 W. North Avenue, Chicago, Illinois
124, 135, 332

HOUSE OF MYSTERY   Sardine Creek Road, Medford, Oregon
256 (2), 257 (2)

ILLUSTRATED LONDON NEWS, LTD.   260-268 Grays Inn Road, London
WC1, England
63-64, 65, 66-67-68, 70, 71, 72, 73, 74, 75

INDIAN TOURIST OFFICE, GOVERNMENT OF   19 East 49th Street, New
York, N.Y.
296-297

INSTITUTE FOR PARAPSYCHOLOGY, THE   Durham, North Carolina
197, 198, 208, 209

KEYSTONE PRESS AGENCY, INC.   170 Fifth Avenue, New York, N.Y.
169, 304

LONDON TIMES, THE   Printing House Square, London EC4, England
68, 69, 77, 260, 261, 262, 263

MANCHESTER EVENING NEWS AND CHRONICLE   3 Cross Street,
Manchester, England
396

MOUNT EVEREST FOUNDATION, THE   Royal Geographical Society,
Kensington Gore, London SW7, England
311 Top

MUSEUM OF THE CITY OF NEW YORK   5th Avenue and 104th Street,
New York, N.Y.
380

NATIONAL INVESTIGATIONS COMMITTEE ON AERIAL PHENOMENA
1536 Connecticut Avenue, N. W., Washington, D. C.
88, 104, 107, 112

NATIONAL LIBRARY OF MEDICINE   8600 Rockville Pike, Bethesda,
Maryland
288, 389, 391

NEW YORK PUBLIC LIBRARY   Fifth Avenue and 42nd Street, New York,
N.Y.
128, 221, 277, 281

NOVA SCOTIA INFORMATION SERVICE   30 West 54th Street, New York,
N.Y.
31, 32, 42

PEABODY MUSEUM   Salem, Massachusetts
174, 175, 178-179, 180, 184, 186, 189

PICTORIAL PARADE INC.   130 West 42nd Street, New York, N.Y.
23, 24   Top

PIX INC.   236 East 46th Street, New York, N.Y.
24 Left, 154, 164-165, 168, 278, 298, 302 Top, 302-303, 303 (2)

PAUL POPPER LTD.   24 Bride Lane, Fleet Street, London EC4, England
151, 152, 157, 307 (2), 313, 314 Bottom

PROFESSIONAL PICTURE SERVICE   147 West 42nd Street, New York,
N.Y.
370

RADIO TIMES HULTON PICTURE LIBRARY   35 Marylebone High Street,
London W1, England
50, 225, 301, 310 Bottom

RYERSON PRESS   299 Queen Street West, Toronto, Ontario, Canada
(Pictures from "The Oak Island Mystery" by Reginald V. Harris)
35, 38, 41, 46

SOVFOTO   25 West 43rd Street, New York, N.Y.
194, 322, 324

ULLSTEIN GMBH/BILDERDIENST   Berlin 61, Kochstrasse 50, Berlin,
Germany
272-273

UNITED PRESS INTERNATIONAL   220 East 42nd Street, New York, N.Y.
24 Center, 25 (2), 81, 85, 106, 115, 155, 160, 166-167, 167, 199, 244 Bottom,
245 Bottom, 253 (2), 279, 310 Top, 311 Bottom, 315 (2), 316-317, 393

UNITED STATES DEPARTMENT OF THE AIR FORCE   Washington, D. C.
95, 96, 97, 98, 99, 101

UNITED STATES DEPARTMENT OF THE COAST GUARD
Washington, D. C.
241, 244, 245, 247

UNITED STATES DEPARTMENT OF THE NAVY   Washington, D.C.
237, 238

WEEKEND MAGAZINE   231 St. James Street West, Montreal, Quebec,
Canada
45

WIDE WORLD PHOTOS, INC.   50 Rockefeller Plaza, New York, N.Y.
82, 91, 100, 105, 110, 116, 195, 203, 314 Top

WORLD BOOK ENCYCLOPEDIA   Merchandise Mart, Chicago, Illinois
318, 318-319, 319, 320, 328 (2)

To my Mother

Preface

Mysteries, like a great many other concepts, are not what they used to be. The word, derived from the Latin *mysterium*, connoted divine revelations, spiritual secrets quite beyond the human ken.

Today, the word *mystery* is applied first and foremost to stories of crime. But crime, no matter how complex, is seldom more than a banal one-dimensional riddle that can be summed up in the phrase, "Who-done-it?" In this collection of mysteries, I have tried to revert to the older and more universal meaning of the term. The mysteries described in this volume do not recount trespasses against a legal code, but are rather happenings, phenomena, and events which defy logical explanation.

This doesn't mean that these bafflements are necessarily earth-shaking. The amount of mystification produced by a phenomenon or event can be quite out of proportion to its basic importance. UFOs, for example, may, according to some opinion, one day influence the fate of mankind; but the forces which generate these UFOs are not one iota more baffling than the forces which caused the movements of a few coffins in an obscure West Indian graveyard. The basis of selection, then, has been the quality rather than the scope of the conundrum.

Another prime consideration was whether these mysterious happenings can be authenticated. There are as many phoney mysteries extant as there are fake slivers of the True Cross. The reader will therefore find no mention in this book of the lost continents, Atlantis and Moo, nor of the allegedly prophetic architecture of the Egyptian pyramids, nor of Joanna Southcote's box, nor of the *loup-garou*, nor of Lincoln's death dream, nor of the angels of Mons, nor of zombies, nor vampires, nor ghosts—for the simple reason that Plato, Conan Doyle, and Charles Fort notwithstanding—there isn't a shred of evidence that any of these alleged marvels have ever existed.

Some of the stories chosen for this book are hardy perennials, solid enough to be prodded and dissected without destroying the bafflement. These reported events form an intellectual itch on the skin of human curiosity, an irritant which we shall continue to scratch until investigation has triumphantly produced a solution. The centuries-old enigma of the Easter Island statues was but yesterday deciphered by Thor Heyerdahl. This may happen with any of the riddles set forth in this book—even perhaps while you are still reading these pages.

Bewilderment may be largely a matter of viewpoint. The "devil dwarf" of the Papuans is our transistor radio of today. To quote a supposedly anonymous proverb, though I rather suspect that it was coined by James Thurber: *If, to Man, a cricket seems to hear with its legs, it is possible that to the cricket, Man seems to walk on his ears.*

JOHN GODWIN

This Baffling World

The Oak Island Enigma

The most fascinating of mysteries are those concerned with hidden treasure. Few topics have so fired the imagination as the prospect of wealth to be acquired by the mere act of finding it. The earliest known forms of narrative entertainment—Chinese fairy tales—contained accounts of secreted hoards, troves usually guarded by a demon or two, and this plot line has retained its audience appeal undiminished down the centuries.

Hidden treasures are known to exist in every portion of the globe, with the possible exception of the Antarctic. Every war, every violent social upheaval, increase the number.

Thus World War II transformed about 40 square miles of the Styrian Alps, Adolf Hitler's "National Redoubt," into a fabled treasure trove. Every second mountain lake in the area is alleged to contain Nazi hoards, cached there during the final convulsions of the Third Reich. No doubt treasures were stashed away by some Nazi bigwigs when the Third Reich disintegrated, but so far the *contents* of these hiding places have come as a sour surprise to treasure hunters.

In the summer of 1959, a team of salvage engineers, financed by a West German magazine, combed Lake Toplitz. They hauled up eight metal cases. In these strong boxes, $35 million worth of British five-pound notes had been crammed—every bank note a forgery! The phoney specie turned out to be part of "Operation Bernhard," a Gestapo scheme aimed at disrupting the wartime economy of the Western Allies by circulating billions of counterfeit pounds and dollars. This fake currency had been manufactured at the nearby Ebensee concentration camp. In April, 1945, when the swastika world was collapsing, the camp's SS guards sank what remained of the money into Lake Toplitz, creating one more legend of submerged treasure. Historically fascinating, but hardly a pot of gold.

Yet the fact remains that fantastic fortunes in coins, jewels, and precious metals, most of them gained illicitly, *have* been hidden away and are still awaiting recovery.

Just off the American mainland, for instance, lie four minute islands that were used as piggy banks by a couple of generations of pirates. Between 1640 and 1730, the boom years of marine knavery, loot estimated to be worth $100 million is believed to have been buried on those specks of volcanic rock. But apart from a few stray gold and silver pieces accidentally found by beachcombers, no one has so far sighted even a glimmer of this wealth—and not for want of trying.

The Florida coast was the hunting ground of a nightmarish gent named Edward Teach, better known as Blackbeard. Before the British Navy put an end to his career, he buried a large portion of his profits on Amelia Island, some 30 miles north of Jacksonville. For 50 years, natives and tourists have been searching for his troves, but to date, the only people to cash in on them have been the sellers of fake treasure maps.

Southwest of Florida, in the Yucatan Channel, lies a sandy little patch called Isla Mujeres, the Isle of Women. A short ferry ride from the Mexican coast, the isle was both home and headquarters of a highly successful Spanish freebooter named Mundaca. Somewhere on the island rests Señor Mundaca's share of a lifetime of looting—some three and a half million silver pesos, according to his own boast. When he died, he left neither a chart nor a will and, so far, in spite of much frantic digging, no one has turned up a peso.

Tiburon (Shark) Island is located in the Gulf of California, barely two miles from shore. Once the haunt of cannibalistic Indians, the island served as a hiding place not only for pirate booty, but for some of the immense quantities of gold which the Aztecs hid from the Spanish conquistadores. But while several authentic letters and documents tell of treasure being stashed on Tiburon, not one contains a map or even a mention of a landmark. The hoards are still there, waiting.

PROSPECTOR ON COCOS ISLAND   *Here is Robert Vergnes, leader of a 1962 French treasure-hunting expedition, which ended in tragedy. The canoe of the prospectors was swamped in a storm, and only Vergnes survived. He lived a Robinson Crusoe existence for two months before being picked up by a passing ship.*

The catch with all these treasures is, of course, the missing map. Yet for one of the richest troves ever assembled outside of Fort Knox, no less than three authentic place maps are known to exist.

Cocos Island, off the Pacific coast of Costa Rica, is barely 20 square miles of wildly tangled undergrowth, surrounded by almost vertical coastline cliffs. Cocos exudes an aura of indefinable malignancy that every treasure hunter has commented on and has been glad to get away from. These treasure seekers include such well-nerved individuals as automobile racer Sir Malcolm Campbell and the redoubtable Count Felix von Luckner.

Most of the island is covered with a thick greenish-brown mass of creepers and entwined branches that block off the sun, keeping the soft

FRENCH TREASURE HUNTERS
These three men, on the beach of Cocos Island immediately after their arrival in November, 1962, met disaster when their canoe capsized in a storm. Only Robert Vergnes (center) survived.

TREASURE CHART
Found hidden inside an old pocket watch, this dramatic find was made by Toronto watchmaker, M. C. Rice.

TREASURE TROVE *Underwater photographer Mike Wilson displays some coins and some cannon he raised from a reef several miles off the coast of Ceylon. The coins, minted in Persia in 1702, are pure silver. The two small cannon are presumably of Dutch origin.*

TREASURE HUNTERS FIND COINS   Arthur McKee and Charles Brookfield are elated with the ingots of silver and the gold doubloons they found on an old Spanish galleon in a coral bed off Key Largo, Florida.

BURIED TREASURE This hoard of silver coins and ingots were found in a garden in Peine, northern Germany, by a local carpenter. The treasure is believed to have been buried around 1379, one of the thousands of caches squirrelled away, throughout the past centuries, in almost every part of the globe.

earth below dark and moist. A stench of rot and decay fills the air, together with the whining hum of thousands of tiny flies. "The first thing
it reminded me of," wrote an American journalist, "was an open grave."

The curiously sinister atmosphere seems to affect even animals. Sir
Malcolm Campbell described how his dog suddenly woke him one night
when he "leaped to his feet with a terrifying howl and dashed to the
open flap of our tent, barking with rage and fear. I have never seen a
dog in such a paroxysm of terror." For three nights running, the dog
repeated this performance, whining and cringing in abject horror. But
although Sir Malcolm scouted the camp each time, he saw nothing except the blackness of the scrub and heard nothing save the drone of
insects.

Covered with a live blanket of ferociously stinging flies, cursed with
a foul humidity that rots the shirts on the backs of explorers, Cocos
Island is one of the most intensely uncomfortable spots on the globe. But
the lure of buried riches is so strong that the Costa Rican government
utilizes the island as a regular source of revenue. Treasure hunters pay a
standard fee for which they get an official charter entitling them to try
their luck anywhere on the island.

According to tradition, the island harbors three distinct hoards. The
existence of the first two is based largely on hearsay; that of the third,
the largest, is documented fact.

Around the turn of the 18th century, Captain Edward Davis was
one of the numerous freebooters who plundered the coasts of Central
America, then called "New Spain." He made Cocos Island his headquarters. He finally vanished without trace after he failed to capture the
city of Porto Bello. In 1709, shortly before his farewell venture, he is
believed to have hidden his accumulated plunder somewhere on the
island. The spot is unknown, but we have a record of the amount involved: 700 bars of gold, 20 water kegs filled with gold doubloons, and
more than 100 tons of Spanish silver reales.

The second treasure belonged to a particularly feared marine gang-
ster named Benito Bonito, who combined gold hunger with sadism. In
1819, he took the biggest haul of his career when he captured a transport
off Acapulco, Mexico, which carried 150 tons of gold. Bonito then sailed

for Cocos, crushed a mutiny among his crew, and then set off on what turned out to be his final plunder cruise. We know he must have left his king-sized swag on the island, because pirate vessels—to whom speed was essential—couldn't afford to sail with 150 tons of gold as ballast. Bonito had dropped anchor in Wafer Bay, at the north face of the island. It was here that later explorers found the horribly splintered skeletons of his rebellious sailors. There is every chance that the gold lies buried near his anchorage. Bonito himself was buried at sea—the result of his subsequent encounter with the British frigate, *Espiegle*.

The island's crowning attraction, however, is the mapped and documented treasure of Lima, a trove which has bedeviled the efforts and hopes of more men than any other hoard in the world.

In 1821, the Peruvian capital was the seat of the Spanish viceroys. Lima was by far the richest city on the continent. In that year, Simon Bolivar, was successfully booting the Spanish forces out of their colonies. Lima trembled at the approach of the revolutionary armies, and church and municipal authorities of Lima met and decided that it would be prudent to dispatch the city's movable wealth to safer regions.

Shipping space, however, was desperately scarce; every available Spanish vessel was filled. So the valuables of Lima's magnificent cathedral were loaded into the English brig, *Mary Dier*. This church treasure was nothing short of breathtaking. There was a life-sized statue of the Virgin Mary made of solid gold and encrusted with diamonds. There were silver candlesticks, jeweled chalices and vestments, wooden cases filled with pearls, rubies, and sapphires. There were figures of saints dressed in cloaks of silver and trunkfuls of gold doubloons. The entire hoard was valued at around $30 million.

It was altogether too much for the *Mary Dier's* Scottish master, Captain Charles Thompson. Instead of sailing to Panama and delivering his cargo to the Spanish authorities, he made for Cocos Island. There he and his crew hid the treasure and departed again, but only after Thompson had drawn a meticulous map of the island and the precise hiding place.

Up to this point, the story is quite clear; hereafter, it grows increasingly murky. Somehow, on the journey from Cocos, the *Mary Dier* was lost with her entire crew, save Captain Thompson. According to some sources, she was sunk by a Spanish warship; according to others, she foundered in a storm. Whatever happened, only Thompson survived. He finally reached Newfoundland on board a whaler, minus his ship, but still in possession of his treasure map.

Treasure maps then, as now, were suspect; and try as he would, the Scotsman could not get a backer trusting enough to equip an expedition to a back-of-beyond spot like Cocos. It was not until 1840—almost 20 years later—that Thompson met two men willing to take the gamble. They were Newfoundlanders named Boag and Keating. Before the trio could sail, Thompson died of what was perhaps conveniently called "a fever." The treasure map passed to Keating.

Five months later, Keating and Boag reached Cocos. Here again, a mist of uncertainty creeps over the story. For reasons never quite explained, their crew mutinied. The leaders, fearing for their lives, hid out on the island, and eventually their ship departed without them.

Two months later, another Newfoundland whaler arrived. No one knows what happened on that dark island in the interim, but the rescue vessel found only one survivor—Keating. He explained that Boag, too, had died "of a fever," although neither his body nor his grave was seen by anyone.

Keating returned to his hometown of St. John—without the treasure. We can only assume that he didn't trust his rescuers sufficiently to let them transport the hoard. But he still had his precious map, and he spent years trying to organize another expedition. When he died in 1873, he hadn't succeeded.

Keating willed the chart to a fellow mariner named Fitzgerald who, however, was quite disinterested. He allowed a couple of copies of the map to be made, but he himself never went a-treasure-hunting.

From here on, it becomes quite impossible to keep track of the string of people who owned this map and tried their luck with it, though we know they included a British army officer, a Newfoundland fisherman, a Royal Navy skipper, a Costa Rican government agent, and Sir Malcolm Campbell.

About a dozen subsequent treasure hunts were staged at Cocos.

Besides being almost bitten to death by the flies, the fortune hunters found skeletons, old weapons, and rotting pieces of marine equipment. The only other thing they discovered was that the carefully drawn treasure map was completely useless.

According to Thompson's chart, he had concealed the entire Lima treasure in a natural cave only a few feet below ground, at the headwater of a creek flowing into Chatham Bay, his anchorage. All the searchers had to do was follow the creek upstream and watch for the landmarks that indicated the cave. But as it turned out, only the bay and the creek were still there. The landmarks, as well as the cave, seemed to have vanished.

It took a tremendous amount of sweat, fury, and frustration before the solution of the riddle dawned on the treasure seekers; and then it was the kind of solution that does no one any good. Cocos is swept by violent tropical storms, and is frequently torn by landslides and earth tremors. Undoubtedly, these cataclysms were quite enough to obliterate a shallow cave, and wipe out every guiding mark.

Such upheavals would also account for the disappearance of the other two hoards. Likely, all three fortunes are still on Cocos, but they are about as traceable as three golden needles in a constantly shifting 20-mile haystack. It is almost as if that evil little island were determined to hold onto the riches planted in its bowels.

The key to all of the treasure troves mentioned so far is simply locating them. Whatever mystery surrounds them can be summed up in the single word *Where?* But there is one hoard the existence of which defies all the rules of treasure hunting. Its exact burial place is known, has been measured and surveyed, and is clearly visible to the most myopic eye. This treasure is located on an easily accessible spot, free from tropical insects and fevers, and so physically attractive that it has been used as a picnic ground for generations.

Yet for 160 years, this buried hoard has resisted all salvage attempts, has defeated picks, shovels, power drills and electronic indicators, and has swallowed up around $1,500,000 in digging expenses without disgorging a cent. The treasure on Oak Island lies there to this day, posing a riddle that all modern technical genius has been unable to solve.

The curtain of this conundrum rose one bright and breezy October morning in 1795. Three young men were paddling their canoe around Mahone Bay, looking for a suitable picnic site. Their names were Anthony Vaughan, Jack Smith and Dan McGinnis (or McInnes, depending on which source you consult).

Mahone Bay is a large, sheltered anchorage on the rugged southern shore of Nova Scotia, dotted with several hundred small islands, most of which are uninhabited and were then unexplored. One of the islands attracted the attention of the youths. It was a mile long and half a mile wide and shaped—very appropriately—somewhat like a question mark. Because of its abundance of tall oak trees, it was known as Oak Island.

The trio landed and began to explore. They came upon a clearing in the middle of which towered a huge, solitary oak. As they came closer, they noticed that one branch, about 15 feet from the ground, had been sawed off, and that the remaining stump bore unmistakable marks of ropes and tackle. Directly below the stump, there was a circular depression in the ground, some 12 feet in diameter, which looked as though something had been buried there.

The boys were local youngsters, brought up on the tales of pirates who had preyed on New England shipping half a century earlier and who had used these isolated Nova Scotian bays as hideouts. Their first thought was of buried treasure; their second, of digging implements.

The three returned the following morning, equipped with picks and shovels. The lads were aglow with the possibility of wealth lying just beneath the surface. They fell upon the curious circle and began to dig with a vengeance. Their excitement mounted when they noticed that they were digging into a well-defined shaft driven into the hard clay soil, the walls of the shaft clearly marked by the traces of pickaxes.

Ten feet down, they unearthed a platform made of solid oak logs. Convinced that the treasure—whatever it was—would appear next, they broke through the six-inch wood. All they found underneath, however, was more hard clay. The digging went on.

A few feet farther, the boys found an old rusty boatswain's whistle. Then, their excitement mounted to feverish heights when they unearthed a copper coin dated 1713. At 20 feet, they came upon another oaken

AERIAL VIEW OF OAK ISLAND   *One of 350 islands in Mahone Bay, Oak Island is three-quarters of a mile long and about one-half mile wide. Smith's Cove is at the lower right. The "money pit" is halfway between the jetty in the Cove and the swamp in the center of the picture.*

platform. They beat their way through that, shoveled out another 10 feet of soil, and reached yet another platform.

For the lads this meant the end of the road—at least temporarily. They were 30 feet down and, with the tools at their disposal, could dig no farther. There was no telling how many more platforms awaited them.

DIGGING EQUIPMENT   *This aerial view shows a crane near left center, the site of the treasure-hunting operations.*

But by now, they were certain they had stumbled on the site of a fantastic hoard. It was just a question of getting the implements needed to dig it out.

That proved more difficult than they had expected. Oak Island, it seemed, had an eerie reputation, macabre enough to make the mainlanders give it a wide berth. The island had reputedly been a fitting ground for the ships of the notorious Captain Kidd and other freebooters, who had allegedly carried out executions on that site and had left the island crawling with evil spirits. There was also a tale of mysterious lights that blinked on and off, and that lured fishermen to their death. All in all, not the kind of island to spend time on, especially not on the word of three adventurous youngsters.

In spite of being rebuffed, the boys refused to abandon "their" treasure; and when McGinnis and Smith married a few years later, they brought their wives to Oak Island to live, so that they could stay near the treasure hoard.

Eventually their perseverance paid off. In 1804, they managed to kindle the interest of wealthy Dr. John Lynds who formed a company which began excavating the hole in earnest, this time with every form of digging apparatus then in use.

Down and down they went. Every 10 feet down, they struck another oaken platform, each of an identical six-inch thickness and each fitted into the shaft with a precision that would have done credit to a mining engineer.

Then, at 93 feet, they came upon an entirely new kind of obstruction—a tier consisting of sandwich-like layers of charcoal, ship's putty, and mats of coconut fiber. When that, too, had been breached, there lay exposed a large flat stone covered with odd markings that looked like mirror writing. Below that—more clay!

At this stage, the excavators decided to knock off for the day. The next day was Sunday. So it was not until Monday morning that they returned to the pit. To their puzzlement, they found, the 95-foot hole filled with 60 feet of water!

There can be no doubt about the tenacity of the diggers; they immediately began a bucket chain to bail out the water. Their intelligence seems more dubious, for apparently they spent no time at all trying to figure out where the water came from. Only after 22 days of bailing, when the water level in the pit showed no signs of diminishing, did they try to guess the origin of the flooding. McGinnis believed they had struck a subterranean spring, although a taste of the water would have disabused him of this theory.

Acting on this assumption, they undertook the backbreaking labor of digging another pit directly beside the original one, expecting to drain out the water into the new channel. They were almost 100 feet down—deeper than they had gone the first time—when there was a thunderous roar. The old shaft had collapsed! And the new one began to fill with water so rapidly that the men had to scramble out for their lives.

This, as far as the company was concerned, was the end. They had used up their capital, and had expended months of grim toil. The total achievement: two waterlogged holes. The only positive result was to have dispelled Oak Island's ill repute, for evil spirts had not been among their tribulations.

The treasure hunters attributed their failure to bad luck. As Smith wrote to a mainland friend: "Had it not been for the various mischiefs nature played us, we would by now, all of us, be men of means." As it later became apparent, bad luck had little to do with the fiasco.

The first searchers had uncovered only three clues. The first was the copper coin dated 1713. The second was the coconut fiber matting, clearly brought to the site from overseas because no such material was made in America. The third was the stone with the strange markings, a clue that might have offered a definite lead. Oddly enough, none of the treasure hunters seemed to have paid much attention to the inscription. Smith kept the stone in his home, treating it more like a souvenir than the possible key to the mystery. It was not until some 120 years later that the slab was taken to the mainland for closer study. The translation was murky. One of the wishful-thinking interpretations ran: "TWO MILLION POUNDS LIE BURIED TEN FEET BELOW." That this was, indeed, the meaning of the inscription is less than likely. Why should anyone who had used so much ingenuity to protect a hoard from interference advertise its presence on a stone slab? Moreover, in that period, an amount would have been stated in guineas rather than in pounds. In any case, the puzzling stone was either lost, stolen, or destroyed some time during the 1920's.

In spite of their initial failures, the discoverers were now more convinced than ever that there *was* treasure in the pit. The only question was how to get at it.

Decades passed. McGinnis died. Smith and Vaughan continued to

COCONUT FIBRE   This piece of matting was found inside the "money pit." During the windjammer era, this tropical material was used as "dunnage" in stowing ships' cargoes. The fibre does not grow in Canada.

work their farms on Oak Island, never losing hope that one day they would be able to lay their hands on the gold.

In August of 1849, a new, well-financed syndicate had been formed in Truro, Nova Scotia. Composed of local businessmen and engineers, this new group undertook the task in a somewhat more scientific manner.

Digging down to the water level of the shaft, they installed a pod auger, a horse-driven drill then used in mining operations, which picked up samples of whatever it passed through. At 98 feet—three feet deeper than the original excavation—the auger passed through another layer of oak, and then penetrated what appeared to be loose metal. Brought to the surface, the bit was found to contain two tiny links of a chain. And the links were *pure gold!*

Down went the drill again. Once more it twirled through loose metal. Then it bit into something harder which, on inspection, turned out to be more wood. Forced several feet deeper, the bit repeated the same sequence—wood, loose metal, wood.

Smith, Vaughan, and the other syndicate members beamed at each other in triumph. The pod auger had proven them right—there *was* treasure in the shaft. Way down there rested two chests, one buried on top of the other, each made of four-inch-thick oak wood, each containing 22 inches of precious metal.

However, the problem of getting at the chests remained. There was that damnable water. As before, bailing proved utterly futile. The only alternative was to sink yet another shaft beside the treasure cache in the hope of draining off the flood. This time the treasure hunters dug down 118 feet, tunneling directly under the mystery pit. The same maddening "mishap" occurred. Water began to pour into the new shaft, rapidly filling it to the same level as the old one.

Only now, faced with another shambles, did the treasure seekers get around to doing what they should have done years before—taste the water. To their amazement, it proved to be salty. Then, watching the shaft, they observed that the water level rose and fell in the same rhythm as the ocean tide. Since it was quite impossible for sea water to seep through the hard clay soil, they suddenly realized what they were up against: a subterranean channel connected the treasure pit with the ocean.

Under these circumstances, they could have bailed till doomsday without reducing the water level by more than a few feet. The only chance was to block the flow at its source.

THE MONEY PIT OF OAK ISLAND   This sketch shows the depth of the shaft to 170 feet at which point drillers struck an iron plate. At the beginning of the shaft, wooden platforms were found every 10 feet to a depth of 90 feet. At 98 feet down, two treasure chests were encountered. It was at this point that the diggers were foiled by a sea water channel which, leading from Smith's Cove, flooded the shaft. At 151 feet down, diggers encountered a cement chamber in which it is assumed the main treasure trove is buried. But here the treasure is guarded by a sea water channel which leads from South Beach; and the flooding of the chamber effectively prevents the removal of the cache.

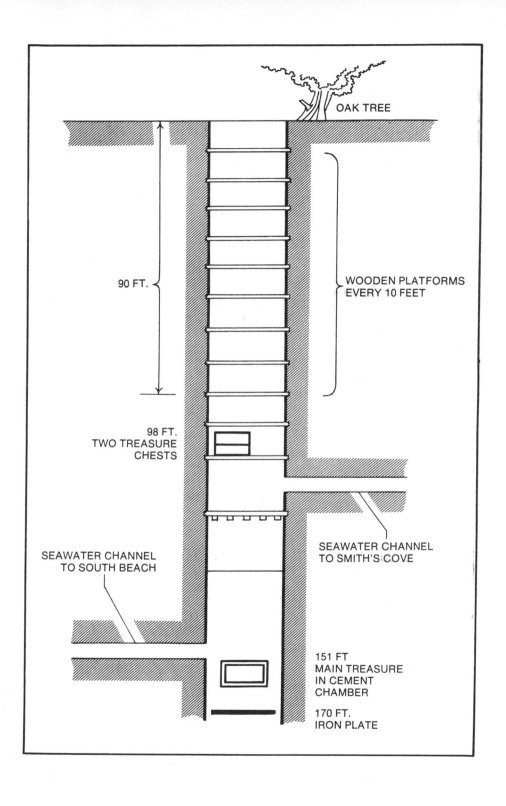

WORK ON OAK ISLAND   This photograph shows operations conducted during 1896 and 1897.

The nearest beach was at Smith's Cove, some 490 feet away from the shaft. As the treasure hunters combed through the sand searching for the inlet, their curiosity turned to awe. For beneath the sand, they discovered a stone floor laid across the entire distance between the high tide mark and the low tide mark. This stone floor was neatly covered with the same coconut fiber they had found in the pit. Underneath the stone floor they came on five drains lined with stones. These drains slanted down from the ocean until they converged on a central channel which ran in a direct underground line to the treasure shaft.

Incredible as it seemed, someone had converted 150 feet of beach into a sponge. As the tide came in, the water was soaked up and held by the thick coconut fiber, then channeled to the pit via the drains. Normally, this mass of sea water would be held back by the pressure of earth inside the shaft; but should anyone dig down into the shaft from above and remove the earth, the pressure would lessen. As marauders neared the treasure chests, the earth above would exert less pressure, the water below more pressure, and the shaft would automatically be flooded.

It was fantastic, unbelievable—but there it was. The treasure pit was protected by the Atlantic Ocean. Let anyone disturb the delicate balance between sea and soil and—whoosh!—the cache would be flooded.

And even now, the treasure seekers were foiled by that diabolically clever designer. The vital question remained: *How would the men who had hidden the treasure go about recovering it?*

Somewhere, in or near the shaft, there must have been a device to keep the hole dry while its contents were dug out—a form of safety catch known only to the designers. It is unthinkable that anyone with the amazing skill of this pit builder would have barred himself from taking out what he had put in. This consideration did not seem to have occurred to the syndicate members. Instead, they went to the huge expense of building a dam at Smith's Cove to stop the sea from filling the inlet at high tide. After that, the shaft could have been pumped out.

Could have been—yes! As it happened, a violent gale roared along the coast when the next tide came in, and the dam was smashed to pieces.

The Truro syndicate was bankrupt! Forty thousand dollars in the red and not a dime to show for it. The members retired to less exciting pursuits. But even while licking their financial wounds, they comforted each other with the thought that at least they had bared the remarkable secret of the mystery pit.

As it turned out, they'd done no such thing. The shaft still held secrets undreamed of.

What they had accomplished was to focus world attention on the riddle of Oak Island. Over the next 40 years, half a dozen attempts were made to get at the hoard, none of which got even as far as the earlier expeditions.

Then, in 1893, an unusually enterprising Nova Scotian, named Frederick Blair, organized yet another syndicate. The new company was determined not to repeat any of the mistakes of their predecessors. When Blair arrived at the scene, he found he would have to start from scratch. The previous attempts, most of them very clumsy, had caused the treasure shaft, as well as the various draining shafts around it, to collapse.

With great astuteness, Blair and his workmen began their operations not at the treasure site, but at Smith's Cove. They drilled a line of holes across the path of the underground channel, filled these holes with dynamite, and blew up the channels, thus effectively blocking the flow of sea water to the shaft. Or so they thought.

Next, they sank a metal pipe down the pit, following roughly the line of the primitive pod auger used by the Truro outfit. Within the protective pipe, their own drill could work much more efficiently.

Once again, a bit chewed down into the mysterious clay hole, deeper and deeper, past the levels of the previous explorations. There seemed to be no need to go farther than the depth of the two treasure chests, but Blair had an idea that the shaft might hold a few additional surprises. And his hunch was right.

At 151 feet the bit carved out something that at first appeared to be soft gray stone. Under chemical analysis, however, it turned out to be cement—seven inches of it. Then came another four inches of wood, then 32 inches of loose metal, followed by more wood, and another layer of cement.

From each of these materials, the bit brought up minute samples, including specks of gold and something that looked like a scrap of parchment. Together, they presented a picture of the pit's anatomy. Clearly, the two chests discovered higher up were merely a blind, cunningly placed there to give whoever came upon them the idea that he had struck all there was to strike. The more valuable treasure rested in the cement chamber, 53 feet farther down the shaft.

As Edward Hooper, one of the syndicate members, wrote to a friend in London: "Never in my life have I known the kind of excitement that gripped us at that moment. We felt that we were about to uncover the most cunningly concealed secret on the face of the earth. The riches down below seemed but of lesser importance, it was the solution of the riddle that had us all agog."

Alas for the hopes of the lyrical Mr. Hooper. Suddenly an ominous gurgling roar was heard from deep within the shaft. Seconds later, a jet of water squirted from the pipe and shot 10 feet into the air, drenching everyone within range.

The water was sea water—but from where? Blair ordered large quantities of red dye pumped down the pipe, then watched the inlet at Smith's Cove for traces of it. There were none, which meant that the underground connection between the Cove and the pit was still blocked. Later that day, however, huge scarlet stains appeared on the beach at the *south* side of the island, *more than 600 feet from the shaft.*

FREDERICK L. BLAIR   *The well-known prospector points to the location of Oak Island in Mahone Bay, Nova Scotia.*

This could mean only one thing: there was another subterranean tunnel in the pit, protecting the cement treasure chamber, quite the same as the discovered channel had protected the two treasure chests.

TOURISTS   The island is frequented by visitors who are intrigued by some of the elaborate machinery on Oak Island.

Blair and his men scoured the south beach, hoping to find the inlet. But neither they nor those who came after ever did.

With dogged persistence, Blair continued drilling, in spite of the constant inrush of water. At 170 feet, after churning through more clay, the bit hit an obstruction it could not penetrate. It was iron plate. This was the deepest point any of the treasure hunters had ever reached.

The iron, which seems to form the bottom platform of the shaft, has never been breached.

But Blair wasn't finished. He commenced new digging operations, although by then, the entire vicinity of the shaft resembled a quagmire. Water pouring in at a rate of several hundred gallons per hour, turned the clay into slippery mud. After weeks of floundering in the black stew, the diggers had lost all trace of either of the two treasure chambers. Now, in fact, they couldn't even locate the position of the original shaft. The treasure hunt had been transformed into a hideously expensive game of blindman's buff.

Blair doggedly wanted to continue. But his syndicate colleagues, having spent $115 thousand, decided to call it a day. Although Blair lacked the resources to carry on single-handed, he bought the treasure trove rights of the island and issued a standing offer to lease these rights to any taker in return for a share of whatever might be turned up.

Until his death in 1951, the tough old Nova Scotian never abandoned hope. He watched one partner after another take up the challenge, watched the excavation methods grow more complex and sophisticated, watched huge sums of money poured into the pit.

In 1909, it was a New York engineer named Harry Bowdoin. Then came heavily financed syndicates from New Jersey, Maine, and Wisconsin. In 1930, a Nova Scotian outfit returned to the island. One by one, each expedition ran into the same obstacles that had foiled their predecessors, and one by one they failed.

In 1935, a real heavyweight picked up the gauntlet. Gilbert Hedden, a businessman from New Jersey, had money as well as considerable mining experience. He launched salvage operations on the largest scale yet.

He laid underwater electric cables from the mainland to Oak Island

and had ample power to run his machines. For a while, the electric pumps managed to beat the inrushing sea water, but his machines could do little against the mud. When the actual digging got underway, Hedden's workmen floundered about almost as helplessly as Blair's had. As far as anyone could determine, the constant drilling, digging, and flooding—plus the several draining shafts sunk all around the pit—had so dislocated the treasure chests that they could no longer be pinpointed closer than within a 100-foot radius. After the game of hide-and-seek in the mud had swallowed $140 thousand, the man from New Jersey called it off.

The pit continued to lure fortune hunters at a steady trickle. There came veteran prospectors and miners, men with divining rods, and even a Scottish lady bearing a map which she claimed to have drawn according to instructions given by the ghost of Captain Kidd.

Most of these treasure seekers stayed just long enough to add their money to the immense quantities already poured into the pit. To some, the shaft became an obsession; even after failure, they couldn't bear to leave the site.

In 1959, an Ontario steelworker named Restall quit his steady job and moved himself and his family to Oak Island. He built a small cabin near the muddy, debris-strewn craterfield that today indicates the treasure site. He spent four years and all of his savings on small-scale digging operations that turned to naught.

This, then, is the story of the most puzzling and maddening treasure cache in the world—the hoard on Oak Island that has defied all of the vaunted technology of the Atomic Age. Perhaps one day, some weekend adventurer traipsing over the terrain will accidentally unearth the key —history yields that kind of humor.

But until that day—which may never come—we can only guess at the exact nature of the treasure and the mysterious mechanism employed by its builders who someday hoped to render the treasure pit an open sesame. We know there is both gold and parchment on Oak Island, but not how much of each. Yet there can be no doubt about the high value of the contents, for nobody undertakes such a Herculean task as a practical joke.

THE RESTALL FAMILY   Robert Restall, who in his early years was a
dare-devil motorcyclist, and his wife Mildred, a former ballet dancer, pose
with their sons Robert, Jr. and Ricky shortly after moving to Oak Island. On
August 17, 1965 tragedy struck when Restall, apparently overcome by the
carbon monoxide fumes from a nearby gasoline power-pump, collapsed and
fell into a 27-feet deep shaft. Rescue attempts by his son Robert, age 24, an
associate, and three workmen proved equally tragic. Three of the rescuers,
among them Restall's son, were also overcome by the fumes and died.

TREASURE SITE   *Even today, thousands of tourists are lured to the world-famous site of the Nova Scotia trove.*

It is the very scope of that task that offers us at least a slender clue to the men who accomplished it. Thanks to the literary skill of Robert Louis Stevenson, we tend to associate treasure islands with piracy. But the longer we consider the structure of the pit the less plausible that theory becomes. The burial of the Oak Island hoard required not only a large number of men working undisturbed for a lengthy time, it also required expert engineering, know-how of a superior order akin to genius. Whoever designed the shaft obviously expected to return one day in considerable strength to salvage the contents. There is not the faintest evidence in history that any bunch of buccaneers was gifted with the craftsmanship that went into the construction of this burglar-proof safe.

The 1713 copper coin found at the site has caused a great many researchers to assume that the treasure was buried around that date. But there is no reason why it shouldn't have been hidden much later—say in 1758. For 1758 was the year the giant French fortress of Louisbourg fell to British attackers after a long and bitter siege during the French and Indian War. Louisbourg, designed to guard the vital mouth of the St. Lawrence River, was situated on Cape Breton Island near the northern tip of Nova Scotia. The fortress contained part of the gold reserve of New France, and if the British had managed to get their hands on it, they would surely have mentioned such a coup in their official records.

There is a strong possibility that the French spirited their gold out of the fortress and transported it 240 miles south to Oak Island. At the time, France's military engineers were undisputedly the best in the world; they would have possessed both the manpower and the skill to construct such an impenetrable cache.

Naturally, the builders assumed they would eventually wrest French Canada out of British hands. They would then return at leisure and reclaim the gold. History—in the person of General James Wolfe—turned that assumption into an illusion. And so posterity has been bequeathed an enigmatic strongbox to which no cracksman has yet found the key.

The Devil in Devonshire

Throughout that gray and clammy afternoon of February 8, 1855, the countryside around the Exmouth estuary in southwestern England resembled a hunting ground. Women, children, and old folks remained hidden indoors, while the landscape was swarming with able-bodied men and dogs. Army muskets, shotguns, pistols, pitchforks, flails, pikes and clubs were everywhere in sight.

The men were trudging back and forth and in circles through the thick snow, peering behind hedges, rustling through undergrowth, scouring embankments, poking into farmyards, orchards, and cemeteries. Their quarry, let it be said, was at least as unorthodox as their methods of pursuit. About 20 per cent of the hunters were searching for a mysterious animal of indefinable shape, about the size of a donkey. The rest, however, were looking for THE DEVIL.

The belief that Satan was stalking around in the immediate vicinity caused the more timid to stay in their houses and barricade the doors. The sturdier grabbed whatever armament they possessed and went after the Evil One—though not quite sure just what they would do if they found him. The majority had no doubt that he was pretty close at hand —for the marks of his cloven hoof were plainly visible in the snow.

The people who staged this hunt were neither backward nor particularly superstitious, and not in the least given to fits of mass-hysteria. They had merely been startled out of their wits by a phenomenon that left the greatest intellects of the country as much at a loss as the local peasantry.

A century ago, the county of Devonshire—proudly known as

"Glorious Devon"—was one of the prettiest and most prosperous sections of rural England. Famous for its potent apple cider and picturesque Channel coast, and already the scene of a thriving tourist trade, Devon had the reputation of breeding a hardheaded, taciturn, and shrewdly conservative species of man, closely resembling the New England Yankee. Here was the last place one would expect to encounter a satanic manifestation, either real or imaginary.

On the night of February 7, an exceptionally heavy snowfall blank-

TOTNES   An artist's drawing of the little town as it looked around 1855.

eted the coastal area in the southern part of the county. The flakes began to swirl around eight o'clock, and the fall continued until close to midnight. After that, no one in the county was astir; nightlife had never been a Devon specialty.

About six the following morning, Henry Pilk, a baker, emerged from his backyard bakehouse in the small town of Topsham. The yard and the street beyond were covered by a white layer of snow, as virginal as a fresh bedsheet. Or almost so. For as Mr. Pilk admired the effect, he noticed a line of the most peculiar prints he had ever seen.

Each print resembled a small horseshoe; and at first, the baker thought they might have emanated from a pony. But then he saw that each print was in line—*each in front of the other*—and therefore, more like the track of a two-footed than a four-footed animal.

The really odd part, though, was that the prints started at the wooden six-foot-high fence, approached close to the bakehouse, and then veered off toward the fence again. Mr. Pilk, apparently not a man of great curiosity, took note of the tracks, then went about his work. He did not trouble to look over the fence, nor did he rack his brain as to the nature of the beast that had visited his yard during the night.

An hour later, his yard was invaded by a neighborhood group which included Albert Brailford, the schoolteacher, a person of consequence. The group had followed the tracks from the street, hoping to catch sight of whatever had left them. Pilk joined them. Together, they trailed the prints *back into the street*.

The group swelled rapidly: housewives, schoolchildren, apprentices, tradesmen, shopkeepers—running up from all directions. As they progressed and word of the hunt spread, citizens called out again and again, announcing newly found evidence. To everyone's growing consternation, the trackers learned that the same hoofmarks were visible outside almost every house in the street, and also in several adjoining streets, and in the fields beyond. Householders and servant girls waved excitedly from garden gates and doorways: "Over here—they're here, too!"

Now the entire town was buzzing with the news. As more and more people spilled out their stories, it became clear that Topsham had been visited by some strange creature with frightening peculiarities: a creature that could, to all intents and purposes, walk through walls!

For some of the tracks led into gardens protected by stone walls 12 feet high. The gates were securely locked and had not been tampered with; the snow on top of the walls lay undisturbed. *Yet the single line of prints advanced straight at the walls and continued on the other side, as if no obstacle had been in its path.*

The searchers gradually coordinated their efforts. It now turned out that almost every house in town had been visited by the strange being. The trail ran mostly along the ground, but sometimes the trail jumped up onto roofs; and occasionally, over snow-covered wagons which had been left standing overnight. The tracks never varied nor faltered nor doubled back; they went on unperturbed, passing each point but once, zig-zagging right and left as if the nocturnal wanderer had peered into every dwelling en route.

And while the inhabitants of Topsham were tracing through their streets, the people of a score of other communities were doing the same. For the mysterious prints were discovered along almost 100 miles of the south Devon coast!

Topsham, situated on the estuary of the Exe River, marked the northern tip of the "printed" region. Totnes, about 97 miles down the coast, was the southern extreme. Between these points, virtually every town and village—and yes! even lonely farmsteads—awoke to find the hoofmarks on doorsteps and roofs. From Torquay, Newton, Teignmouth, Luscombe, Dawlish, Powderham, and a dozen other places came news of the prints. Peasants found them on solitary hayricks; clergymen, in churchyards and cemeteries; squires, on the drives in front of their mansions. Similar prints were discovered along lonely beaches, in stretches of woodland, on main streets, in market squares. All of these prints must have been made during the previous night, but no one in the area could remember either seeing or hearing anything that might yield a clue to their maker.

The sightings grew weirder by the hour. At Mamhead, a local physican named Benson followed a line of the prints across an open field and up to an 18-feet-high haystack which was blanketed in snow. The

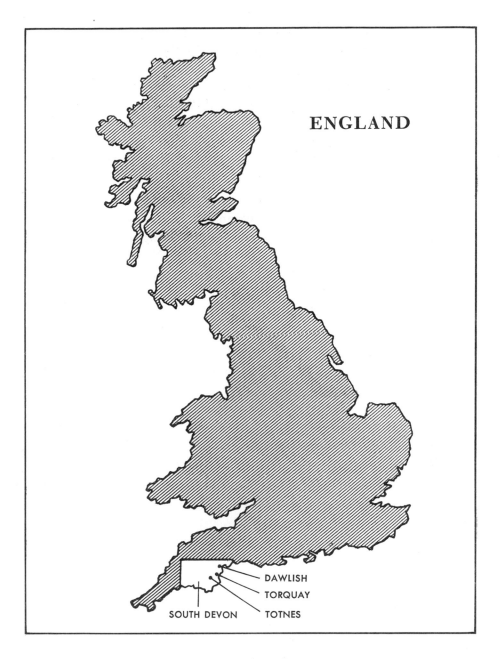

ENGLAND

DAWLISH
TORQUAY
SOUTH DEVON   TOTNES

*MAP SHOWING DEVONSHIRE DISTRICT   The unshaded
part of this map of England indicates where Devonshire lies.*

snow mantle was unmarked—but the tracks continued on the other side, as if whatever had caused them had simply stepped over the huge obstacle in its path.

In the same parish, two "hunting gentlemen" spent a couple of hours pursuing the hoofmarks through thick and thorny gooseberry bushes and dense hedges. Although seasoned trackers, the two men found no signs denoting the passage of a furred animal through the vegetation. They found only the mysterious tracks, which ceased abruptly at one point, as though the creature had suddenly flown off. But half a mile further in the same direction, they sighted them again—this time on the roofs of a row of cottages. From this eminence, the tracks descended back to earth, and then went on—in a straight line—until they reached the streets of Mamhead.

Nothing, it seemed, could halt the progress of the unknown creature. Between Powderham and Lympstone lay the Exe River estuary, unfrozen, and almost two miles wide at this point. Yet the trail led up to the western bank and continued on the opposite shore, starting right at the water's edge, as if the thing had either swum or stepped across. The same had happened at the Teignmouth estuary, six miles further south, where the trail led straight into the water and appeared again on the other side.

The prints were easy enough to follow, since they looked like no other marks left in the snow. Even town folks, who had never done any tracking in their lives, had no trouble distinguishing these prints from those of bird or of animal traces. The weird prints stuck out like signposts; and before they gradually faded away, several hundred people, up and down the coast, had made sketches of them. The shape of the drawings varied slightly, but the outline and dimensions were virtually identical, thus:

The hoofmarks definitely resembled those of a donkey. They were convex, and measured four inches by two and one-half inches. The distance between each print—that is, the length of the creature's step—was an unvarying eight inches, and this was true whether or not the trail lay across level ground, through thickets, or over rooftops. This by itself was an extremely odd fact since animals, like humans, vary their strides according to circumstances.

But even more puzzling was the continuous single line of the prints. Every quadruped progresses by placing its feet right and left, leaving a distinct double track. Even bipeds, like birds and humans, do not place one foot in front of the other, unless walking a tightrope. But this was exactly what the thing seemed to have been doing—walking along some invisible single line that stretched in intricate convolutions from Totnes to Topsham.

The first general reaction to the phenomenon was simply curiosity. As long as the prints were fresh and undisturbed, the locals clearly enjoyed the exciting game of discovery and guesswork; everyone putting in his or her ha'penny's-worth of opinion. In due course, it was comfortably agreed, their learned betters would come up with a sound explanation.

But as the day wore on and the tracks began to blur, the excitement gave way to apprehension, and finally to stark fear. The blurring process caused little indents in some of the marks, giving rise to the disturbing rumor that the tracks were those of a *cloven hoof* (which they were not). Satan, as everyone knew, was the possessor of such a hoof, and also the only critter that might conceivably walk through walls and step over rivers and hayricks. The news spread by word of mouth, and then from village to village, that last night the Devil had wandered around south Devonshire, peering into every house, presumably to mark down future victims.

Within hours, the tracking game became a grim all-male affair. Oldsters, youngsters, and womenfolk retired to their homes and barred the doors. Some went so far as to board up the windows. Simultaneously, hundreds of volunteers armed themselves as best they could, called out their dogs, and proceeded to comb the countryside, quite ready to tackle the Evil One, though armed with little but agricultural implements for the most part.

At least one person came close to paying with his life for the uproar. Daniel Plumer, known around the village of Woodbury as "Daft Danny," was a harmless imbecile who decked himself in layers of chicken and goose feathers and who lived by begging and stealing, and spent most of his waking hours shambling around the woods imitating bird and animal noises. Though the locals all knew him, the people from Topsham did not. About 30 Topshamites, bristling with guns and cudgels, flushed him out of a thicket, saw his unearthly figure galloping off, and promptly gave chase.

Afterwards, nobody could quite explain just what he thought he was chasing, but all were in bloody earnest about it. They caught the gibbering Danny, tore off his feather costume and were in the process of clubbing him to death, when Squire Bartholomew rode up and restored order. Since Bartholomew also happened to be the local magistrate, he was able to rescue "Daft Danny" by placing him in the village lockup until the excitement blew over.

By late afternoon, the tracks had vanished. But the countryside was still milling with armed search parties, men on horseback, and baying hounds. Rumors ripened faster than the prints faded. Some folks swore they had seen the sinister hoofmarks glowing like live coals in the snow. Others had heard devilish laughter echoing through lonely glades. Still others had seen a gigantic horned shadow looming over ancient Powderham Castle. The most widespread story had it that the prints evaporated before your eyes when you looked at them, only to reappear magically the moment you turned your back.

People dreaded the coming of darkness. The majority were convinced that IT was sure to return the next night to perpetrate . . . well, no one knew just what. Two companies of Royal Fusiliers were allegedly marching down from Exeter to patrol the county during the night. But what could a soldier do against a creature that walked through brick-walls? In fact, no fusiliers or any other kind of soldiery were marching anywhere.

Having combed the landscape without finding anything, the members of the search parties retired to their houses and stayed there. The inns were empty, because few dared risk a walk home after dark. But nearly every house and cottage kept its lamps or its candles burning that night.

What disturbed people most was undoubtedly the bewilderment of their "betters." In everyday matters, the Devon rustics were a pretty independent lot, but they were also products of a rigid class structure; they looked to the gentry for enlightenment concerning anything untoward—like steam engines, comets, balloons, or war. And while the educated minority smiled at the notion of Satan stomping the neighborhood, they were as clueless as the yokels.

England has always been a hotbed of amateur naturalists, a country whose newspapers devote acres of space to correspondence concerning the hibernation habits of frogs, and the exact date and location of the year's first cuckoo call. Devonshire had rather more than her share of zoological dabblers—many of them retired missionaries, sea captains, colonial army officers, and game hunters. As a group, these people possessed a formidable knowledge of animal lore, all of which was brought to bear on the mysterious hoofprints. But the net result was a huge zero.

The more obvious theories—the footprints were made by a donkey, or a pony, or a horse—had to be scuttled immediately. Everyone was familiar with the tracks of these animals. But the thought that the tracks might have been made by one of the less common creatures, such as an otter, a deer, a beaver, a fox, or a stoat, had likewise to be discarded, since neither the prints nor the method of locomotion of these animals bore the slightest resemblance to the tracks. There simply wasn't any four-footer capable of leaving a single trail.

A bird, of course, would have been able to surmount obstacles like garden walls and haystacks and to fly across the rivers involved. But who had ever heard of a hoofed bird? A hoofed bird that can walk a single line for 97 miles?

Even more than the actual prints, it was their pattern that mystified. All animals, quadrupeds or bipeds, have a discernible purpose in their wanderings. Usually, the animal is in search of food. The trail, however, ruled out any kind of foraging or grazing. The trail indicated a steady, uninterrupted forward progress without any wayside stops for feeding.

A migratory animal, then? This theory was even less feasible. No migrating beast would choose to follow a zig-zag course leading through umpteen towns and villages, methodically touching every isolated farm-stead and country house in between.

Having drawn a blank with every other species, the guessers in-evitably turned to Homo Sapiens. Squire Bartholomew expressed what many were thinking, when he said: "Animal—balderdash! Some blasted hoaxer did it."

Yes, there was something mechanical about the trail that indicated a device rather than a walking creature. The constant single line, the precise eight-inch interval between each mark, the equal clarity of every print, certainly did suggest that a contraption of some sort had been per-ambulated over the countryside with no other purpose than to create bamboozlement.

What's more, this was the Victorian heyday of the prankster, and the practical joker, the great era of ghost impersonations. England's so-cial climate was at that day particularly favorable to elaborate gags ex-ecuted by gentlemen with much leisure—always providing that they were indeed, "gentlemen." Lesser breeds ran a decided risk of being tagged "disturbers of the peace," and then run off to jail. And though Queen Victoria was notoriously unamused by such antics, society, as a whole, found them side-splitting. In London, the upper crust was still laughing about young Chester Hetherington, one of the Carlton Club bloods, who had conned the Royal Navy into giving him a 12-gun salute by appearing as the Crown Prince of Ethiopia. Society was still tickled about the story of the elderly, but quite incorrigible, Lord Pengbourne, who threw a magnificent dinner party at his Sussex mansion to which he invited a local poetry society. At the conclusion of the banquet, only Lord Pengbourne himself was able to rise from his chair; the others were, literally, glued to theirs.

The possibility of a hoax was, therefore, considered quite early in the situation. It would have taken only moderate ingenuity to work up a gadget that would leave those bewildering hoofmarks in the snow—say a wheel with hoofs affixed at eight-inch intervals, that could be trundled along the ground. Or better yet, a print marker that fitted over the hoaxer's own shoes!

But these brainstorms were swiftly put to rest by the technical impossibilities they entailed. For the perpetrator of such a stunt would have had only about six hours of darkness in which to execute his prank. He would have had to start after midnight when people had gone to bed—and would have had to finish before six in the morning—when the countryside was astir again. In order to leave his prints over the area involved, he would have had to move at a rate of more than 16 miles per hour, regardless of obstacles encountered—a patently impossible proposition for any man.

What about several men—a whole swarm of pranksters working in unison? Even that conjecture did not stand up to scrutiny. How would such men have vaulted across garden walls without disturbing the snow on top? How would they have leapt over haystacks and have walked over sloping roofs? And why—if they had used any means beside their feet—were there no tell-tale tracks, save those hoofmarks?

At first, only southern Devonshire was exercised by these questions. But soon, most of Great Britain joined in. Several London newspapers, including the authoritative *Times*, ran the story, resulting in an immediate trickle of visitors to Devonshire. Some came armed with big game rifles; others, with sketch books and magnifying glasses. All were eager to encounter the mysterious beast or at least its tracks. All were disappointed. There was plenty of snow during the days that followed, but the phantom prints never did reappear.

It took almost a week before the district returned to normal, and even then a great many rustics carefully avoided the lonely trails on which the marks had been found. They were, the saying went, "Devil's Walks," and not to be trodden on lightly. Farmers went armed whenever they left their homes. For weeks, the folks of that district anxiously scanned the landscape every morning to see whether the hoofmarks had recurred.

Many local clergymen textured their Sunday sermons around the mystery prints. Although none went so far as to declare Satan directly responsible, several hinted darkly at "ominous signs in our midst" or at "the irrefutable presence of the Great Enemy—visible to all who have eyes to see." The more credulous scared the living daylights out of their parishioners. The message went forth that the hoofmarks were the consequence of the rife drinking, swearing, and licentiousness in the congregation, and were to be taken as a dire warning from Heaven.

This, however, was not the opinion of the Rev. Musgrave of Mamhead, who sent his sketches of the marks to the British Museum, the Zoological Society, and the director of Regent's Park Menagerie in London.

Rev. Musgrave also wrote a lengthy communication to the *London Illustrated News,* in which he expounded a theory of his own. The tracks, he declared, were those of a kangaroo, which had escaped from some circus or animal show in the vicinity. Such an animal was quite capable of leaping over haystacks and walls; a kangaroo hopped on two legs; and, he concluded, did so fast enough to cover 97 miles in one night.

The Reverend's pencil sketches were beautifully executed; but unfortunately, his knowledge of the marsupial didn't match his artistry. For while a kangaroo does, indeed, hop on two legs, it keeps its legs parallel at all times, thus leaving a distinct double trail. A big one could conceivably clear a 12-foot wall, but such an animal would be no more able to leap along a sloping rooftop than it could swim an icy two-mile estuary. What's more, there is not the faintest similarity between the imprint of a kangaroo's nailed toes and the hoofprints that were seen.

Though the Rev. Musgrave may have been wide off the mark, his deduction was certainly more intelligent than that of Richard Owen, then regarded as England's greatest living naturalist. Mr. Owen was among the dozens of people who communicated their guesses to the *London Illustrated News.* His particular stab was based on a drawing sent to him by "an esteemed zoological friend." From it, Mr. Owen gathered that the tracks were the work of a large number of badgers, aroused from hibernation by hunger, who had gone scouring the countryside in search of nourishment. This must rank as one of the most spectacularly silly deductions on record, quite in keeping with the string of asininities with which Owen later tried to refute the teachings of Charles Darwin.

The Devonshire farmers were old hands at badger hunting and perfectly familiar with that animal's prints as well as with its habits. Though the learned Mr. Owen's reference to a "plantigrade quadruped" might have had them stumped, and while they may not have known that this meant "flatfooted four-legger," they certainly were aware that badgers have paws—not *hoofs*—and that the food forays of badgers do not take them zig-zagging, in single file, through city streets.

Not everyone was willing to offer his solution to newspaper readers gratis, so to speak. One authority, signing himself "W.W.", put out his theory in the form of a pamphlet which sold for twopence, and apparently sold in the thousands. Titled "The Swan With The Silver Collar," this publication had a charming Hans Christian Andersen air about the cover, which was fully borne out in the contents. According to this writer, a handsome, but rather fatigued swan turned up in St. Denis, France, five days after the Devonshire scare. The bird was wearing a silver collar with an engraved inscription that identified it as belonging to Prince Hohenlohe of Germany. From this slender evidence, the author deduced: The swan's feet had been padded so that each foot was shaped like a donkey's hoof. This had been done in order to prevent the swan from damaging the flower beds in the Prince's garden. With these padded members, the swan had "undoubtedly" left the mysterious marks. The author, however, did not go so far as to reveal why a swan, capable of flying the English Channel, should have promenaded 97 miles up the Devon coast.

The guessing game was now in full swing and there was barely a beast or bird, alive or extinct, which was not designated by some letter-writer as the perpetrator of the prints. The list read alphabetically from auk to zebra. In between, there were giant leaping rats, gargantuan rabbits, bears walking upright, escaped circus dromedaries, migrant penguins, and even an aurochs, an outsized bison that hadn't been seen alive since the Middle Ages. None of the sponsors offered any idea as to what might have become of the animal *after* it had completed its nocturnal jaunt.

Most of the guesswork wasn't worth printing; but the far-flung interest did arouse more astute speculation. An English lecturer at Heidelberg University wrote to the *London Illustrated News* that he had discussed the puzzle with a Russian colleague. The Russian had told him that similar prints had appeared several times along the Galician border in Poland and that the local peasants wouldn't follow them or even go near them, since they belonged to some unknown creature.

Another reader drew attention to an account left by the Antarctic explorer, Sir James Ross, some 15 years earlier. In May, 1840, Captain Ross's ships anchored off Kerguelen Island, a bleak and inhospitable rock lying northeast of the Antarctic circle, and believed to be inhabited only by seals. A surveying party put ashore came across "singular footsteps belonging to an ass or a pony" which the search group tried to follow, only to lose sight of the prints on rocky ground. According to Ross, the marks were "three inches in length and two and a half in breadth, having a small and deeper depression on each side, and the shape of a horseshoe."

Kerguelen, now a French possession, has been thoroughly charted. But no beast that might have left such hoofprints has been encountered there. In fact, there is no sub-antarctic animal who would leave such hoofmarks.

The "devil's hoof marks" never again appeared in Devonshire, nor in any other locale in the British Isles. Nobody so far has been able to establish even the frailest of links between the baffling hoofprints found in Eastern Europe, and those found on the fringe of Antarctica, and those seen in southern England. Perhaps there is no such link.

REPORT OF FOOTMARKS IN DEVONSHIRE   In a letter to the "Illustrated London News," dated February 24, 1855, there appeared this eyewitness account of the strange footprints in Devonshire. The writer, who claims to have spent five months in the backwoods of Canada, cannot think of any bird or beast that might have left such a trail. The writer also discounts any disfiguring effects on the tracks caused by atmospheric changes.

(This facsimile and the others which follow are enlargements of the original text in the "Illustrated London News" which were printed to a width of three inches.)

FOOT-MARKS ON THE SNOW, IN DEVON.

(From a Correspondent.)

As many of your readers have perused, I have no doubt, with much interest, the paragraph which appeared in several of the papers of last week, relative to the mysterious foot-marks left upon the snow during the night of Thursday, the 8th, in the parishes of Exmouth, Lympstone, and Woodbury, as also in Dawlish, Torquay, Totnes, and other places on the other side of the estuary of the Exe, in the county of Devon, extending over a tract of country of thirty or forty miles, or probably more; and as the paragraph I allude to does not fully detail the mysterious affair, it may probably be interesting to many to have a more particular account—which I think this unusual occurrence well deserves.

The marks which appeared on the snow (which lay very thinly on the ground at the time), and which were seen on the Friday morning, to all appearance were the perfect impression of a donkey's hoof—the length 4 inches by 2¾ inches; but, instead of progressing as that animal would have done (or indeed as any other would have done), feet right and left, it appeared that foot had followed foot, in a *single line;* the distance from each tread being eight inches, or rather more—the foot-marks in every parish being exactly the same size, and the steps the same length. This mysterious visitor generally only passed *once* down or across each garden or courtyard, and did so in nearly all the houses in many parts of the several towns above mentioned, as also in the farms scattered about; this regular track passing in some instances over the roofs of houses, and hayricks, and very high walls (one fourteen feet), without displacing the snow on either side or altering the distance between the feet, and passing on as if the wall had not been any impediment. The gardens with high fences or walls, and gates locked, were equally visited as those open and unprotected. Now, when we consider the distance that must have been gone over to have left these marks—I may say in almost every garden, on door-steps, through the extensive woods of Luscombe, upon commons, in enclosures and farms—the actual progress must have exceeded a hundred miles. It is very easy for people to laugh at these appearances, and account for them in an idle way.

At present no satisfactory solution has been given. No known animal could have traversed this extent of country in one night, besides having to cross an estuary of the sea two miles broad. Neither does any known animal walk in a *line* of single footsteps, not even man.

Birds could not have left these marks, as no bird's foot leaves the impression of a hoof, or, even were there a bird capable of doing so, could it proceed in the direct manner above stated—nor would birds, even had they donkeys' feet, confine themselves to one direct line, but hop here and there; but the nature of the mark at once sets aside its being the track of a bird. The effect of the atmosphere upon these marks is given by many as a solution; but how could it be possible for the atmosphere to affect one impression and not another? On the morning that the above was observed the snow bore the fresh marks of cats, dogs, rabbits, birds, and men clearly defined. Why, then, should a continuous track, far more clearly defined—so clearly, even, that the raising in the centre of the frog of the foot could be plainly seen—why then should this particular mark be the only one which was affected by the atmosphere, and all the others left as they were? Besides, the most singular circumstance connected with it was, that this particular mark removed the snow, wherever it appeared, clear, as if cut with a diamond or branded with a hot iron;—of course I am not alluding to its appearance after having been trampled on, or meddled with by the curious in and about the thoroughfares of the towns. In one instance this track entered a covered shed, and passed through it out of a broken part of the wall at the other end, where the atmosphere could not affect it.

The writer of the above has passed a five months' winter in the backwoods of Canada, and has had much experience in tracking wild animals and birds upon the snow, and can safely say, he has never seen a more clearly-defined track, or one that appeared to be less altered by the atmosphere than the one in question. Marks left upon thin snow especially may after a time blur a little, but never lose their distinctive character, as every one will know who has been accustomed to follow the track of the American partridge.

Should you think the above likely to interest your readers, or draw from any of them a better solution of this most singular occurrence than has at present been given, perhaps you will allow it a place in your most interesting journal. I send you a copy of the foot, taken from the snow, and also a succession of the steps, to show you the manner of progressing.   SOUTH DEVON.

PROFESSOR OWEN'S LETTER   Addressed to the "Illustrated London News" by the highly esteemed naturalist, Richard Owen—who hadn't seen the actual prints—the writer baldly declares that the prints were made by a badger. In the second-last paragraph Mr. Owen accuses "the assertor" of failing to go over the ground "with a power of acute and unbiased observation"—a quality the great naturalist himself seems to have scuttled.

THE ILLUSTRATED LONDON NEWS

[MARCH 3, 1855.

PROFESSOR OWEN ON THE FOOT-MARKS IN THE SNOW IN DEVON.

(*To the Editor of the* ILLUSTRATED LONDON NEWS.)

AN esteemed zoological friend has submitted to me a carefully-executed drawing of one of the more perfect impressions left in the snow at Luscombe, South Devon, on or about the 8th of last month. It was of the hind-foot of a Badger. This is almost the only plantigrade quadruped we have in this island, and leaves a foot-print larger than would be supposed from its size. The Sketch, of which you have given a Cut in p. 187 (Feb. 24th), gives a correct general idea of the shape and proportions of these foot-prints, but without the indications of the pads on the sole, and the five small claws, which the drawing sent to me exhibited. Such perfect foot-prints were rare, because those of the fore and hind-foot are commonly more or less blended together, producing the appearance of a line of single footsteps; which appearance, if a bear had been abroad in the five winter months spent by your Correspondent in Canada, would have shown him was not peculiar to the foot-steps of man, but characteristic of other plantigrade mammalia, though they may be quadrupedal. The badger sleeps a good deal in his winter retreat, but does not hibernate so regularly and completely as the bear does in the severer climate of Canada. The badger is nocturnal, and comes abroad occasionally in the late winter, when hard-pressed by cold and hunger: it is a stealthy prowler, and most active and enduring in its quest of food.

That one and the same animal should have gone over 100 miles of a most devious and irregular route in one night is as improbable as that one badger only should have been awake and hungry out of the number concealed in the 100 miles of rocky and bosky Devonshire which has been startled by the impressions revealed by the rarely-spread carpet of snow in that beautiful county.

The onus of the proof that one creature made them in one night rests with the assertor, who ought to have gone over the same ground, with a power of acute and unbiassed observation, which seems not to have been exercised by him who failed to distinguish the truly single from the blended foot-prints in question.

Nothing seems more difficult than to see a thing as it really is, unless it be the right interpretation of observed phenomena.   RICHARD OWEN.

I HAVE read with great interest the paragraph in your last publication giving an account of the most extraordinary prints in the snow, which have occasioned such excitement and fomented so melancholy a mass of superstitious folly in the villages lying southward of Exeter, on either side of the river Exe.

Permit me, however, to state that the outline accompanying your intelligent Correspondent's recital of the circumstances hardly conveys a correct idea of the prints in question. As an amateur accustomed to make most accurate drawings from nature, I set to work soon after these marks appeared and completed the accompanying exact fac-simile of those that were visible on the lawn of our clergyman's garden in this parish. He and I traced them through a low privet hedge, by a circular opening of one foot diameter. On applying a rule, the interval between each impression was found to be undeviatingly eight inches and a half. On the same day a mutual acquaintance, familiar with natural history, and not long since returned from the Pacific Ocean, measured the intervals between similar prints in his garden, above a mile and a half distant from the Rectory, and found it to be exactly eight inches and a half. This, in my opinion, is one of the most remarkable and confounding circumstances we have to deal with.

In the course of a few days a report was circulated that a couple of kangaroos had got loose from a private menagerie (Mr. Fische's, I believe) at Sidmouth. Few of us had had opportunities of seeing the impression made on sand or loam by the hinder feet, or hocks rather, on which this animal sits; and we were not unwilling to give credence to the suggestion that the exotic quadruped (walking, when it does walk, as a biped; but bounding over vast lengths of space more like a chamois) might have been loose and vagrant in the neighbourhood, and left the strange impress here referred to. Still, it was quite inexplicable that the animal, considering the scale of the foot, should leave, in single file, one print only, and, as has been already observed, with intervals as exactly preserved as if the prints had been made by a drill, or any other mechanical frame.

A scientific acquaintance informed me of his having traced the same prints across a field up to a hay-stack. The surface of the stack was wholly free from marks of any kind, but on the opposite side of the stack, in a direction exactly corresponding with the track thus traced, the prints began again! The same fact has been ascertained in respect of a wall intervening.

No animal with cushion paw, such as the feline tribe—diminutive or large (cat or tiger)—exhibit, could have made these marks; for the feet of most quadrupeds tread in parallel lines, some widely divaricated, others approximating very closely. The ass, especially, among the animals daily seen, approaches the single line. The fox leaves round dots in a single line; the stoat two and one alternately. Moreover, the feline tribe leave concave prints; whereas, in each of these mystic prints, the space enclosed by the bounding line was convex, as in the print of a patten.

Early in the week we were informed that two cranes had been shot at Otterton, below Budleigh Salterton, and that these were the mystical printers; but the well-informed in zoology at once rejected this offered explanation. Within the last four-and-twenty hours, a very shrewd and intellectual neighbour of mine, about six miles distant, wrote me word that a gentleman in the parish adjoining his own had traced these peculiar prints through his garden-walks into a six-inch gutter, and there he saw the marks of *claws*. This has induced some to suppose them to be the track of a catamountain. Two other gentlemen, resident in the same parish, pursued a line of prints during three hours and a half, marking their progress under gooseberry-bushes and espalier fruit-trees; and then, missing them, regained sight of the impression on the roofs of some houses to which their march of investigation brought them. These gentlemen "swear to claws." Upon which my correspondent (a member of the Society of Antiquaries) observes, "We incline to believe they must be otters', driven out in quest of food. Our friend felt toe-marks at the contracted part of the print, though they were not discernible by the eye."

Some "chiel amang" the congregation where I was discoursing three Sundays since had evidently been "taking notes, and, faith! he prented them" (as Burns would say); and though, without incurring the charge of the slightest approach to irreverence, I found a very apt opportunity to mention the name of kangaroo, in allusion to the report then current. I certainly did not pin my faith to that version of the mystery, nor call upon others to receive it *ex cathedrâ*; but the state of the public mind of the villagers, the labourers, their wives and children, and old crones, and trembling old men, dreading to stir out after sunset, or to go out half a mile into lanes or by-ways, on a call or message, under the conviction that this was the Devil's walk, and none other, and that it was wicked to trifle with such a manifest proof of the Great Enemy's immediate presence, rendered it very desirable that a turn should be given to such degrading and vitiated notion of a superintending Divine Providence; and I was thankful that a kangaroo was "in the wind," as we should say, and serving to disperse ideas so derogatory to a christianised, but assuredly most unenlightened community. I was reminded, nevertheless, by one pertinacious recusant, that it is written that Satan should be unchained for a thousand years, and that the latter days are at hand. Still, mine was a word in due season, and did good.

The generality of such of us as can reason dispassionately on view of a phenomenon which seems, as yet, to be without precedent or parallel, incline to believe it must be a bird of some unfamiliar tribe, wandering and hopping over this region: but all inquiry seems to be fruitless. I have addressed communications to the British Museum, to the Zoological Society, to the keepers of birds and beasts in the Regent's-park menagerie; and the universal reply is, they are utterly unable to form any conjecture on the subject, however correctly the impressions had been copied.

I am emboldened to address you with more than the ordinary confidence of a correspondent " well up in his facts," inasmuch as I am living in the centre of the district where the alarm, so to speak, was first given. Sir L. Newman's Park, at Mamhead, is exactly opposite to my own residence. Starcross Tower is an object of the picturesque, and beautiful to gaze upon from my study window; and Powderham Castle gleams in the sunshine, half a mile further up. These are on the other side (west) of the river Exe, two miles in its breadth; and the marks were as abundant throughout the places just specified, and their neighbourhood—Kenton, Dawlish, Newton, &c.—as here at Exmouth, Withecombe Ralegh, Lympstone, Woodbury, Topsham, and the vicinity of Bicton, and Budleigh. There are many "travelled men," and deep-thinkers, too, among us, far from being

Credulous to false prints

(as *Isabella* says to *Angelo*); but—eager as we are to ascertain the exact point of knowledge in natural history at which the elucidation of this unprecedented mystery might commence—our anxiety as zoologists, or as students or connoisseurs in any one of the λογοι (or sciences), is a feeling of apathetic indifference in comparison with our regret for the prevalence and evil-working of that gross and incredible superstition which is raging like endemic disease among the lowest class in every direction; and I shall have every cause to rejoice, if, on view of what has now been laid before you by pen and pencil, any one of your numerous readers and abler contributors should succeed in solving the difficulty, and remove thereby a dangerous, degrading, and false impression.

Withecombe, near Exmouth.   G. M. M.

REPORT FROM "THE TIMES," DATED MARCH 6, 1855
The excitement caused by the mysterious footprints is evident in this story.

THE MYSTERIOUS FOOTPRINTS IN DEVONSHIRE. —The interest in this matter has scarcely yet subsided, many inquiries still being made into the origin of the footprints which caused so much consternation on the morning of the 8th ult. In addition to the circumstances mentioned in *The Times* a little while since, it may be stated that at Dawlish a number of persons sallied out armed with guns and other weapons for the purpose, if possible, of discovering and destroying the animal which was supposed to have been so busy in multiplying its footmarks. As might have been expected, the party returned as they went. Various speculations have been made as to the cause of the footprints. Some have asserted that they are those of a kangaroo, while others affirm that they are the impressions of the claws of some large birds driven on shore by stress of weather. On more than one occasion reports have been circulated that an animal from a menagery has been caught; but the matter at present is as much involved in mystery as ever it was.

ACCOUNT IN "THE TIMES" OF LONDON OF FEB. 16, 1855
This story concerning Reverend Musgrave's sermon on the Devon-
shire hoof prints alludes to his suggestion that they might be those
of a kangaroo.

EXTRAORDINARY OCCURRENCE.—Considerable sensation has been caused in the towns of Topsham, Lympstone, Exmouth, Teignmouth, and Dawlish, in the south of
Devon, in consequence of the discovery of a vast number of
foot-tracks of a most strange and mysterious description.
The superstitious go so far as to believe that they are the
marks of Satan himself; and that great excitement has
been produced among all classes may be judged of from the
fact that the subject has been descanted on from the pulpit.
It appears that, on Thursday night last, there was a very
heavy fall of snow in the neighbourhood of Exeter and the
south of Devon. On the following morning the inhabitants
of the above towns were surprised at discovering the foot-
marks of some strange and mysterious animal, endowed
with the power of ubiquity, as the footprints were to be
seen in all kinds of unaccountable places—on the tops of
houses and narrow walls, in gardens and courtyards, enclosed by high walls and palings, as well as in open fields.
There was hardly a garden in Lympstone where these footprints
were not observable. The track appeared more like that of a
biped than a quadruped, and the steps were generally eight
inches in advance of each other. The impression of the
foot closely resembled that of a donkey's shoe, and measured
from an inch and a-half to (in some instances) two and a-half
inches across. Here and there it appeared as if cloven, but in
the generality of the steps the shoe was continuous, and,
from the snow in the centre remaining entire, merely showing the outer crest of the foot, it must have been convex.
The creature seems to have approached the doors of
several houses, and then to have retreated, but no one has
been able to discover the standing or resting point of this
mysterious visitor. On Sunday last the Rev. Mr. Musgrave
alluded to the subject in his sermon, and suggested the possibility of the footprints being those of a kangaroo; but this
could scarcely have been the case, as they were found on
both sides of the estuary of the Exe. At present it remains
a mystery, and many superstitious people in the above towns
are actually afraid to go outside their doors after night.

EDITORIAL IN THE "INVERNESS COURIER"   The "Illustrated London News" reprinted this contemporary editorial from a
Scottish newspaper in its issue of March 10, 1855.

WE find the following in the *Inverness Courier:*—" The footprints seen in this neighbourhood were traced for a considerable way across
the fields, and at the Longman, and again at the Crown, near the house
of Abertarff. Many of our townsmen went to see the phenomenon, and one
brought home a lump of the snow, in which the foot-prints were strongly impressed, exhibiting it as a very curious and mysterious occurrence. The cloven
hoof had an ominous and by no means prepossessing look! Fortunately, however, an observant naturalist had already examined the foot-prints and decided
the point. Some animal, probably a hare or polecat, had traversed the field at
a gallop with its feet close together. The paws had become slightly filled with
snow, so that only the round form was impressed, and the open space between
them left a slightly-raised and pointed mark like the centre of a cloven hoof.
This gentleman followed the track till, on ascending a slope, the animal appeared to have slackened its pace to a trot, and then left upon the snow distinct
impressions of its four feet. Further on, the animal seems to have sat down on
the snow, and again its four feet were distinctly traced. Nothing more was de-
sired—the mystery was traced.

LETTER BY THOMAS FOX   This letter appeared in the "Illustrated London News" of March 10, 1855, accompanied by drawings
which purported that the strange footprints were those of a leaping
rat.

BALLINGDON, near Sudbury, Suffolk, March 3, 1855.

The foot-marks described by your Devon Correspondent are made, in my opinion, by the poor despised and insignificant rat. My brother lives in a house a quarter of a mile from Sudbury, surrounded by fields and gardens: he called my attention to the foot-marks of rats about his garden, and we found they had laid siege to his potato clamp. Tracing the depredators, he exclaimed, the Devonshire donkey has been here! and, on examination, I found the foot-marks exactly to agree with those described in the ILLUSTRATED LONDON NEWS for last week. We found the marks of no other mammalia, except of the rabbit, and no one would suppose they could all be made by the same kind of animal. The snow being drifted, and, consequently, of varying depths, afforded me an opportunity of observing the cause

of the variety of the foot-marks. Where the snow was only one inch deep, marks were very distinct: in one they were caused by the rat walking slowly on all his toes; in another track he is evidently trespassing on the heel, as does the bear, the rabbit, and the squirrel; in another track the donkey-shoe form is more clearly defined, which is caused by the snow being deeper. The rat is an expert climber, though far inferior to the squirrel, whose conformation his greatly resembles: they are provided with a very powerful but short forearm, the muscles of which are strongly developed.

It is well known that when these little animals leap or bound along they alight upon their four feet very close together, and the large muscles of their short arm cause the *ulnæ* to be far apart and nearly touching the ground, and in their descent form in the snow the semi-circular part of the donkey shoe; and the toes of the hind-feet approaching near to the *ulnæ* or elbows of the forearm, complete it by forming its two sides. The impression between the heels and the shoe is made by the rat's tail. I should have said the distance from the toe of one impression to the heel of the preceding one was eight inches. THOMAS FOX.

———

LETTER BY JABEZ ALLIES *In his communication to the "Illustrated London News," dated March 3, 1855, the writer suggests the footprints were ornithological in origin.*

THE FOOT-MARKS IN THE SNOW, IN DEVON.

(We select the following from several additional communications upon this inquiry) :—

In addition to what I said in my letter of the 28th ultimo, relative to the " Foot-marks in the Snow in Devon," it appears to me that, as the " snow lay very thinly on the ground at the time," as stated by your Correspondent, such was the reason why the inner part of the tracks was not so clearly defined as the outer part of them ; therefore the outline reversed would look like a donkey's track, as stated in my previous letter ; and I presume the heel of the tracks has been taken for the forepart of them.

If birds made the tracks, they probably were either web-footed ones or waders—most likely the latter, as they could run much swifter and better across the country.

Dr. Buckland, in his " Bridgewater Treatise," vol. ii.. p. 39, in speaking of tracks in new red sandstone, set forth in plate 26A of that work, says—" None of the footsteps appear to be those of web-footed birds ; they most nearly resemble those of Grallæ (waders), or birds whose habits resemble those of Grallæ. The impressions of three toes are usually distinct, except in a few instances ; that of the fourth or hind-toe is mostly wanting, as in the footsteps of modern Grallæ."

Now, if the foot-marks in the snow were made by waders, the shallowness of the snow is a sufficient reason why the impression of the fourth or hind-toe was not made (as in the cases noticed by Dr. Buckland), and with respect to web-footed birds their hind-toe is very small.

The size of the tracks in the snow—namely, four inches by two inches and three quarters—shows that they must have been made by very large birds (if they are attributable to them), and the probability is that some waders were frozen out by the severity of the weather from the shores of the rivers or estuaries of the sea, and that they ran over South Devon in the night of the 8th ult. in search of food, and afterwards mounted aloft, as cranes do, before the dawn of day.

If the bird theory is correct, perhaps some one skilled in ornithology may, from the size of the tracks, and the distance (eight inches) of the stride between them, give some idea what species of bird it was.

Tivoli House, Cheltenham, 3rd March, 1855.   JABEZ ALLIES.

EDITORIAL IN "BRIGHTON GUARDIAN" *This editorial, which appeared on February 29, 1855, was reported in the "Illustrated London News" of March 10, 1855.*

We agree with a Correspondent that the following attempted solution, from the *Brighton Guardian* of Feb. 29, between its jest and earnest, is calculated to envelop the subject in deeper mystery :—

Is it not possible—nay, probable—that these are the footsteps of that animal so accurately described by Biom Heriolfson, the Icelandic navigator, who visited the coasts of Labrador, A.D. 1001, and to whom, with Lief, Baron Humboldt, in his "Cosmos," attributes the discovery of America ? The records of this event are both numerous and authentic, and have received ample confirmation from the researches of Rafn, the greatest Northern scholar of our times. Biom Heriolfson describes an animal, which he terms the Unipede, or Uniped, as having a foot similar to that represented by the copy given in the ILLUSTRATED LONDON NEWS, with the exception of an almost imperceptible division in the outer and inner circles of the hoof. The character of the limb was, in his opinion, a stranger phenomenon than its singleness, for it partook rather of that of a quadruped than of that of a bird. He informs us that the wings appeared to radiate from the middle of the back with the feathers spreading out in a manner similar to those in the tail of a peacock ; but they were slightly divided into two equal parts when the bird was in motion. Moreover, the uniped had the power, when alarmed or excited, of erecting a single crest of feathers above the head so peculiar and striking that an opinion prevailed among the learned of Iceland that this animal was the unicorn, hitherto considered fabulous. Let it be remembered that the inhabitants of Iceland, during the eleventh, twelfth, and thirteenth centuries, created and maintained, amidst its snows and volcanic fires, a literature which would have honoured the happiest climes of Europe. Biom Heriolfson, in completing his description of the uniped, states that the organs of vision approximated so closely that they had the appearance of a double eye. This bird, he affirms, flew, or rather ran, with incredible swiftness, touching the ground frequently and at equal distances. Thus the footsteps would be in a direct line. In conclusion, your readers may rest assured that the dimension of the tail of the uniped is just one half of that of a great dodo.

*WRITER EXPLAINS SOURCE OF FOOTPRINTS   In the issue
of the "Illustrated London News" of March 3, 1855, this correspondent from Topsham proposes that the prints were made by an otter.*

As much interest has been excited by these extraordinary foot-tracks, I beg to offer you a few remarks in explanation of what I have observed in this neighbourhood (Topsham).   Myself and another medical friend bestowed considerable time in endeavouring to discover the peculiarities of this most singular impression.   The outline, certainly, in all cases resembles that of a hoof, which has given rise to the idea of its supernatural origin among the ignorant; but, on more minute examination of the tracks, we could distinctly see the impressions of the toes and pad of the foot of an animal; a rough draft of which I showed to a friend of mine in Exeter, and, without any comment on my part, he recognised it as that of the otter, being well acquainted with that animal and its habits.

I have enclosed you a rough Diagram of the impressions which we observed within the hoof-like tracks; the outside toes were larger than the rest.   I am not acquainted with the otter myself; but of this I am fully convinced, that the animal, be it what it may, is of low stature, from the tracks having shown it to have passed uninterruptedly under the branches of shrubs, &c., not more than eight or nine inches from the ground; and in a neighbouring village it went through a six-inch pipe drain.   It must be borne in mind that most rivers have been frozen over for some weeks, and therefore the otters have thus been prevented from obtaining their usual food—namely fish; and when such is the case, they ramble many miles in search of other food.

The otter is not a rare animal in this neighbourhood, and frequents the streams near Exmouth, Lympstone, Woodbury, Budleigh, Topsham, Clyst, the river Exe (in all which parishes tracks have been seen), as well as Dawlish, Torquay, Totnes, &c.   The tracks in this parish we observed going in contrary directions; we did not notice any in a direct line, but in alternate steps, forming two parallel lines of steps.   We also saw tracks on a low wall, and over the tiles of a linhay, and in several instances it had visited the summer-houses and tool-houses of gardens; in all of which portions of the same characteristics were more or less traceable, the ball or pad in the centre being more frequent than the others.   Its visits have been repeated in some localities of this town.

Topsham, Feb. 26th, 1855.

LETTER TO THE "ILLUSTRATED LONDON NEWS" OF MARCH 3, 1855   Here the writer offers the conclusive opinion that the footmarks were made by the humble toad.

Saint Mary's Church, Torquay, Devon, 3rd March, 1855.

Having seen in the ILLUSTRATED LONDON NEWS sketches of the foot-prints made in the snow in this neighbourhood by some animal unknown, and as various conjectures are made as to what animal has thus travelled over fields and gardens, and after going clean over housetops has not been stayed by a tidal river two miles wide, I send you an attempted explanation of the affair. There are certain times and seasons for the pairing and breeding of animals accurately fixed by Nature. The green plover is frequently caught in the snow in Scotland after his arrival in that country, and he must bear it as best he can, and why should not other animals have to face the snow-flake in the breeding season, and have to travel a weary way before they can make their beds and lay them down in peace? This, I am persuaded, is the hard fate of the animal who has caused such unwonted prints upon the snow in Devon; Is a infer from the simple fact of finding the marks of the animal first, and then finding the carcass with the evident marks of a violent and sudden death in the track. It was neither bird nor beast that made the marks, but a reptile; not only putting his feet and claws (for he had claws) to the ground, but his belly too; hence the puzzle of the large print made in a line by his four feet and his belly all at once, every time he hopped. At the twenty-first milestone from Exeter, and third from Torquay, a large toad was found by me in the turnpike-road, crushed to death by a carriage-wheel; the track of the same was well defined for some distance along the road, and was exactly as described by your Correspondents and illustrated by you.

The time for frogs and toads to spawn in Devon is rather earlier than in the north. Frogs are scarce here, but toads are not; and as Shaldon village lies against a steep hill, the houses admit toads to travel over them easily; and all toads that are to breed must travel to the water to do so, be the distance more or less; and as nobody turned out this unfortunate toad to seek his mate and meet his death, it has no doubt been the fate of others like him to have had a trip on the snow-flake.   ALEX. FORSYTH.

EDITOR'S NOTE   After this book was set, the news item on this page appeared in the "Times" of London in the issue of Tuesday, January 16, 1968— striking evidence of the continued interest in the mystery of the strange hoofprints encountered in Devonshire over a century ago.

THE TIMES TUESDAY JANUARY 16 1968

THE COURSE OF NATURE

DEVIL'S HOOFMARK —BY A MOUSE?

MYSTERY IN SNOW 113 YEARS AGO

FROM A CORRESPONDENT

The exhibition of footprints of famous people in a factory safety campaign hardly breaks new ground: years ago the wild animals and birds of Britain won the distinction of a public display of their footprints, when Mr. Alfred Leutscher, the Essex naturalist, wrote a book on the subject, complete with footprint photographs and drawings from nature.

One file in Mr. Leutscher's records on animal footprints has now grown bulky—that labelled "Devil's Hoofmarks". His explanation that a wood mouse could have caused the mysterious hoofprints in the snow which caused such a sensation in Devon long ago has not gone unchallenged by some observers, though it is generally accepted as a highly likely theory in weightier scientific quarters.

That Devon affair, reported in The Times of February 16, 1855, became almost a legend, and still is. Footprints were found at Topsham, Lympstone, Exmouth, and other places which might well have been made by an abominable snow dwarf. They resembled the imprint of a small hoof about 2¼in. across: superstitious people at once saw them as the marks of Satan himself, for sometimes they were even cloven.

The creature seemed to have approached doors and then gone away. Its imprints went up and along walls, over roofs, across high-walled courtyards, and vanished at the foot of walls only to reappear at the other side: clearly the devil could walk straight through a solid wall. People became afraid to go out at night, a local parson spoke reassuringly on the matter from the pulpit, and an armed party sallied out from Dawlish to settle the hash of the mysterious stranger. "As might be expected, the party returned as they went", was the dry comment of The Times report.

Many other theories

Many other theories have been put forward since Mr. Leutscher gave his explanation, ranging from a kangaroo to a mooring ring trailing on a rope attached to an escaped balloon. The critic who pointed out that the Devon imprints covered about 100 miles and that this was an impossible feat for one small animal, invited the reply that there was no reason whatever to assume a single animal was responsible, in a county where the wood mouse is abundant.

Mr. Leutscher put his theory to the London Zoological Society: he pointed out that an animal when hopping lands with all four feet in a bunch, and in soft snow, especially when it is melting, the result is a U-shaped impression — the "devil's" footprint. There is only one British animal small enough to have made those Devon tracks—the wood mouse, which can certainly climb and leap. Mr. Leutscher has in fact found wood mouse footprints in snow in Epping Forest near his home which exactly conform to the sketches of the Devon imprints.

Things in the Sky

Back in 1952, when I was a young and comparatively innocent reporter on an Australian newspaper, I saw what appeared to be the most dramatic snap ever taken of a Flying Saucer. It was being offered for sale by an understandably excited photographer from the Sydney suburb of Balmain, who claimed to have taken the picture while the thing was hovering just a few feet over his roof.

The picture showed a gleaming white object which looked like a piece of crockery. There were three rows of portholes plainly visible, with something that looked like a termite's antenna waving on top. Definitely the stuff tabloid front pages are made of.

However, before buying the shot, the editors decided to dispatch a fact-finding commission to the scene of the sighting. Fifty per cent of the commission consisted of me. The other half was a veteran crime reporter, 300-odd pounds of beef and bristle, with eyes that could curdle fresh milk. And while I, agog with enthusiasm, was busily scribbling atmosphere notes, my partner surveyed the landscape with the bleakest skepticism.

He pulled the photographer aside and placed a paw the size of a ham on his shoulder. "You know, mate," he said amiably, "if this turns out to be a hoax, I'll wring your bloody neck."

The gentleman promptly turned the color of yogurt, mumbled something about a joke being a joke and, anyway, so help him, he wouldn't have accepted any money for the picture. The Flying Saucer, it turned out, was a modernistic Danish lampshade, appropriately painted, and rigged up above his roof by invisible wires.

My reason for relating this banal episode is that it contains, in a nutshell, most of the factors that drive serious researchers to distraction. Here was a hoaxer—and there must be hundreds of the breed—hoping to cash in on a matter of intense public concern. Here was an eager reporter (me) ready to swallow every blessed word of the yarn. The exposure, of course, tended to cast doubts on the authenticity of *any* sightings and on *any* photographs of any Flying Saucer.

Usually in these matters there is the crank element. Let anyone breathe the word "saucer" and up will pop some citizen who might even claim to have ridden in a weird space vehicle, steered by little green men with pink eyes, who conversed fluently in pig-Latin.

In that same year of 1952, a record total of 1,501 skyborne "something" were reported from places as far apart as Scotland and St. Helena. Since systematic counting began in 1949, more than 10,000 sightings have been noted, "seen" by close to a quarter of a million spectators.

Only 58 per cent of the objects reported were of a disk shape; the rest were said to look like a huge cigar or like an egg or like a floating dome. This makes the journalistic tag "Flying Saucer" misleading. The U.S. Air Force settled on the much more valid label of "Unidentified Flying Object" or UFO.

But whatever name we bestow on these hovering or zooming whatizits, the UFOs constitute the most controversial phenomenon in the world today. UFOs have brought about a unique situation: hundreds of thousands of people claim to have seen something which hundreds of thousands of other people insist do not exist.

The first vague reports of UFO sightings came from Sweden, Norway, and France shortly after the end of World War II. The reports received fairly wide publicity in the European press, but caused hardly a stir in America.

Then, on June 24, 1947, a young businessman named Kenneth Arnold was piloting his private plane above Mount Rainier, Washington, when he saw, clearly outlined against the snow-covered mountain, nine silvery disks flying in formation at very high speed. After landing at Yakima airport, Arnold reported what he had seen—or thought he had

KENNETH ARNOLD   In June, 1947 this Idaho businessman made the first recorded report of a UFO sighting in America. Arnold described the object as "saucer-shaped," after which newspapers promptly coined the term "Flying Saucer."

seen—using the term "saucer-shaped" to describe the objects. Newspapers immediately pounced on the story, and the term "Flying Saucers" was born.

A surprising number of people believed that Arnold had conceived the shape of his disks from reading H. G. Wells' *War of the Worlds*. But in that pioneer science-fiction classic, the Martian invaders didn't actually fly at all; they were shot to earth in giant projectiles, and they then proceeded to conquer the earth with their three-legged walking "fighting machines."

Arnold's experience unleashed an epidemic of saucer-sightings throughout the United States. The skeptics dubbed the rash of reports as "discomania," and almost laughed the UFO believers out of existence. Mass delusions, after all, were nothing particularly new. A few centuries earlier, much larger segments of the population had been constantly seeing horned devils, ghosts, witches on broomsticks, werewolves, and vast assortments of leprechauns.

In August 1914, half a million otherwise sober Londoners swore that Russian troops had marched through their city, clearly recognizable as such because they "had snow on their boots," and this in spite of the fact that the nearest Russian soldier was 1,100 miles east of the British capital.

As recently as 1938, a radio broadcast by Orson Welles about spacemen resulted in thousands of New Yorkers "seeing" Martians in the streets, and phoning the police to come to the rescue. In certain sections of the Metropolitan area, terror ran rampant and some people even prepared to evacuate. No credibility gap here.

The tendency among more sophisticated Americans was to regard "discomania" as a form of summer sickness, and to predict that the fever would wane with the approach of fall. However, instead of petering out, the rash of UFO sightings increased. Reports of flying objects kept pouring in at a rate of 15 to 20 per week; and along with the reports, came a steady trickle of pictures. Taken mostly by amateur photographers, these snaps ranged in quality from the dimmest blurs to remarkably vivid pictures of — what? Some photos showed flashing streaks which resembled comets or fireballs; others, flat discs, hanging in the sky at a slant; still others, resembled ironing boards. A few looked like inverted cones.

Radio Listeners in Panic, Taking War Drama as Fact

Many Flee Homes to Escape 'Gas Raid From Mars'—Phone Calls Swamp Police at Broadcast of Wells Fantasy

A wave of mass hysteria seized thousands of radio listeners throughout the nation between 8:15 and 9:30 o'clock last night when a broadcast of a dramatization of H. G. Wells's fantasy, "The War of the Worlds," led thousands to believe that an interplanetary conflict had started with invading Martians spreading wide death and destruction in New Jersey and New York.

The broadcast, which disrupted households, interrupted religious services, created traffic jams and clogged communications systems, was made by Orson Welles, who as the radio character, "The Shadow," used to give "the creeps" to countless child listeners. This time at least a score of adults required medical treatment for shock and hysteria.

In Newark, in a single block at Heddon Terrace and Hawthorne Avenue, more than twenty families rushed out of their houses with wet handkerchiefs and towels over their faces to flee from what they believed was to be a gas raid. Some began moving household furniture.

Throughout New York families left their homes, some to flee to near-by parks. Thousands of persons called the police, newspapers and radio stations here and in other cities of the United States and Canada seeking advice on protective measures against the raids.

The program was produced by Mr. Welles and the Mercury Theatre on the Air over station WABC and the Columbia Broadcasting System's coast-to-coast network, from 8 to 9 o'clock.

The radio play, as presented, was to simulate a regular radio program with a "break-in" for the material of the play. The radio listeners, apparently, missed or did not listen to the introduction, which was: "The Columbia Broadcasting System and its affiliated stations present Orson Welles and the Mercury Theatre on the Air in 'The War of the Worlds' by H. G. Wells."

They also failed to associate the program with the newspaper listing of the program, announced as "Today: 8:00-9:00—Play: H. G. Wells's 'War of the Worlds'—WABC." They ignored three additional announcements made during the broadcast emphasizing its fictional nature

Mr. Welles opened the program with a description of the series of

Continued on Page Four

ORSON WELLES   The young director, who in a broadcast dramatized H. G. Wells' "War of the Worlds" and caused panic among his radio listeners, is surrounded the following day by reporters who question him about the startling reaction of the public. Mr. Welles expressed regret that so many of the radio audience had been led to believe that the earth was being invaded by Martians. Above is the report that appeared in the New York Times of Monday, October 31, 1938.

Soon, there was hardly a newspaper or magazine in the United States that had not run several saucer pictures, along with a saucer story.

With this publicity there grew a sense of trepidation, the Cold War becoming chillier every day. What if these things stirring around above us were Russian reconnaissance machines of a hitherto unknown type?

While speculation was raging, the Pentagon and the U.S. Air Force maintained a poker-faced neutrality. They would neither admit nor deny the existence of UFOs. The Air Force went to some pains to point out that most of the sightings involved untrained spectators who could have mistaken any number of aerial manifestations for flying objects; the reports "were simple misinterpretations of natural phenomena." This verdict, presumably, applied to the photographs as well.

But what if the observers were themselves airmen? In May, 1948, two Eastern Air Lines pilots flying a DC-3 had a startling encounter with this "natural phenomenon." Captain C. S. Chiles, a veteran with thousands of flying hours, sighted what he described as a wingless aircraft, 100 feet long, shaped like a cigar, and without any protruding surfaces. "Whatever it was," Chiles reported, "it flashed down toward us, and we veered off to the left. It veered to its left and passed up about 700 feet to our right and a little above us. Then, as if the pilot had seen us and wanted to avoid us, it pulled up with a tremendous burst of flame from the rear, and zoomed into the clouds, its prop wash or jet wash rocking our plane."

Here was the first recorded account of amazing maneuverability, implying that at least some of these UFOs were steered by an active intelligence.

FLYING SAUCER IN SICILY　　　*Standing on a bridge in Taormina, these observers stare at two UFOs.*

Those UFO Spotters Persist Despite the Official Pooh-p...

F...

By Joseph R. Hixson
The Herald Tribune Staff

was supposed to be ever, the alarums and excur... s redoubled. More than a ... ago the Northwestern ...versity astro-physicist who ...onlights checking flying ...

The Air Force denied any radar sightings, pooh-poohed fuzzy photographs and what happened? Letters from saucer believers poured into newspapers across the country. People saw hovering, lighted objects in New Haven, Conn.: Lakewood N. J...

Congressional investigation of UFO's.

The flap in Washington reached the point where Defense secretary Robert S. McNamara had to make a formal denial of the existence of radically new flying devices during his testimony on the ...

ings. The Defense Secretary promptly did. And he also denied that saucers could be secret U. S. flying machines.

It was nat... question shoul... laps of scient... Baltimore co... best methods landing on ... other planet...

Dr. Edwar... ...tive secretar... Aeronautics ...cil said, ... pilots rep...

"(UFO's); that's why I take the train."

At the same meeting, as... tronomer John S. Hall of the ...ell Observatory in Arizona ...te of Dr...

More Myste...

Sightings Zoom Faster Than Flying Saucers

Mysterious flying objects ...ere observed in the night ...y last night and early today ...y scores of law enforcement ...fficials and citizens in widely ...eparated sections of the coun...

At Ann Arbor, Mich., Washtenaw County Sheriff Deputy Thomas Dorrance said he and other deputies early today watched a zigzagging, blinking object change color from red ...

Passaic, N. J., also saw the lights.

"I saw flickering red lights up there," said John Baxley of the Temppe City, Calif., sheriff's substation. He said the object he saw had at least

...rown, know ...scinated b ...more step ... scientifi ...gist, a p ...astronom

study pro...

Air Force scientists who investigate reports of unidentified flying objects had their work cut out for them last night.

Scores of persons, including police, reported seeing the mysterious objects last night in widely scattered sections of the country, according to United Press International.

A Bangor, Maine, man fired his pistol at a glowing object —and hit it.

"I could hear the elderberry bushes scraping —

UFO Expert Has Feet on Ground

By GEORGE CARMACK
Scripps-Howard Newspapers

WASHINGTON, March 29—Even in Washington where the press conference is a way of life, the one staged by Maj. Donald E. Keyhoe was special.

The retired Marine had several things going for him as he faced newspapermen and TV cameras in the National Press Club yesterday.

His subject has been a sure-fire hit for 20 years—"Unidentified Flying Objects," which to the major's disgust the public keeps calling flying saucers.

Called Swamp Gas

The questions were numerous. The conference was still going strong after an hour and 45 minutes and reporters with early deadlines were sneaking out like drama critics at a Broadway opening.

Keyhoe and his fellow board members urged the United States to "establish a nationwide tracking network and make public the recorded UFO speeds, shapes and maneuvers."

Ford Backed

They urged an end to what they called official secrecy and backed Ford's demand for an investigation.

Keyhoe expressed a personal opinion that a reasonable hypothesis about the UFOs was that they came from somewhere outside the earth.

He and other members of his board gave case after case of reports of sightings and claimed they had many instances where the same flying object was locked on by radar, seen by human beings and photographed.

They told of a sighting near Grottoes, Va., ...which the object had taken off with a power- ...d later "DuPont engineer" ...found it "highly

Dext... g obje...

a child ...tions on ... hav... d. Res... ...ect wa... exture ...re and ...nning...

McNamara Sinks Saucers As Out of This World

WASHINGTON, March 31 ...PI) — Flying saucer fans, ...word from the top at the ...ntagon is that there aren't ...—either ours of somebody ...e's.

...hat's what Defense Secre...y Robert S. McNamara told ...gressmen yesterday. Gen.

McNamara said he was sure this wasn't the case.

Gallagher then asked McNamara is he could "categorically deny" the possibility that unidentified flying objects reported seen in Michigan and elsewhere had extra-terrestrial implications.

would have an intense interest in any such manifestation because of its security aspects.

The defense chief said all the UFO sightings had been investigated by the military and there was no evidence to support the theory they might be controlled vehicles from outer

87 Coeds & 2 Others See Unidentified Flying Object

Hillsdale, Mich., March 22 (UPI)—A civil defense director, an assistant dean and 87 coeds reported today that they watched a glowing object zip past a Hillsdale college dormitory and hover in a swamp for hours.

Their description of the eerie object seen here last night tallied closely with that of one seen by more than 50 persons, including 12 policemen, near Ann Arbor, Mich., the previous night.

The witnesses said they watched from the second floor of a girl's dormitory. Mrs. Kelly Hearn, assistant dean of women, had the coeds take notes. They and William Van Horn, 41, Hillsdale County civil defense director, said the object dimmed its lights when police cars approached.

maker, cou... porter for ... and a you... morning h... a large obj... still and th... the air.

By his ... man." He ... tified flyi... sighting h... telephone ... residents ...

"I got ... recalled th... next guy. ... was the a... so stunne... capacity t... to think, ... evidence

---

NEWSPAPER REPORTS *This medley of headlines illustrates the intense preoccupation of the American press with UFOs.*

hs

OM OUTER SPACE?

Most are explained

Craft Sighted UFO probe pushed

By Robert R. Brunn
Staff correspondent of
The Christian Science Monitor

Washington

ble in more than a dozen states, per-
utting their lawns for the first time at
t, are heralding the return of the
season. All of them have reported in
weeks sightings of "unidentified flying
s."

e see "flying saucers." Others see
y glowing objects hovering and flitting
h the spring night air.

matter how puzzling or fanciful, how-
these strange incidents continue to be
rs of governmental concern.

Harold Brown, for

Outside Experts May Study UFOs

By United Press International
WASHINGTON.

tion, has explained all but 646
of the 10,147 flying saucer re-

Cops Chase Flying Saucer From Ohio to Pennsylvania

Ravenna, Ohio, April 18 (AP)
—"We were close, closer than I
ever want to be again," said a
deputy sheriff who chased an
unidentified flying object from
Ohio into Pennsylvania.

Hundreds of persons in both
states reported seeing the "brilliant and shiny" object early
yesterday morning.

Police Chief Gerald Buchert
of Mantua, about eight miles
north of Ravenna, said he took
a picture of the object from his
front yard but the Air Force
told him not to release it.

Buchert said it looked like
"two table saucers put together."

Portage County Deputy
Sheriff Dale Spaur

object were very distinct.
"Somebody had control over it,"
he said. "It wasn't just floating
around. It can maneuver." He
said the only sound coming
from the object was a steady,
faint humming, like an electric
transformer.

The Federal Aviation Agency's air traffic control centers
at Oberlin and Pittsburgh said
they sp
jects or
Patr
East P
the obj
it by
imately
alerted

Was Hors Killed by Colo. UFO

ALAMOSA, Colo. (AP)—Did
Snippy the horse come out second best in a tangle with a flying saucer?

Mr. and Mrs. Berle Lewis, owners of the 3-year-old Appaloosa
whose mutilated—and reportedly radioactive—carcass was
found in a remote area of southern Colorado's San Luis Valley,
declare firmly that's what happened.

Others, with varying degrees
of expertise in the field of unidentified flying objects, disagree.

"I discounted everything else
after it [the carcass] came up
radioactive," said Lewis, a car-

On the Trail of a UFO

NORA EPHRON

Last year, John Ful-
ler took a trip to Exe-
ter, N. H., to see a
couple of men about a
flying saucer.

Fuller, a columnist
for the Saturday Re-
view, playwright, free-
lance writer and tele-
vision documentary-

have been a more unlikely re-
sk: to interview two policemen
who claimed that in the early
Sept. 3, 1965, they had sighted
pulsating red lights, standing
ving incredibly rapidly through

estimony, Fuller is "a cautious
d no previous interest in uniden-
cts; his interest in the Exeter
en prompted by some startling
sations he had had with Exeter
oing his bi-monthly column.
"Incident at Exeter" (Putnam's).
f his change from skeptic

New York recently from his summer home in
Martha's Vineyard.

"My assumption," he said, "is that the Air
Force knows all about the subject, knows that
they exist. The difference between what the Air
Force says officially and what the pilots tell me
off-the-record is frightening.

"Why won't they admit it? First, it's a matter
of ego. The off-the-record report is that they ha
done everything they can to come near th
things and they can't do it. One naval author
clocked one of them as going 3000 knots in
atmosphere—over 3000 mph. Second, they mi
have instructions not to disrupt the populati
My feeling is that an uninformed public is m
worse off than an informed public. Third, they
tangled in such a web of fabrication I don't kr
how they're ever going to get out."

What does Fuller think the UFOs are? "
interplanetary theory holds up best," he said

* * *

John G. Fuller — the middle name is Gr
after Ulysses S., a friend of his great-grandfa
—was born in Philadelphia and raised on
Main Line, one of three children of a dentist.
family is descended from Dr. Samuel Fulle
surgeon who came over on the Mayflower, th
Fuller admits the fact with some embarrassm

In the fall, Fuller's second book on unid
fied flying objects will be published. It conc
the story of a New Hampshire couple—the
a prominent leader in the NAACP, his wi
social worker—who had encountered a UFO a
undergone hypnoanalytic therapy with a highly

UFOs Harmless (So Far)

The Air Force's investigating astro-
physicist has described the recent rash of
unidentified flying objects in Michigan as
a phenomenon related to escaping swamp
gases. At least he did not say it was
case of hot air. Such sightings have bee
all over the world for
years, whic
that these
rected by

But an
flying sa
persons who reported sighting
noting
evidence
(or fro
these
persons,
ill (or
policemen,
Michigan,
sistant dean
the objects.

Air Force Begins UFO Investigation

An Air Force investigating
team trudged through soggy
farm fields and interviewed
persons who reported sighting
of flying unidentified flying objects in
southern Michigan. Sightings
were reported three times
within a week in the area
around Ann Arbor. Scores of
including farmers,
University coeds and an as-
women

Two months later, at 2:30 P.M., July 7, 1948, the telephone rang in the office of Colonel Guy Hix, Commanding Officer of Goodman Air Base, Kentucky. At the other end of the wire was a State Trooper from nearby Madisonville. In a voice he was trying hard to keep cool and official, the policeman informed the colonel that he had just seen a gigantic UFO flying toward the base.

The colonel, his aide, Major Woods, and five other officers rushed to the control tower. About four minutes later, they saw a huge metallic object hovering over the field. It was shaped like a disc, its cone-like top glowing a crimson-yellow. At the moment, it seemed to be hardly moving.

Colonel Hix sounded the alarm. Three F-51 pursuit ships took off from the field. The trio was commanded by Captain Thomas Mantell, who immediately radioed down that he had "that thing" directly in

GLOWING DISC-SHAPED UFO   This time exposure, made by James Lucci, is on file at NICAP. Witnesses estimated that the object in the sky had a diameter of 45 feet.

front of him. A few minutes later, the captain's voice came through again: "I'm at 10,000 feet and pursuing it. It's going up and forward now as fast as I am—that's 360 m.p.h. I'll pursue it as high as 20,000 feet."

The other two aircrafts returned to base and both pilots reported that they had seen the disc streaking upward. Their commander was close behind. But not another sound came from Captain Mantell. Shortly after five o'clock, the wreckage of his plane was found scattered over a three-mile area.

The Air Force spent almost 18 months investigating the occurrence. Then an incredibly meager statement was issued: "Captain Mantell had probably blacked out at 20,000 feet from lack of oxygen." This may very well have been the case. But what lured him to that height was quietly ignored.

That same year, the Air Force released a document that caused a hubbub of excitement. Called *Project Grudge Report,* it dealt in some detail with the reports of Unidentified Flying Objects since the end of World War II, both in Europe and America. The document made no direct statement as to what these objects might be, but the *Project Grudge Report* pointed out that intelligent beings might conceivably exist on planets other than ours, that technological progress on such celestial bodies might have begun thousands of years ahead of us, and that such a civilization might now be scouting the doings on planet Earth. The report ran:

> *"Its members might observe, that on earth we now have A-bombs and are fast developing rockets. In view of the past history of mankind they should be alarmed. We should expect at this time, above all, to behold such visitations."*

The immediate effect of this statement was to set a firecracker under America's lunatic fringe which soon became increasingly vocal and unbelievably imaginative. Instead of merely sailing through the sky, saucers were now suddenly landing all over the place, disgorging crews of those famous little green men who all seemed to have rehearsed the phrase that was to become a cartoon classic: "Take me to your leader!"

Men and women—an astonishing number of them in southern California—were approached, kidnapped, made love to, stunned or taken for a joyride by those saucer crews. Several individuals even claimed to have been whisked off to Mars, occasionally even to Jupiter.

For, to the originators of these tales, the *Project Grudge Report* was "documentary evidence" that the saucers were spaceships, manned —sometimes womaned—by extraterrestrial creatures.

Throughout America, "contactees" proliferated like fungi. Contactees were folks who had not merely sighted UFOs, but had been in some form of contact with their crews. Such contacts were for the most part oral; but occasionally, the contact became very physical indeed, for a number of ladies blamed their sudden pregnancy on those friendly visitors from outer space.

Contactees rushed into print with their experiences, first in the specialized magazines; later between hard covers.

Dean of the contactee-authors was a gentleman who insisted the saucers came from Venus. Their crews had told him so. He produced fascinating hand-drawings of these Venusians, handsome creatures with shoulder-length hair, wearing Eisenhower jackets and ski pants.

A British writer related that the first expedition from Venus arrived on earth in the year 18,617,841 B.C. He not only gave that precise date, but he also revealed that the commander of the landing party was named Sanat Kumara, which he obligingly translated from the Venusian as meaning "Lord of the Flame."

By and large, though, contactees preferred to stick to good old Mars. A lady realtor in Los Angeles announced that what we called Martians were actually angels, beings "of almost unimaginable beauty." The reason why so few people caught a glimpse of them was that they were visible only to "the pure in heart and spirit." The lady was taken for a spin in an angelic saucer, during which she learned that the UFOs were standing by in order to prevent an atomic war. If a conflict seemed about to erupt, the Martians would "step in and nip it in the bud."

Several Mid-Western contactees favored the theory of UFOs as anti-catastrophe guards. Instead of guarding us against a nuclear war, they suggested that since the earth might be in imminent danger of

*FLYING OBJECTS OVER MICHIGAN   Picture,
taken southeast of Ann Arbor with a sub-miniature
camera by Washtenaw County Deputy David Fitz-
patrick on March 16, 1966, shows two strange objects
in the sky.*

keeling over on its side — a chilling prospect they called "Polar Flip Disaster"—the saucers were standing by to somehow prevent that disaster.

On a more earthy level was the encounter of a Newark Valley (N.J.) farmer who was approached by a group of figures completely encased in silvery one-piece suits. The leader addressed the farmer in fluent English, proclaiming: "We are from the planet known as Mars." What they were after, however, was nothing more dramatic than a bag of fertilizer. They needed it, they explained, in order to rehabilitate the Martian agricultural system. Other reports, just as zany, found their way into print.

However, for the most part, the hand of the hoaxer was fairly unmistakable. In Chicago, two young mechanics briefly electrified the press by "finding" the shattered remains of a space saucer on a deserted stretch of the shore of Lake Michigan. On examination, all the discovered parts turned out to have derived from quite earthly, though elderly, automobiles.

From Georgia, came the story of a truck driver who claimed to have run over and killed a "spaceman." In evidence, the driver produced the 20-inch-long body of a hairless, shriveled creature weighing about four pounds and faintly resembling a man. It didn't take the police long to establish that the body was that of a monkey whose hair had been shaved off and whose tail had been amputated—but not before the story had gone over a national wire service.

These tales and several hundred other fiascos were publicized by radio and by newspaper, mostly in a dead pan style that a large number of people mistook for sober reportage. All this served to generate a climate that was not exactly conducive to serious evaluation of the UFO phenomenon; recoiling from this barrage of idiocy, the reaction of the U.S. Air Force was to clam up tight.

A drastic change took place in the early 1950's. Until then, Air Force personnel were pretty much at liberty to discuss the subject with journalists and to even write about UFOs themselves. Then, by the strict order, AFR 200-2, members of the service were forbidden to talk in public about UFO sightings and were not permitted to release information on the subject. "Only if it has been positively identified as a familiar or known object" is comment permissible, read the order.

Another paragraph of the same regulation states that servicemen "will not contact private individuals on UFO cases, nor will they discuss their operations with unauthorized persons unless so directed, and then only on a 'need-to-know' basis." A final paragraph deals with the handling of UFO reports and photos.

No reason for this crackdown was given. Air Force spokesmen merely hinted that the order might have been deemed necessary to keep certain advanced aircraft secret. The YF-12 jet, for instance, was still in its testing stages. An airman, seeing the machine splitting the sky at two-and-one-half times the speed of sound, might mistake that craft for a UFO and spread description of a plane which was still classified as secret.

Unfortunately, AFR 200-2 had the effect of excluding the public from whatever concrete information the Air Force was gathering. And this exclusion in itself spread suspicion that the facts might be of such a startling nature that the powers that be simply did not dare release such information to the people.

In 1950, the U.S. Air Force organized a special department charged with the investigation and correlation of everything connected with UFOs. Called *Project Blue Book*, it is quartered in a single room on the second floor of a windowless concrete structure at the Wright-Patterson Air Force Base in Ohio. Every Air Force base in the United States also has a UFO officer whose task it is to conduct an investigation of every sighting reported in his area. The facts are then sent to the *Project Blue Book* center where a team of scientists and technicians analyzes the report and compares it to other data. Final analysis of each report is then forwarded to the Pentagon.

All these reports are considered classified material. The method by which they are evaluated is not revealed to any outside scientific body. Occasionally, a summing-up report is released, which reveals conclusions derived from a batch of investigations, but never reveals the incidents on which such conclusions are based.

A 1965 report revealed that there had been 887 reported sightings

that year. Of these, 245 were identified as being of astronomical origin:
210 aircraft; 36 balloons; 152 satellites; 126 hoaxes, hallucinations,
fireworks, etc. Eighty-five were judged to supply insufficient data; 17
were still being processed. *But 16 were listed as genuinely "unidentified
objects!"*

In that same year, the Air Force announced that it had drawn three
firm conclusions from the work of *Project Blue Book*. These were:

> 1. *That no unidentified flying objects has ever posed a
> threat to national security.*
> 2. *That no evidence has been submitted to indicate that
> unidentified sightings represent technological developments
> beyond the range of our scientific knowledge.*
> 3. *That there is no evidence that the sighted objects are of
> an extraterrestrial nature.*

These conclusions would have been considerably more comforting
if the Air Force had also revealed how they were arrived at. As it was,
they sounded somewhat akin to a government proclaiming "We are
winning the War," without adding what it was it chose to regard as
indications of victory. In any case, the conclusions stood in stark contrast to what the authorities had allowed to slip out before clamping on
their news blackout.

In July, 1952, for instance, when UFOs were observed in the sky
above Washington, D. C., the Department of Defense had called a news
conference, conducted by Major General John Samford. The general
said that UFOs seemed to have "unlimited power—that means power
of such fantastic higher limits that it is theoretically unlimited—it's not
anything we can understand."

In 1956, a private organization, the *National Investigations Committee on Aerial Phenomena* (NICAP), was formed with the sole purpose of throwing light on the UFO riddle. With headquarters in Washington, D. C., supported by roughly over 10,000 members who live in
the United States and in 30 foreign countries, NICAP is a far cry from
the crackpot outfits that had dominated the saucer scene in the early

years. Admiral R. H. Hillenkoetter, who had headed the CIA from 1946 to 1950 was on its Board of Governors and today the Board includes such personalities as Dewey J. Fournet, formerly one of the Air Force's UFO specialists; J. B. Hartranft, head of the Aircraft Owners and Pilots Association; and Rear Admiral H. B. Knowles. Members of NICAP include German rocket scientist Hermann Oberth, and Albert Chop, an official of the National Aeronautics and Space Administration.

In 1967, Major Donald E. Keyhoe became NICAP's director. A dedicated combination of gadfly and crusader, Major Keyhoe is convinced that the government's refusal to disclose the UFO facts it has collected imperils national security. A former flying officer in the Marine Corps and a technical writer on aviation, Keyhoe has turned his organization into a shadow replica of *Project Blue Book,* minus the restriction of AFR 200-2.

PROJECT BLUE BOOK   Here is the cover of the Air Force report, covering the investigation of unidentified flying objects. Prior to 1948, "Project Blue Book" was known as "Project Sign" and also as "Project Grudge." The facsimile pages from the "Blue Book" which follow indicate the concerns and the position of the Air Force toward UFOs. UFO sightings are listed and classified, statistics are cited, and the "Men from Mars" theory entirely deflated.

PROJECT

BLUE

BOOK

1 MARCH 1967

Reports categorized as INSUFFICIENT DATA are those for which one or more elements of information, essential for evaluation, are missing. Some examples are the omission of the duration of the sighting, date, time, location, position in the sky, weather conditions, and the manner of appearance or disappearance. If an element is missing and there is an indication that the sighting may be of a security, scientific, technical, or public interest value, the Project Blue Book Office conducts an additional investigation and every attempt is made to obtain the information necessary for identification. However, in some instances, essential information is requested from the observer and is never received; therefore, no further action can be taken.

The third and by far the smallest group of evaluations is categorized as UNIDENTIFIED. A sighting is considered unidentified when a report apparently contains all pertinent data necessary to suggest a valid hypothesis concerning the cause or explanation of the report, but the description of the object or its motion cannot be correlated with any known object or phenomena.

TYPES OF UFO IDENTIFICATIONS AND EVALUATIONS

There are various types of UFO sightings. Most common are reports of astronomical sightings, which include bright stars, planets, comets, fireballs, meteors, auroral streamers, and other celestial bodies. When observed through haze, light fog, moving clouds, or other obscurations or unusual conditions, the planets, including Venus, Jupiter, and Mars, have been reported as unidentified flying objects. Stellar mirages are also a source of reports.

Satellites are another major source of UFO reports. An increase in satellites reported as UFOs has come about because of two factors. The first is the increase of interest on the part of the public; the second is the increasing number of satellites in the skies. Positive knowledge of the location of all satellites at all times enables rapid identification of satellite sightings. Keeping track of man-made objects in orbit about the earth is the responsibility of the North American Air Defense Command Space Detection and Tracking System at Ent AFB, Colorado. This sophisticated electronics system gathers complex space traffic data instantly from tracking stations all over the world.

Other space surveillance activities include the use of ballistic tracking and large telescopic cameras. ECHO schedules of the South/North equator crossings are prepared by the Smithsonian Institution at Cambridge, Massachusetts. From the data produced by these agencies, satellites mistakenly reported as UFOs can be identified quickly. Some of these are visible to the naked eye.

Aircraft account for another major source of UFO reports, particularly during adverse weather conditions. When observed at high altitudes and at some distance, aircraft can have appearances ranging from disc to rocket shapes due to the reflection of the sun on their bright surfaces. Vapor or condensation trails from jet aircraft will sometimes appear to glow fiery red or orange when reflecting sunlight. Afterburners from jet aircraft are often reported as UFOs since they can be seen from great distances when the aircraft cannot be seen.

The Project Blue Book Office has direct contact with all elements of the Air Force and the Federal Aviation Agency civil air control centers. All aerial refueling operations and special training flights can be checked immediately. Air traffic of commercial airlines and flights of military aircraft are checked with the nearest control center, enabling an immediate evaluation of aircraft mistakenly reported as UFOs. However, since many local flights are not carried, these flights are probable causes of some reports.

Balloons continue to be reported as UFOs. Several thousand balloons are released each day from military and civilian airports, weather stations, and research activities. There are several types of balloons - weather balloons, rawinsondes, radiosondes, and the large research balloons which have

2

CONCLUSIONS

To date, the firm conclusions of Project Blue Book are: (1) no unidentified flying object reported, investigated, and evaluated by the Air Force has ever given any indication of threat to our national security; (2) there has been no evidence submitted to or discovered by the Air Force that sightings categorized as UNIDENTIFIED represent technological developments or principles beyond the range of present-day scientific knowledge; and (3) there has been no evidence indicating that sightings categorized as UNIDENTIFIED are extraterrestrial vehicles.

The Air Force will continue to investigate all reports of unusual aerial phenomena over the United States. The services of qualified scientists and technicians will continue to be used to investigate and analyze these reports, and periodic reports on the subject will be made.

The Air Force takes no stand on whether or not extraterrestrial life could or does exist. Scientists believe that it is entirely possible that the universe contains life on planets other than our own. No evidence yet exists that there is other life. The Air Force continues to extend an open invitation to anyone who feels that he possesses any evidence of extraterrestrial vehicles operating within the earth's space envelope to submit his evidence for analysis. Initial contact for this purpose is through the following address:

> PROJECT BLUE BOOK INFORMATION OFFICE
> SAFOI
> WASHINGTON, D.C. 20330

Anyone observing what he considers to be an unidentified flying object should report it to the nearest Air Force Base. Persons submitting a UFO report to the Air Force are free to discuss any aspect of the report with anyone. The Air Force does not seek to limit discussion on such reports and does not withhold or censor any information pertaining to this unclassified program.

TOTAL UFO (OBJECT) SIGHTINGS

(Compiled 15 Feb 67)

YEAR	TOTAL SIGHTINGS	UNIDENTIFIED	SOURCE
1947	122	12	Case Files
1948	156	7	Case Files
1949	186	22	Blue Book, Page 108
1950	210	27	Case Files
1951	169	22	Case Files
1952	1,501	303	Blue Book, Page 108
1953	509	42	Case Files
1954	487	46	Case Files
1955	545	24	Case Files
1956	670	14	Case Files
1957	1,006	14	Case Files
1958	627	10	Case Files
1959	390	12	Case Files
1960	557	14	Case Files
1961	591	13	Case Files
1962	474	15	Case Files
1963	399	14	Case Files
1964	562	19	Case Files
1965	887	16	Case Files
1966	1,060	30	Case Files
TOTAL	11,108	676	

ARRIVING FROM MARS BY UFO?

In recent years there have been many reports of unidentified flying objects (UFO's), especially since the first Soviet Sputnik went up on October 4, 1957. From time to time the question has been raised as to whether the UFO's might have come from Mars or Venus, perhaps bearing intelligent beings. Usually the answer to this question has been simply a guess which depended to a considerable extent on what the individual wanted to believe. Most scientists have been inclined to doubt that the UFO's came from Mars or Venus, preferring to credit the sightings to natural phenomena which are not as well known as they should be.

There is a logical approach to this question as to whether or not UFO's have come from Mars or Venus. It is well known that if some one on the earth wants to send a space vehicle to Mars or Venus, there are specific favorable times, times when a body can be launched so that it will travel along a minimum-energy orbit, arriving at the path of Mars (or Venus) just as that planet comes to the same point. For example, favorable times for launching a rocket to travel to Venus have been listed as Oct. 27, 1965, June 5, 1967 and January 11, 1969, and for Mars, December 23, 1964, January 26, 1967 and February 28, 1969. (SPACE HANDBOOK, Gov't Printing Office 1959.)

Of course, there are similar favorable times for launching a space vehicle from Mars (or Venus) to the earth, and for each of these launching times, there would be a corresponding arrival time at the earth. These favorable arrival times come at intervals of about 584 days for Venus and about 780 days for Mars. Actually, in each case, the interval is a close approximation to the synodic period of the planet; for Venus, the synodic period varies from 579.8 to 587.8 days, and for Mars, from 767 to 803 days.

One could then choose intervals of 20 days, say, ten days on either side of a favorable arrival date, and look to see how many UFO's were sighted in each such "favorable arrival interval", here named fai, (plural fais). If there were no increase in the number of UFO's in these fais, then it would be unlikely that any considerable number of UFO's had been arriving from Mars or Venus.

Someone is certain to raise the question as to whether or not a Martian or a Venutian would elect to travel in a minimum-energy orbit. Here I shall assume that intelligent beings from any part of the universe will choose to travel by means and paths that will minimize the expenditure of energy.

This fai approach to the problem can be carried a step farther. One can make a list of the UFO's observed in the fais, and look at the record of each to see if the UFO was observed travelling in the direction it would have if it came from Mars (or Venus) in a minimum-energy orbit. Roughly speaking, a space vehicle from Mars should overtake the earth from behind and one from Venus should be overtaken by the earth. Thus one could determine whether the path of approach was associated with the proper radiant point in space; here we use the term in the sense in which it is used in connection with meteors.

Now to look at the evidence! A list of UFO's sighted between September 8, 1956 and December 31, 1963 was examined. Nine fais of 20 days were found in this interval, 5 for Venus and 4 for Mars. Circular paths were assumed for Venus, Earth and Mars in computing travel times for space vehicles, but no particular difficulty is encountered if one elects to allow for the eccentricities of the various paths. In table I below, the number of UFO's reported in each fai of 20 days is given, and is to be compared with the average number of UFO's per 20-day interval outside the fais, namely, 1.88.

DONALD EDWARD KEYHOE   *The retired U. S. Marine Corps Major is director of the National Investigation Committee of Aerial Phenomena (NICAP).*

NICAP has its own top-flight team of scientists to evaluate information. Moreover, NICAP has been able to utilize reports quietly leaked to it by personnel who have found the Air Force's censorship intolerable. Through Keyhoe's group, some of the most startling UFO incidents of recent years have reached the public's ears.

There is the still unexplained loss of a jet fighter on November 23, 1953. That day, a UFO had been sighted over Lake Superior, on the U. S.-Canadian border. An F-89 was ordered up from Kinross Air Force Base, Michigan, to take a closer look at the strange thing in the sky. The jet, piloted by Lieutenant Felix Moncla, apparently chased the object for some distance over the lake. Then, suddenly, the Kinross Air Base lost radio contact with Moncla. And nothing has ever been heard or seen of either Moncla or his plane since! An extensive search of the area failed to find any trace of wreckage.

Later, the Air Force announced that the unidentified object was in reality a Canadian airliner. NICAP, however, contradicted that statement. Keyhoe claimed that his organization had received letters from the Royal Canadian Air Force stating categorically that no Canadian aircraft of any sort had been in the vicinity at the time.

Which is where the matter rests. We don't know why or how Lieutenant Moncla disappeared. Nor do we know how anyone could have mistaken a commercial airliner for a UFO.

Even more puzzling was the Air Force's behavior in the "Killian Case." On the night of February 24, 1959, Captain Peter Killian and First Officer John Dee were at the controls of an American Airlines DC-6, en route to Detriot. While over Pennsylvania, both pilots suddenly saw three huge, disc-shaped objects, brilliantly lighted, flying in formation beside their plane. After keeping pace for a few minutes, the strange trio put on speed and disappeared into the darkness. *The objects were observed, not only by the two pilots, but also by the passengers of the airliner.*

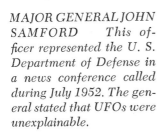

MAJOR GENERAL JOHN SAMFORD   This officer represented the U. S. Department of Defense in a news conference called during July 1952. The general stated that UFOs were unexplainable.

Captain Killian told some newspaper reporters about his experience, and the story hit the papers. Almost immediately, and for no apparent reason, the Air Force stepped in, and a spokesman explained that what Killian had actually seen were three *stars*.

The captain, a veteran flier, stuck to his guns. His version was corroborated by his co-pilot, as well as by several of the passengers. The Air Force bluntly insisted Killian was wrong. The Air Force kept on berating the captain's report—and with increasing vehemence—even after two other commercial pilots volunteered that they, too, had sighted the UFO trio during the same night and in the same area.

By degrees, the argument grew bitter. At stake for Captain Killian was his professional standing. If his eyesight was that bad, he really shouldn't be put in charge of a commercial plane. And if Captain Killian could see well enough, then at the very least, the position taken by the Air Force assailed his veracity. More pilots, both commercial and private, entered the fray, declaring that they frequently encountered UFOs on that particular route. At least four sightings had previously been reported.

The furore reached all the way to Congress where several voices demanded that Killian be invited to state his case before a House Committee. At this point, the Air Force switched theories. Their spokesmen now explained that the UFOs Killian saw had been a tanker refueling three B-47 jets in flight. The star version was dropped. But NICAP pointed out that all flight refueling operations are automatically reported to the Air Defense Command. How, then, that the Air Force suddenly discovered that such an operation had taken place that night along Killian's route? And even if such an operation had occurred, no experienced pilot could possibly have mistaken four standard aircraft types for three UFOs.

But the issue was not pressed any further. About a week later, the whole uproar suddenly ceased. Killian stopped arguing. According to Major Keyhoe, Mrs. Killian told NICAP that American Airlines, acting on Air Force instructions, had forbidden her husband to continue the debate. The interesting point here is not whether the U.S. Air Force had used pressure to muzzle an opponent—but *why?* Killian was, after all, a

CAPTAIN PETER KILLIAN This officer was allegedly muzzled by the U. S. Air Force, after he reported an encounter with three disc-shaped objects, while he was at the controls of a commercial DC-6, en route to Detroit in February, 1959.

civilian. It should have been a matter of total indifference to the U.S. Air Force if he had claimed to have seen flying giraffes. Why *wasn't* it?

There is no cut and dried explanation. It evidently seems to be part of U.S. Air Force policy to more or less laugh off UFO reports by non-fliers, but to jump with both feet on any such claim made by an airline pilot.

Perhaps, because a commercial pilot makes an uncomfortably convincing witness, for a flier is familiar with mirages, meteorites, searchlight reflections, condensation trails, and a host of other optical or atmospheric symptoms that might fool ground folk. An airline pilot's eyesight is checked regularly; and a pilot is rigorously barred from imbibing liquor before a takeoff. A pilot knows just about every kind of hardware in the sky; he is not likely to mistake a satellite for a saucer. Above all, a commercial flier is just about the very last person in the world to try a UFO hoax, for his job depends on his emotional stability. If anything, airline pilots are over-cautious in their reports; sometimes only their very close friends ever get to hear about some of their more curious flight encounters.

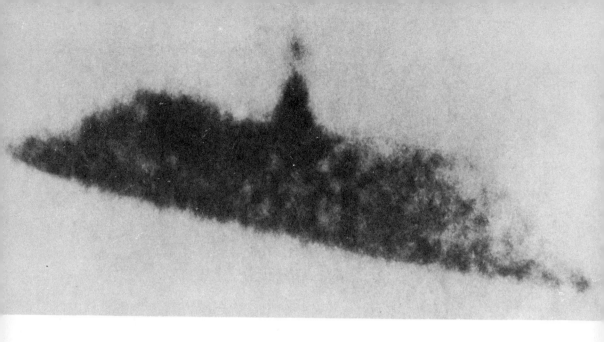

UNIDENTIFIED FLYING OBJECT   *This classic saucer shape was photographed by farmer Paul Trent near McMinnville, Oregon, in May, 1950.*

Yet an astonishing number of pilots have seemed willing to risk ridicule and grounding. When Dr. Edward C. Welch, executive secretary of the National Aeronautics and Space Council, traveled to a 1966 conference in Baltimore by rail, he told reporters: "So many airline pilots report seeing UFOs—that's why I take the train." Dr. Welch's remark may have been a joke, but the fact that so many airline pilots have reported sightings is anything else but. For instance, on a February night of 1965, the captain and crew of a trans-Pacific jetliner, bound for Japan, found themselves being "paced" by three gigantic football-shaped craft, glowing vivid red in the darkness. The shapes themselves seemed to glow, but no jet or other form of exhaust or propulsion was visible. For 30 minutes by the clock, the objects flew alongside the airliner, keeping close formation. Then, they suddenly accelerated to several times the plane's speed and climbed out of sight in a matter of seconds.

An almost identical encounter was reported by the pilots of a German airliner flying over the North Sea. This time the glowing football shapes shadowed the aircraft for over an hour. The pilots estimated them as being more than 600 feet in length. Their glow changed from bright red to yellowish. They took their leave with equal abruptness. "They flicked off so fast that we seemed to be standing still by comparison," the German pilots related.

Both the changing colors and the fantastic rate of speed of such UFOs have been commented upon again and again. British Air Force personnel and Chilean Air Force personnel stationed in the Antarctic have reported flying objects alternately glowing white, yellow, green and orange, moving forward and sideways, with equal ease and speed.

Probably the most famous pilot to encounter a UFO was TV celebrity Arthur Godfrey. On the night of June 17, 1965, he and his co-pilot Frank Munciello were flying their light aircraft near Philadelphia. Suddenly a glowing round object appeared near the plane's right wing, forcing Godfrey to bank sharply to avoid a collision. He immediately radioed the Philadelphia tower of the Federal Aeronautics Administration, asking whether any air traffic was scheduled near him. The reply was firmly negative. Nevertheless, the shining disc was still there. Then,

ARTHUR GODFREY Radio and television star is shown as he looked in 1951, when he was a commander on active duty in the Naval Reserve.

according to Godfrey's and Munciello's report, the UFO fell back, flew a circle behind their plane, and easily drew level with the *left* wing. For the next few minutes Godfrey did his best to shake off the glowing shadow, banking and pulling away. But his efforts were useless. The disc followed every maneuver almost playfully, matching its speed with that of the twin-engined plane. After hanging on for as long as it pleased, the UFO shot ahead and disappeared.

Similar reports have come in from airmen in Brazil, Argentina, Britain, France, Spain, Canada, and Australia. And as one Aeronautics Administration official estimated: "For every UFO report handed in by an Air Force or airline pilot, there are probably a dozen encounters kept quiet for fear of being considered odd or inebriated."

A curious thing about saucer sightings is that they seem to come in batches. The first wave of UFO alarms broke out in 1947, reached its climax in 1952, and then faded down to a trickle of items buried in the back pages of newspapers. The second rash appeared early in 1965, and is still going strong.

SAUCER OVER BRAZIL   *This picture was taken by professional photographer Almiro Barauna at Trindade Island, in January 1958.*

SAUCER SIGHTING   *This is an enlargement of the photograph shown*
on the opposite page.

At a Washington press conference, General Samford was asked whether he could explain this great variance in sightings over the years.

The general answered: "There are many reasons why this volume of sightings goes up and down; but we can't help believing that, correctly, one of the reasons for this volume is that man is doing a great deal more."

Although phrased somewhat confusingly, the general's reply left little doubt as to what he meant. Things from outer space were looking us over, the frequency of their appearances being governed by our activities on earth. Judging by airmen's reports, the salient feature about UFOs seem to be their curiosity. Although capable of literally flying rings around any of our conventional aircraft, the UFOs reportedly spend considerable time *observing* planes—by keeping pace alongside our aircraft or trailing them over great distances.

Or do they? The U.S. Air Force doesn't think so. When the second wave of UFO sightings broke, the Air Force proceeded to demolish each report almost as quickly as it popped up. The explanations, at times, came through so fast and so pat they gave the impression of having been prepared in advance.

On the night of September 3, 1965, two patrolmen of Exeter, New Hampshire, accompanied a very excited young man back to an open field over which he claimed to have seen a UFO. Officer Eugene Bertrand, an Air Force veteran, was pretty sure that all the agitated youngster had seen was a helicopter—until Officer Bertrand caught sight of the object himself! It was hovering in complete silence about 100 feet from the ground, a vaguely rounded shape ringed by brilliant red lights that flickered on and off, casting a vivid scarlet glare over the field. The three men watched the thing for several minutes, judging it to be about 80 feet in diameter. Then the shape moved away, but stopped at intervals, the red lights continuing to pulsate until the visitor finally disappeared toward the ocean.

Bertrand notified the Pease Air Force Base. That night, half a dozen other residents of the area reported sighting the silent form. Their descriptions tallied with that of the police officer. Among them were two motorists who had stopped their cars when the UFO passed them, only a few feet overhead.

The explanation of the Air Force was simple: weather balloons—either the same one, or several in the same vicinity. Some of these balloons are quite huge, they explained, and are covered with running lights. The balloons move soundlessly, and since they are steered by the wind, they may hover one moment, and they may rapidly dart off the next. To anyone not familiar with their appearance, these balloons may look like phantoms, particularly at night.

The only flaw in the Air Force's statement is that weather balloons, after being released, drift up, to an altitude of 100,000 feet. They have not been known to float around near ground level.

In March 1966, on the night of Sunday the 21st, Frank Mannor, a Michigan farmer, was alerted by the howling of his dogs. His house stands on a rise overlooking a piece of swampland, some 12 miles north-west of Ann Arbor. Even from a distance, Mannor and his son could see a faint reddish glow hanging over the swamp. As they approached, they spotted "a thing about as long as an automobile, rough like coral rock." It was hovering a few feet off the ground in a patch of mist. As the two men gazed, it suddenly turned blood red, giving off the glow they had seen from a distance.

Mannor raced back home and telephoned the nearby Dexter village police. Soon a dozen policemen and deputy sheriffs, plus about 40 villagers, were swarming toward the marsh. While they were still approaching, the glowing object rose higher and zipped away over their heads. It flew toward the road where Patrolman Robert Hunawill was waiting in his radio car. He saw the object sweep over his car, then circle over the swamp, where—according to his statement—it was joined by three other objects. The four lights, flashing red and white glows, then disappeared toward the west.

The following night identical changing lights were watched by the dean and 87 coeds from the windows of the Hillsdale College dormitory. The college people were joined by the local civil defense director who took notes while the shape, now red, now white, hovered over the area for nearly three hours.

During the same night, scores of other locals—policemen, farmers, motorists, men and women—reported sighting the object. At times, the thing came perilously close to the ground; at other times, it seemed to be about 1,000 feet up.

This time the Air Force dispatched their most respected UFO investigator to southern Michigan, Dr. J. Allen Hynek, astronomer and director of Northwestern University's Dearborn Observatory. Dr. Hynek inspected the area, and before voicing an opinion, sifted through the reports of more than 200 people.

"It is easy to dismiss the cases of birds, balloons and the like," he ventured, "but when good solid citizens report something puzzling, I believe we have an obligation to do as good a job as we can. I regard our 'Unidentifieds' as a sort of blot on the escutcheon. Somehow, we scientists should be able to come up with answers for these things."

Dr. Hynek's answer in this case was marsh gases—blobs which un-

*DR. J. ALLEN HYNEK
The professor has been
long associated with the
U. S. Air Force in government investigations of unexplained flying objects.*

der certain conditions glow in vivid colors and drift through the air, carried along by the faintest breeze—an explanation with a couple of gaping holes in it. For farmer Mannor had lived right beside the swamp for almost 40 years, and he was quite familiar with marsh gases, friar's lanterns, will-o'-the-wisps, etc. So were his six dogs, who never before had howled at the sight of jack-o'-lanterns. So, for that matter, were the policemen from Dexter, all of whom agreed that the objects they saw definitely didn't *drift* through the air, but *flew, circled* and *swooped* under what could only have been their own power.

Anyway, there were no swamps near the scene of the next sighting, which occurred in broad daylight. Shortly after 5:00 A.M. on the morning of April 17, Patrolman Wayne Houston of East Palestine, Ohio, received a police broadcast alerting him to the presence of a UFO in his area. Half an hour later, he saw the object hovering in the air. "As near as I can describe it, it looked like a partially melted ice cream cone, a wedge-shaped affair with the pointy part of it being down," he said. Houston proceeded to chase the thing in his patrol car, following it along Ohio Highway 14, then along Pennsylvania Highway 51 where it finally put on speed and left him behind.

A few hours later, a brilliant and shiny object, looking like "two table saucers put together," appeared over Mantua, Ohio. The local police chief, Gerald Buchert, snapped a picture of it from his front yard. He later told reporters that an Air Force representative had told him not to release the photograph.

The same object, or one looking exactly like it, was chased in two separate cars by Deputy Sheriff Dale Spaur and his partner, William Neff, of Portage County. The hunt went on for 86 miles and lasted an hour and a half, ending in Conway, Pennsylvania, near Pittsburgh. Spaur said he clocked the UFO travelling at speeds up to 103 miles an hour. "Somebody had control over it," he added. "It wasn't just floating around—it could maneuver."

Hundreds of people in both states also sighted the same object and deluged police stations with their reports. On this occasion, the Air Force's only comment was that none of the air base radar screens along the route had recorded any objects which corresponded with the reports.

By then, however, UFO alarms were pouring in at such a rate that local authorities hardly had time to register them. Police Officer Joe Baldwin at San Marino, California, received more than 30 calls within an hour. All callers reported slowly rotating lights in the sky. "At least five patrolmen and as many firemen saw them," said Baldwin. "They appeared to circle around a central hub, and were spaced about one-and-one-half yards apart. You could distinguish each light separately."

Another UFO flurry kept New Jersey on edge for three days running. One of the observers was James Novello, a former Air Force pilot with 6,000 hours of flying time behind him. "The thing I saw had a kind of rim about it, and the core looked like an old-fashioned light bulb which was ready to flicker out," he said. He estimated that the object was 100 feet long, and about 1,500 feet up in the air.

Some 300 people in Bryan, Texas, reported watching a "star-like thing that repeatedly changed colors."

FLYING SAUCER   *One of the clearest and most impressive photographs ever taken of a UFO, this snapshot was made by highway inspector Rex Heflin while motoring on a highway near Santa Ana, California. The framework of Heflin's windshield is visible.*

At Tomah, Wisconsin, a radio newsman Wayne Eddy gave his listeners a running description of an object he was watching during a broadcast: "It's of a red, green, and white coloring that sort of goes on and off," he narrated. "It's hovering high in the sky—very high—and it seems to zip from side to side."

Simultaneously, scores of sightings were reported from widely separated parts of the globe. In Perth, Western Australia, amateur photographer Benedek, in the process of snapping night views of the city, took some startling UFO pictures. "I noticed a bright light descending from a great height," he told reporters. "It was radiating a light greenish glow, and had an exhaust trail of the same color. Its shape, as well as I could judge it, was slightly oval. I took a picture of it. Then, when it reached a height of about 20 feet above the water, it slowed to a speed of roughly five miles per hour, and I took another picture. I was preparing to take one more when the object shot up into the air vertically with enormous speed, and disappeared within a few seconds." Benedek's color snaps bore out his words. The thing he had photographed was certainly neither a weather balloon nor a blob of swamp gas.

The Japanese captain of a Toa Airlines Convair reported being "followed or shadowed" by a "strange, elliptical luminous object," which flew close to his plane and apparently caused his radio to blank out for several minutes.

Meteorological stations in both France and the Portuguese Azores, manned by trained observers, reported watching UFOs for periods of more than an hour, and described the objects as "lens-shaped and glowing." Incidentally, both stations commented on the erratic behavior of their radio equipment and electro-magnetic clocks during the times that the objects hovered in their vicinities.

In the midst of this UFO invasion, NICAP's Major Keyhoe called a press conference at the National Press Club in Washington. Keyhoe, flanked by six prominent members of his board of governors, faced a most skeptical audience. The newspapermen who gathered there were ready to cast the major as the leading character in a weekend humor piece. But they didn't. For the major, it turned out, was very impressive and came armed with a boxful of evidence. Easily avoiding all attempts to trap him into any kind of "little green men" statements, he and his aides presented a stream of UFO case histories, verified by scientists, airmen, police officers, naval personnel, and other fairly unflappable eyewitnesses.

The most dramatic revelation concerned the observed landing of "a round, metallic craft about 125 feet in diameter" in a field near Staunton, Virginia, four days before Christmas, 1964. The object blasted off after a brief touchdown. Keyhoe produced a statement by Du Pont engineer Lawrence Cook, one of two men who later went over the landing site with Geiger counters. "It was hot—highly radioactive," Cook stated.

Asked for his personal opinion as to the nature of UFOs, the major answered dryly: "It is a reasonable hypothesis that they come from somewhere outside the earth."

He and his fellow board members then urged the United States to establish a nationwide tracking network, and to make public the recorded UFO speeds, shapes, and maneuvers. Above all, they urged an end to official secrecy. Following Keyhoe's conference, Congressman Gerald Ford of Michigan demanded a government investigation of the phenomena which had invaded his home state. His constituents were in the throes of discomania.

The investigation—or *rather* a whole series of them—have in fact been going on for almost 18 years. The catch lies in the phrase *"make public."* For although a number of Congressional hearings on the subject have been held, these investigations were never held openly. Since the material presented to the Congressional bodies was classified as secret, neither the contents nor the conclusions of these investigations have been publicized.

On every previous occasion, the Air Force fought tooth and nail to prevent an open hearing. This time, Congressman Ford's request was neatly countered by Air Force Secretary Harold Brown, who proposed, instead of an open investigation, to set up observation teams of experts —geophysicists, astronomers and psychologists—who would report their findings to the Air Force Systems Command. *Later* these findings *could* be printed in full and made available to the public. *Note the key words "later" and "could."* The proposal left the entire matter to the ultimate discretion of the U. S. Air Force, and served to put off a full-scale Congressional open hearing.

The reason advanced by the Air Force was that a public inquiry was unwarranted. Nearly all of the sightings could be explained as gases, light reflections, birds, mirages, balloons, satellites, stars, condensation

A THING IN THE SKY   *This photo of a UFO was taken by a government employee near Holloman Air Development Center, New Mexico, on October 16, 1957. This picture was released by the Aerial Phenomena Research Organization, after months of close scrutiny.*

trails, hallucinations, or hoaxes. Perhaps so. But if so, why should such harmless manifestations remain classified as secret. Does the Air Force believe that UFOs may be dangerous?

There is, of course, the possibility that UFOs are caused by some unknown, but perfectly innocuous, natural force. For centuries, sailors lived in superstitious awe of St. Elmo's fire—a natural phenomenon which, during certain storm conditions, makes the spars and masts of a ship flicker with eerie lights. Today, we know that St. Elmo's fire is a form of static electricity; but it took some 2,000 years to discover its nature.

DR. WILLIAM MARKOWITZ   During 1958, the professor was director
of time service at the U. S. Naval Office in Washington, D. C.

Ball lightning, which has been seen during thunderstorms since the
dawn of history, is also known as fireballs. Glowing grapefruit-sized
blobs of fire have been reported as dancing along fences, drifting through
open windows, falling down chimneys, and finally exploding with a
bang. Such phenomena were regarded by some early 19th-century scientists as purely imaginary. Today, however, science knows that ball
lightning exists, and that the phenomenon is the result of a change
during a thunderstorm in the electrical conductivity around a ball of air.

    In the case of the UFOs, it is entirely conceivable that we are simply
facing some sort of yet obscure aerial phenomena; but it is likewise conceivable that the "things" may indeed be visitors from some extraterrestrial civilization. With an estimated 50 billion solar systems in our galaxy,

and around 200 billion systems in other galaxies, it would be sheer arrogance to *assume that* only our speck of earth has managed to develop intelligent life. *If in fact* such life does exist on other stars, we may also *assume* that such life would generate the same brand of curiosity that makes us send astronauts into space. Conceding the possibility of UFOs being alien space vehicles, the question arises why their crews have not established direct contact with us. Here again, we may not be so presumptuous as to pattern all other intelligent beings as necessarily functioning along known lines, or possessing human motivations or human responses. Such beings might differ so radically from us in physical makeup as to render communication with us biologically impossible. They may have found our verbal intercourse as incomprehensible as we find the antenna talk of ants.

There is, as yet, not the slightest indication that UFOs—whatever they may be—represent a danger. Their role, so far, seems to have been merely observational. However if some reports prove true, such objects could be potentially lethal, if only because we do not possess any aircraft which can even remotely match their speed and maneuverability.

Writing in the 1964 edition of the *Encyclopaedia Britannica,* Dr. J. Allen Hynek stated that:

> *U. S. Air Force investigators long recognized that most originators of UFO reports are sincere, interested in the welfare and security of their country, and honestly puzzled by the sightings they report. Their subsequent readiness to ascribe a UFO to extraterrestrial sources, their emotional attachment to this explanation, and their reluctance to take into account the failure of continuous and extensive surveillance by trained observers to produce such sightings is surprising. It appears unreasonable that space craft should announce themselves to casual observers, while craftily avoiding detection by trained observers.*

Apparently, this statement did not take all the facts into full consideration. A report by a professional aviator like Captain Peter Killian, cannot be brushed off as a muddle-headed aberration of a hysteric. Apparently, the professor in January, 1966, altered his position somewhat, for in the *Journal of the American Association for the Advancement of Science,* Dr. Hynek wrote that it was "unequivocably false" to say that UFOs are "never reported by scientifically trained people," nor that "UFOs are never seen at close range. I have in my files several hundred reports which are fine brain teasers, and which easily could be made the subject of profitable discussion among physical and social scientists alike."

A little later, Major Hector Quintinalla, Air Force Chief of *Project Blue Book,* said that he did not know of a single case in the U. S. Air Force files of a confirmed report of a landing and lift-off. Combining these two statements, it would seem that the position of the experts connected with the United States government is that although reports of unidentified flying objects have come in from respected individuals, there is no such report which indicates that aircraft from outer space have ever landed on this planet.

Dr. William Markowitz, professor of physics at Marquette University, writing in a September issue of *Science,* a weekly journal published by the American Association for the Advancement of Science, confirms this position. He states that there is no logical reason for believing that UFOs are intelligently guided vehicles of extraterrestrial origin. Nevertheless—and here is the crux of the matter—Professor Markowitz goes on to flatly declare that he does not "take issue with reports of UFO sightings and will not try to explain them away." *"I agree"* states the professor, *"that unidentified objects exist."*

Pooh-poohing the thesis that creatures from outer space are casing Earth, Dr. Markowitz writes:

> *"We, ourselves, look back on an era when many people believed in the existence of centaurs, mermaids, and fire-breathing dragons. I am afraid that 21st-century scientists will contemplate with wonder the fact that, in an age of science such as ours, the United States Air Force was required to sponsor repeated studies of UFOs."*

This cynicism, however, is not shared by all scientists. The *New York Times* of Sunday, December 10, 1967, reported that Professor Feliks Zigel of the Moscow Aviation Institute had recently stated that the most characteristic type of UFO sighted by Russians could be described as follows:

> *"A luminous orange-colored crescent flying with its outward bend forward. Its surface is only a little duller than that of the moon. The horns of the crescent throw out jets, sometimes with sparks. The outer contour of the crescent is sharp, and the inner contour blurred and wavy."*

The Soviet scientist went on to say that such a sighting was made in the Ukraine during September, 1967, and that the reports that came to him contained the information that when the flying object was approached by a plane, the crescent dwindled into a disc. Soviet astronomers in Kazan set the diameter of the crescents that they observed at 500 to 600 meters, and they estimated the speed of these objects at better than three miles a second.

While cautioning that such reports require verification, Professor Zigel went on to say:

> *"The main task is to organize systematic study of the phenomena from astronomical and meteorological observatories. It will then become possible to determine whether the objects are of protoplasmic origin or come from another planet. The second hypothesis merits serious consideration to my mind."*

It is clear that Dr. Zigel, the Soviet professor and the thoroughly skeptical Dr. Markowitz, the American professor, do not exactly see eye to eye, yet there is one crucial point on which they both agree: *There are objects flying about in the skies whose source remains unexplained.*

The 'Ancient' Prisoner

At the stroke of three, the massive oaken gates of the prison fortress swung open. There were barked orders, the rumbling of drums, and the thunder of wheels and hoofs on cobblestones. Lines of pikemen and musketeers froze in salute as the carriage of Monsieur de Saint-Mars, newly appointed Governor of the Bastille, rolled into the courtyard.

Behind his coach came a heavily curtained litter carried by four servants. The moment the two vehicles halted, the Governor did a highly unorthodox thing. Without acknowledging the salute, he rushed over to the litter and personally supervised the procedure that followed. Two sergeants of the entourage helped out a man, stood him between them, and Governor leading, marched him straight to the Bertaudiere Tower.

The soldiers in the yard got no more than a fleeting glimpse of the prisoner. They saw only that he was tall and white-haired—and that his face *was masked by a black velvet cloth!* Then the tower gate slammed behind him. They never saw him again.

It was Thursday, September 18th, 1698. That day the Bastille of Paris received its most famous and least known inmate.

The fortress held him only five years; then the graveyard of St. Paul took him forever. With the possible exception of the Marquis de Sade, no one incarcerated in the infamous Bastille aroused as much excitement, speculation, and controversy as the man whose features remain as enigmatic as the reason for his imprisonment.

Chief instigator of the commmotion was Alexander Dumas, who

with but a spoonful of historical ingredients, cooked up one of the greatest romantic thrillers in literature. It was Dumas who transformed the
piece of cloth in front of the prisoner's face into "a visor of polished steel
soldered to a helmet of the same nature, which altogether enveloped the
whole of his head"—thereby giving the prisoner his classic title in his
book *The Man in the Iron Mask*.

The title stuck long after the original descriptions of the man were
forgotten. The title breathed an aura of macabre mystery. When George
Bernard Shaw was once asked which historical conundrum he would
most like to solve, he replied: "The first to come to my mind is who was
'The Man in the Iron Mask?'"

But outside the fertile brain of M. Dumas, there never was a man
in an *iron* mask. But there *was* a prisoner who frequently—though not
continually—had to wear a velvet face covering, and whose jailers went
to fantastic lengths to keep his identity hidden.

The mask was by no means unique in the annals of penal barbarity.
In 19th century England, as well as in Italy, certain types of convicts
were forced to wear black hoods over their heads whenever they mingled with other inmates. This was a method of psychological torture
designed to produce the feeling of complete isolation, cutting such a
prisoner off from other humans, condemning such a prisoner to faceless
anonymity. Such treatment crushed morale quicker and more
thoroughly than the stocks or the treadmill.

But to all accounts and purposes, the French authorities had no
such aim in masking the man in the Bastille. They didn't propose to de-
moralize him. Every contemporary description alleges that he was
treated with great consideration and courtesy; he was not subjected to
any of the brutalities that were part of prison life 300 years ago.

Apparently, the purpose of the mask was to prevent the prisoner
from being recognized. The same objective ran through everything concerning him for most of the 34 years of his confinement. He was even
buried under a name that wasn't his, and even that name was deliberately misspelled.

In the voluminous correspondence concerning him, his real name
was never written out. He was sometimes "the man you sent me;" oc-

casionally, "the person in the Tower;" mostly, "the Ancient Prisoner." It is this that makes this sinister riddle so fascinating. For this man, shut up for half a lifetime without the semblance of a trial, was not a forgotten nobody rotting away in oblivion: he was the subject of long and detailed letters passing back and forth between the King of France, the Ministers of War and Finance, and his warden. Now and then, these letters contained inquiries into the prisoner's state of health and well-being; but over and over again, they reiterated the Royal Command that he must not be allowed to talk nor communicate with anyone, that he must be threatened with instant death if he tried to talk to his jailers about anything other than his requirements for personal comfort. He was to become a shadow figure without nexus to the outside world.

And the powers in charge very nearly succeeded in making him that.

Historians have since been able to gain a pretty good idea of who the mystery man was; they are still as baffled as ever as to *why* he was treated as he was.

No hint of an answer can be found in all the years of correspondence dealing with the Ancient Prisoner. The only explanation is the casual mention that he had, somehow, incurred "the King's displeasure."

The king was Louis XIV, also known as "Le Grand Monarque," or "Roi Soleil." The royal displeasure could be a terrible thing for the individual it struck. For the fourteenth Louis represented the ultimate of royal absolutism, the creator as well as the victim of a personality cult comparable only to that surrounding the God-Pharaohs of Egypt. His much-quoted "L'Etat: c'est Moi" was the monstrous boast of the ages. Yet the statement was merely a statement of fact. Louis *was* the state. Every official was *his* official, every soldier *his* soldier, every subject *his* subject. He ruled the strongest, the richest and the most influential country of Europe as he would his private household. He was responsible only to himself; accountable, only to God.

But the system that gave him limitless power also forced him into a role which resembled that of the leading dancer in a perpetual intricate ballet. From the moment the King opened his eyes to the moment he retired, he was the centerpiece of an elaborate and never-ending,

THE MAN IN THE IRON MASK   *This painting by A. de̊Neuville,
engraved by C.LaPlante, depicts the myth given currency by Alexander
Dumas in his book entitled* The Man in the Iron Mask. *Dumas describes the prisoner's visor as having been made "of polished steel
soldered to a helmet of the same nature . . ."*

ritual. His morning toilet required the presence of 33 courtiers and valets, each with a distinct function laid down by the manual of etiquette that stipulated who was to unfold the royal shirt, who to select the royal ruffles, who to tie the royal garters, and who to pay His Majesty the first compliment of the day. He was not even permitted the privilege of his own company while performing the most private of functions, but had to remain ringed by attendants while squatting on what was politely called the "commode."

It would take a strong man to endure this wearisome rigamarole, day after day, for any length of time and still retain a measure of judgment. And Louis was a very strong man. He took it for 72 years—the longest reign in recorded history—and he proved to be a remarkably shrewd, hard-working, and capable sovereign. He had all the virtues of a top business tycoon, including early rising and the knack of delegating authority while retaining power. He was quite impervious to flattery. He had been trained in political intrigue by the Machiavellian Cardinal Mazarin, who also taught the monarch rigid self-control.

Though Louis could be utterly ruthless, he derived no pleasure from cruelty. None of the brutalities he ordered were based on anything save coolly calculated purpose. The "Sun King" was definitely not a creature of whims.

Which is why his treatment of the masked prisoner is doubly mystifying. We can ignore the stereotyped phrase about "the King's displeasure." Louis had other means of demonstrating annoyance—banishment, death by slow torture, and so on, which he could impose on whoever he chose. He must, therefore, have had some good reason to keep this particular man alive for 34 years, unharmed, but in limbo.

During the prisoner's lifetime, there was a certain amount of discreet speculation about what was going on. The speculation became bolder after Louis died. The question reached the level of a full-scale investigation after a later monarch, Louis XVI, was guillotined. The governing body of the French Revolution would have loved to uncover yet another juicy piece of monarchial villainy. The Revolution set its best researchers and archivists on the prowl.

The document hunters came upon the private journals of a certain

THE PRISON OF SAINT MARGUERITE   *This fortress stands on
an island one mile out in the Bay of Cannes.*

Etienne du Jonca, who was a lieutenant of the Bastille garrison during
the entire five years of the Ancient Prisoner's confinement in that prison.

The lieutenant described the arrival of the new Governor, how he
brought the masked captive with him from his previous command of
the island fortress of Saint Marguerite in southern France. This occurred
in 1698. Du Jonca only saw the mystery man when he was moved into
a tower cell. Otherwise, he was "waited upon"—fed by a sergeant from
the Governor's own entourage.

Du Jonca learned that the prisoner was allowed to hear Mass, his face hidden by the velvet cloth, and that he wore the same mask whenever the Bastille chaplain visited him. But the most remarkable fact, from du Jonca's viewpoint, was that the prisoner was not officially listed in the fortress records!

On November 19, 1703, du Jonca noted the unknown man's death. He passed away "about ten o'clock at night, without having a serious illness, and was buried at the graveyard of St. Paul."

The researchers promptly went through the burial register of the Church of St. Paul and found the following entry: "On November 19, one Marchioly, aged 45 or thereabouts, died in the Bastille, whose body was buried in the churchyard of St. Paul, his parish, the 20th of the present month. The register was signed by M. Rosarge, Major of the Bastille, and by M. Reilhe, surgeon major."

Who was this man Marchioly? It didn't take the archivists long to discover that no such man existed. The name, it seemed, was the deliberately obscured version of another name, which had, indeed, belonged to another one of Louis's prisoners, a Count Ercole Antonio Mattioli, State Secretary of the Duke of Mantua. The duke was up to his ears in debt. Louis XIV proposed one of those little deals that were the hallmark of his foreign policy. He would pay the Italian's debts in return for the fortress of Casale, an important strategic stronghold.

The money was paid, in gold coin, to Signor Mattioli. But the money never reached the duke. The State Secretary, it appeared, kept the lucre for himself. The duke refused to believe that the money had been paid; consequently, he refused to hand over Casale. Short of declaring war, there was nothing Louis could do.

But double-crossing the "Sun King" was, at best, a somewhat risky undertaking. Seven months later, in the spring of 1679, Louis got even. He despatched four of his court cavaliers to Mantua; they seized Mattioli one dark night, bundled him into a coach, and drove him back across the French frontier. There he was handed into the custody of M. de Saint-Mars, on the island prison of Saint Marguerite.

As far as the investigators of the Revolutionary Tribunal were concerned, here was the solution of the riddle. Louis did not wish anyone to learn about his revenge, and he therefore ordered Mattioli to be kept masked until the day he died. It was a neat solution—precisely what Louis had wanted posterity to conclude!

No, the key to the true identity of the Masked Man was not to be found in the archives of the Bastille nor in the archives of any other prison, but only in the files of the Ministry of War.

These records were a hideous mess: mountains of papers, prints, accounts, letters strewn everywhere, sheafs of writing stuffed behind cabinets, more papers piled up in stacks in the cellars, the hideous result of five years of rampaging by agents of the Revolution.

Only under Napoleon did the staff get around to the Herculean task of reclassification.

LA BASTILLE   Originally a fortified gate erected for the defense of Paris in 1370, this stronghold grew along with the city. Successive monarchs added new walls, buildings and bastions. The various portions of the Bastille, as shown here, date from different centuries. Under Louis XIV, the main function of this compound was that of a prison. The towers, containing the roomy cells, were 100 feet tall; the surrounding moat, 80 feet wide. The whole structure resembled a city within a city. By 17th century standards, accommodation for some prisoners was considered luxurious.

Only then was correspondence unearthed that showed that Mattioli was *not* the "Man in the Mask." The new crop of investigators found letters, and official copies of letters, that had passed between the Minister of War and Saint-Mars over a period of 34 years about the unknown prisoner. This correspondence began a good 10 years before the kidnapping of the Italian. Sprinkled in between were copies of notes that could only have been dictated by King Louis himself, and what was found added up to something much darker and more delicate than the jailing of a foreign crook.

Saint-Mars, who began his career as a subaltern officer of the King's Musketeers, seems to have been an ideal keeper of VIP prisoners. He was tactful, courteous, level-headed, and about as talkative as a clam. While invariably polite to his charges, he followed orders to the last comma. His eternal vigilance and single-minded attention to the instructions passed to him were the reason for the complete success of the masquerade decreed by his sovereign. There is no indication that he ever attempted to discover Louis' motives. Like other, more infamous, jailers after him, Saint-Mars just followed orders. He had reached the rank of major and command of the fort of Pignerol when he received what is believed to be the first note dealing with the mystery captive. It was dated July 19, 1669, and sent by the Minister of War, the Marquis de Louvois:

> *"The King has commanded that the man named Eustache Dauger be sent to Pignerol. It is of the utmost importance that he should be most securely guarded, and that he shall by no means give information about himself to anyone at all. You will prepare a cell that does not adjoin any place that can be approached by anyone, with double doors to be shut, for your sentries not to hear anything. You will, yourself, once a day take him sufficient food, and you must on no account listen for any reason at all to what he may want to say to you, but always threaten to kill him the instant he speaks of anything but his necessities."*

Eustache Dauger? The name didn't mean anything and wasn't

meant to. It was merely another bit of camouflage, this time for the benefit of the jailer. Hence the warning that Saint-Mars was not to listen to any personal revelations the prisoner might want to make.

You can almost hear the Prussian heel-click of perfect obedience in the major's reply:

> *"Monsieur de Vauroy handed over to me the man named Dauger. As soon as I had put him in a very secure place, I told him, in the presence of M. de Vauroy, that if he should speak to me or anyone else of anything but his necessities, I would immediately run him through with my sword."*

But along with this rule of silence went some mitigating conditions, laid down by the King, passed on by the Minister, and obeyed to the letter by the jailer. Accordingly, the prisoner was always to be "addressed in a mannerly fashion," was to be given as many prayer books as he wanted, was to be permitted to hear Mass on Sundays and feast days, and was to have the comfort of a priest for confession "three or four times a year if he so wishes." He was also to be given musical instruments "one at a time"—no mean privilege in the 17th century.

The instructions and reports go on and on. Both the King's concern and the Minister's interest over the prisoner are astonishing. Once Saint-Mars reported that his charge "suffered a mild fever." Immediately he is requested to inform the War Ministry of any worsening of the condition and he is ordered to render the prisoner every possible aid—this in an age when captives were left chained to the wall until their legs withered.

But the most remarkable aspect was the major's remarks on the prisoner's behavior. Time and again, Saint-Mars comments on the man's "pleasing docility," his "sweet nature," his "Christian submission to the will of God and his King." This, then, was no individual who felt himself unjustly or cruelly treated. If anything, it would appear he expected worse. Once, through some laxity of the guards, a servant was able to approach the prisoner and ask him questions. On being interrogated by Saint-Mars, the servant swore that the man had merely shaken his head silently, and had refused to reply.

THE "SUN KING"   Louis XIV, best known for his pronouncement
"L'etat c'est moi" ("I am the state"), mounted the throne of France at the
age of five and occupied it for 72 years—the longest reign in recorded history. Hard-working and shrewd, methodical and ruthless, Louis XIV was
the most powerful monarch of his time and the center of a personality cult.
His appetite for foreign conquest almost matched his taste for mistresses.

In 1678, Saint-Mars had his reward in the form of a promotion. He was appointed Governor of the fortress prison of Saint Marguerite, in the Bay of Cannes, the heart of today's French Riviera. When he moved there, he took his silent prisoner with him; the rest were left behind at Pignerol.

A few months later, Count Mattioli was delivered into his keep there, and was registered under his correct name in the fortress record. Thus while the light-fingered Italian and the mystery prisoner were lodged under the same roof for a time, they were surely not the same person.

Mattioli was mentioned by name on numerous occasions. On the other hand, "Eustache Dauger"—whose crime nobody knows—faded out for good. His name never crops up again. From then on, he is always referred by labels such as "the Man in the Lower Tower," or—in later years—as "the Ancient Prisoner." Mattioli is believed to have died on Saint Marguerite around 1694. The unknown had more than a decade of incarceration ahead of him.

In all the 20 years the unknown prisoner spent on Saint Marguerite Island not a single record indicates that he was forced to wear a mask. Saint-Mars used other means to keep him unrecognized. When the special prisoner attended Mass, he was obliged to sit behind a special curtain arrangement rigged up in the prison chapel. When the priest came to his cell to hear his confession, all communication took place through a small slit in the inner door of the cell, which remained locked while the outer one was opened.

The first time the mask is officially mentioned is during his transfer to the Bastille. Saint-Mars was ultimately promoted to the Governorship of France's most important prison. The move necessitated a journey through three-quarters of the kingdom. The Governor traveled by coach; his prisoner was carried behind him in a litter, which slowed down their progress considerably. Now we come upon the first verified eyewitness accounts of the famous black velvet cloth.

There were several overnight stops at rural inns. During these stopovers, the arms-clanking, plume-waving martial splendor of the convoy attracted much attention. The peasants gathered in droves to watch the masked prisoner being escorted from his litter; but they were kept at a distance by the drawn swords of the prisoner's escort.

One Charles Brisot, landlord of an "auberge" at Digoin, has left the following description of the strangest dinner he ever served:

> *"The prisoner was led to the small private room behind the taproom and guards were posted outside the door. When I entered with the tray containing their supper, I found the masked man sitting upright in his chair, the wine beaker before him. The Governor sat facing him across the table. He had two pistols lying on the table in front of him and handy to his fingers. As I passed, I could see that they were cocked and ready. He motioned me to place the food on the table, but neither he nor the prisoner spoke a word. I put down the supper in haste, and bade them a good appetite. I do not know how the prisoner supped, as his whole face was clothed, but I must presume that he was permitted to remove the mask as soon as I had taken my leave."*

There is a story, quite apocryphal, that during his journey the Masked Man seized an unguarded moment to scratch his name and birthplace on a tin plate with his knife. He then threw the plate out of a tavern window, hoping to tell the outside world who he was. The plate, the tale goes, was found by a shepherd, who immediately returned it to one of the guards. He was taken before Saint-Mars, apparently in hopes of a reward.

The Governor glanced at the plate and then at the shepherd.

"Have you read this?" he asked.

"No, esteemed sir," said the shepherd. "I cannot read."

"Then go and praise God for your ignorance," said the Governor softly, putting his pistol away.

The most remarkable thing about this story is that nothing like it is ever known to have happened. The mass of correspondence containing the smallest details of the prisoner's activities does not include a single hint at an attempt at communication or escape. To use Saint-

Mars's phrase, the prisoner was "a lamb"; he apparently remained a lamb during the entire term of his captivity.

Little can be added about the five years the Masked Man spent in the Bastille. The inquiries and reports about him continued. We learn that he was shifted from one tower to another, that his cell was so placed that he could see the sky but not the ground through his barred window, and that he occasionally played the lute and the bass fiddle to while away the hours.

One day, after having been confessed by M. Giraut, the chaplain, the prisoner died suddenly and quietly. He had spent an estimated 34 years in solitary confinement.

As soon as Napoleon's researchers confirmed that the Masked Man was not Mattioli, the quest began to discover *who* he was. There had been a host of rumors in circulation long before the nationalization of the royal archives made serious research possible. Most speculation veered heavily toward illegitimacy in high places, implying that the Masked Man was the bastard son of a) King Charles II of England b) Cardinal Mazarin c) King Louis himself. Very intriguing, these guesses, but quite out of keeping with the prevailing social mores of the day.

Neither of the two monarchs nor the extremely worldly cardinal had the slightest reason to deny or conceal their "love children." Bastardy was an accepted feature of the "Age of Splendor," both in the highest and in the lowest circles. Every legitimate royal offspring was carefully accounted for, giving no one casually conceived on the "wrong side of the blanket," the least hope of becoming a claimant to the throne. And the diplomat-churchmen of the time were expected to keep mistresses in much the same spirit as a 19th century Anglican bishop was expected to keep a riding stable.

Dumas's "The Man in the Iron Mask" is based on a much sounder premise. In the novel, the prisoner is an illegitimate brother of Louis XIV, a man bearing such striking resemblance to the king that he can impersonate him. Louis, not wishing to kill anyone of the blood royal, has him permanently imprisoned and permanently masked. The novel is so ingeniously laced with historical facts and plausible half-truths that a

THE MAN IN THE IRON MASK   *This drawing by Vierle shows the prisoner playing a musical instrument.*

great number of readers became convinced of its authenticity, a fact which Dumas, who felt justifiably vain about his inventive powers, rather resented. Actually, the theory put forward in the novel doesn't bear much examination. At the time of his arrest, the Ancient Prisoner was a man in his late twenties. If he had resembled the King as closely as alleged, he would have been a famous personality wherever he might have spent his years of liberty. His profile would have greeted him from every silver coin; every peasant, milkmaid, and tradesman would have recognized him. It would, at that advanced stage of his life, been quite impossible to spirit him away, without stirring up a tornado of gossip.

No, it was the very obscurity of the prisoner, the utterly blank page of his background, that made him such an arcanum—as difficult to trace as a victim of amnesia found naked.

Apart from his name and approximate age, the only thing known about him was that he had been secretly arrested by the Town Captain of Dunkirk, on a warrant signed by King Louis himself—a warrant which, contrary to established practice, did not mention his particular transgression. The captain had then personally conveyed the prisoner clear across France, and had handed him over to Saint-Mars, in the citadel of Pignerol.

For over 60 years, French scholars have combed through municipal and parish records, searching for someone called Eustache Dauger, born in the 1630s, and last heard of at, or on his way to, the Channel Coast. They came across several Daugers, but none named Eustache, a fairly rare Christian name. Was the name, then, fictitious?

Not completely. For some odd reason, the cover-up names used in the case always bore some similarity to the original.

When historians finally tracked down their man, they found him in the archives of the so-called "Chambre Ardente." This was a secret criminal court set up by the King and presided over by the incorruptible lieutenant of Paris police, de la Reynie. Its only function was to investigate and try poison cases. On all accounts, this court was one of the busiest tribunals in the country. There was a sound reason why it operated in secret. The crimes this court dealt with were committed chiefly by the higher ranks of the nobility and by the clergy, men and women with illustrious titles and close connections with the royal court. Had they ever been held in the open, as things were set up, such trials would have rocked the general public. Louis could study the evidence gathered by the indefatigable de la Reynie and his detectives and decide, at leisure, who was to be executed, who to be let off with a slapped wrist, and who was to be helped to escape abroad. And the common people, the multitude known as "The Great Unwashed," were none the wiser.

This was a very good thing for the sake of the established social order. For some of the activities uncovered by the "Chambre Ardente" came close to being incredible. It wasn't merely that France's secular and clerical aristocracy poisoned each other wholesale—the court dealt with 442 cases in the space of four years—but the manner in which they did so defies belief.

Louis's "Age of Splendor" has also been called the "Age of Arsenic." And with every reason! In Paris alone, there were some 200 or more female merchants whose stock in trade consisted of poisons and love philtres, sold to steady customers who used them to alternatively attract and liquidate their relays of bed companions.

The poisons were of a very primitive kind: mostly arsenic, antimony, henbane, and aconite, which had to be administered in large quantities. (For the really lethal stuff, like prussic acid, strychnine, curare or beryllium did not appear until a couple of centuries later.) The results were somewhat uncertain. The prudent thought it wise to try out the dosage on lesser fry before tackling the important victim. Thus, the death by poison of, say, an aristocratic husband was often preceded by the demise of two or three base-born humans who served as test cases.

Each murder case tried by the "Chambre Ardente," therefore, usually involved two, five, or a dozen or more victims. One must agree that the exclusion of the general populace—from which three-quarters of the victims were drawn—was an advisable precaution.

The "cause célèbre" of the day, the one that staggered even the fairly unflappable Louis, was the trial of Madame de Brinvilliers. In her case, the monarch waived the French law that forbade the torture of members of the nobility and permitted the "painful question" to be put to her for seven hours running.

Madame was small and plump, with a mass of chestnut hair, alabaster skin, and the "sweetest voice in Christendom." She spoke fluent Latin and Greek, and wrote exquisite verse, but compared to her Lucrezia Borgia would seem as mild as Blondie Bumstead. The number of her lovers and her victims were about even. Her lovers included her two brothers, her five boy and girl cousins, her confessor, her children's tutor, and the 12-year-old son of her coachman. Among her victims were numbered at least five of the sick paupers at the "Hôtel Dieu" on whom she tested her arsenic sweetmeats, her father, both her brothers, and nine or so of her casual acquaintances. She also tried, unsuccessfully, to poison her elder daughter, her tutor-lover, and her husband, the Marquis de Brinvilliers. The Marquis survived, semi-paralyzed for life and had to be helped to his seat to watch her being beheaded.

Madame was no lone wolf. In most of her undertakings, she was aided by her steady paramour, one Gaudin de Sainte-Croix, and also by a group of fellow-spirits which included a young, dishonorably discharged cavalry officer named Eustache d'Auger!

There it was, the name of the "Ancient Prisoner," easily recognizable in spite of the lobotomized "d."

Young d'Auger, who hailed from Picardy, had not been involved in Madame's later career. He vanished from the scene years before Madame's execution in 1676. But d'Auger had assisted her during several of the Black Mass celebrations that horrified her judges far more than her homicide record. Not so much for the sacrilege involved, but *because several of the participating ladies eventually became royal mistresses.*

It is very difficult in this day and age to convey the meaning and purpose of the Black Mass, and to explain the hideous fascination this perverted rite held for thousands of church-going Catholics. In 17th century France, the celebration of the Black Mass reached the proportions of an underground cult, attracting a vast lunatic fringe that included priests and nuns, scholars and courtiers, as well as the demimonde.

Imp. lith. de Delpech.   Lebrun del.^t

M.^{rlle} D'AUBRAY M.^{quise} DE BRINVILLIERS.

Dessiné d'après nature au moment où elle allait au supplice.

Tiré du Musée Royal de France.

THE MARQUISE DE BRINVILLIERS   The most notorious poisoner of her time, she was the eldest daughter of the civil lieutenant of Paris. She murdered her father and an estimated 17 others, including both her brothers. This drawing by Le Brun shows her on her way to her public execution, when she was 46 years old. Her legendary beauty succumbed to decades of debauchery plus five consecutive hours of the "water torture." She was beheaded, her body burned, and her ashes scattered to the winds.

Basically, it was a quest for power. And since the power of Good, that is the power of Established Religion, seemed entirely on the side

du mesme Jour lundy 19 me de
novembre 1703 le prisonnier
Inconneu toujours masque dun masque
de velours noir que Monsieur de
St mars gouverneur a mené avec
que luy en venant des illes ste marguerite
quil gardet depuis lontamps lequel
setant trouue hier un peu mal en
sortant dela messe il est mort
le jourduy sur les dix heures du
soir sans auoir eu unne grende
maladie il nesepeut pas moins
mr girault nottre homonier le
comfessa hier sur pris desamort
il napoint reseu les sacremens
et nottre homonier la excorte un
momant auend que de mourir
et se prisonnier Inconneu gardé de
puis si lontamps aeste enterre
le mardy a quattre hures dela
pver midy 20 me novembre dans
le semetiere St paul nottre pa
Je apris du voisse ou sur le registre mortuel
depuis confant gpe adoune un nom ausy Inconneu #
nome sur leregistre
mr de marsilie   Monsieur de rosarges maior
que on apaié   et ur veil sieurgien qui hont
40 # sans   signe sur le registre
demant

PAGE FROM THE JOURNAL OF ETIENNE DU JONCA   *This is an enlargement of one of the original reports relating to the "Masked Prisoner" made by the King's lieutenant in the Bastille. It describes the death of the mystery man in these words: "On the same day, November 19, 1703, the unknown prisoner, always masked with a mask of black velvet, whom M. de Saint-Mars, the Governor, brought with him on coming from the Ile Sainte-Marguerite, whom he had kept for a long time, the which happening to be a little ill yesterday on coming from Mass, he died today, about ten o'clock at night, without having had a serious illness; it could not have been slighter . . ."*

of Established Government, the ritual took the form of an appeal to the Power of Evil. The Black Mass was Satanism, devil-worship. Here was a desperate attempt to do a bit of manipulating by those who felt that they were being eternally manipulated. The special attraction for women lay in the fact that they were the most manipulated of all. The female devotees felt that their only path to power led over the person— and bed—of some powerful male. The Black Mass, therefore, was frequently designed to cast an erotic spell over such a power figure, to eliminate rivals for his favor, and to render the participant irresistible to him.

The technical details of the ritual are as unprintable as those of the Mau-Mau Oath. The Black Mass was an obscene reversal of the Christian Mass, with a few trimmings added. The altar was a naked woman; the incense, dung; the "holy water," urine; and so forth. An ordained priest had to officiate. It was his task to desecrate the Host, and to intone certain Latin prayers to Satan in wordage of the vilest sort of obscenity. At the peak of the ceremony, the priest cut the throat and slit open the belly of a living baptized infant, drenching the worshipers in the blood.

At this moment, the female appellant would bring herself to a sexual climax, gasping out pleas like: "May the King's juices flow hot only for me!" "Let the Queen's womb shrivel!" "Make Madame de la Valliere grow dry and leathery!" "May the King thirst for my breasts and hunger eternally for my loins!"

We don't know just how many women reached the King's couch via this chamber of horrors. At least two—so believed—Olympe Man-

PAINTING OF LUDOVICUS MAGNUS   Louis XIV, referred to in the Latin as the "Great Louis," was painted in his lifetime by a contemporary artist named Geuslin. The above is a copper engraving made in the 17th century by Vermuelon of the original painting.

cini and Madame de Montespan. With the prize so dazzling and competition so fierce, some court ladies were willing to employ *any* means to gain the attention of Le Grand Monarch. Especially, when sacrificial infants were dirt cheap; the starving denizens of the Paris slums were willing to sell their babies for two dollars a head.

It was never discovered what role Eustache d'Auger played in the Black Mass. We know that he was the first of Madame de Brinvilliers' coterie to be arrested. Her beau, Sainte-Croix, died in 1672 from inhaling the fumes of his own poison pot. Another of the group, one La Chaussée was broken at the wheel in March 1676; Madame's pretty head rolled four months later.

D'Auger, alone, was never put on trial. He was simply tucked away for the rest of his natural life. One can merely venture a guess at the reason for this peculiar treatment. One or more of Louis's mistresses might have interceded on his behalf—perhaps, one of the ladies he introduced to the ghastly ritual and who felt obliged to him for her subsequent elevation. Perhaps such influence saved his neck.

But why the king chose to keep him unrecognized for all those years, both before and after his death, that *why* defies guesswork. A realization of his hellish past might account for the otherwise unaccountable resignation of the masked prisoner to his fate. Moreover, compared to the wheel, the block, and the thumbscrews he did, after all, get off lightly.

Those Who Walk on Flames

There are in this astounding land heathen wizards who can make serpents dance to the flute, while others will cause a tree to grow before your very eyes. Others still can cast a spell upon a length of rope so that it stands upright like a candle in the empty air. They will also permit themselves to be entombed beneath the ground, remaining thus buried for a great period of time and yet emerge again hale in body and spirit. Such men will also take their ease reclining upon boards studded with sharp nails or they will drive cruel spikes and daggers and swords into their own flesh, but do not bleed or suffer. And then there are those who are able to walk on flames and yet do not burn. . . .

The above is an extract from a letter penned in February 1703, by James Buckfield, junior clerk of the East India Company in Madras, to his sister in England. Chances are that Mr. Buckfield never actually saw more than one or two of the marvels with which he regaled his sister in far-off Bristol. The rest he probably knew only from hearsay. But his letter is remarkable insofar as it constitutes the first record to list virtually the entire bag of tricks that came to be known collectively as *jadoo,* the magic of the Orient.

Jadoo is a kind of pidgin-Urdu denoting the black arts in the broadest sense. A *jadoo-wallah* can be anything from a sleight-of-hand entertainer to a genuine fakir. But to the Europeans who picked up the word jadoo meant a specifically Eastern brand of legerdemain for which they could find no rational explanation.

The first Eastern trick to arouse European wonder—and still the most popular—was snake charming. A poisonous reptile is made to dance— that is, sway back and forth—to the tune of a flute. The snake is supposed to become so entranced by the snake charmer's music that it "gets rhythm" and forgets to bite.

Now it so happens that snakes are stone-deaf; they pick up sound vibrations from the ground, but they can't hear anything transmitted by air. The sole purpose of the flute is to attract a crowd.

The snake is invariably defanged; no *samp-wallah* in his right mind would face a reptile still in possession of its armament. The defanged snake will not bite because its mouth is sore; none the less, instinctively it will still spar for a striking position. And therein lies all the mystery of snake charming. As the performer raises the lid of the snake basket he kicks the side, and the reptile rears up. Then, while blowing his gourd pipe, the charmer sways his body from side to side, and the snake follows his movements—just as it would even if the *samp-wallah* weren't playing anything at all. The moment the performer stops swaying, the snake does the same. Snake charmers usually perform with cobras because they are more sluggish than the faster moving kraits and vipers.

Snake charming, practiced from Morocco to Thailand, is probably the most widespread of the *jadoo* acts, but is always performed with deaf and defanged creatures.

The "Growing Tree Trick"—also known as the "Mango Miracle"— is uniquely Indian, or at least was until Western magicians copied it and thereby made the stunt unfashionable in its country of origin. Some European and American exponents of the occult still proclaim this trick to be one of the "genuine wonders" of the East.

This spectacular trick can only be done with a mango. It takes half an hour or more to perform. The spectator sees the magician squat down and plant in the ground a mango pit the size of a large chestnut. He then erects a tripod of three long sticks over the spot, which he elabor- ately covers with his cloak, thus forming a rough tent. After reciting prayers over the structure, the magician whips away the cloak and reveals a little green shoot struggling out of the ground. The cloak goes back; more prayers follow; and next time there is a sapling growing under the tripod. Finally, after yet more prayers, the cloak is removed once again. And behold—a mango tree—two-foot high—complete with several fruits which the magician plucks and hands to the audience for consumption.

This trick is tremendously impressive but incredibly simple once you know how it's done. Like every other good piece of stage magic, this trick requires a lot of practice and an effective spiel, but nothing more. The success of the act depends on the uncanny dexterity of the performer and the rubber-like qualities of the mango plant. This particular plant can be rolled up into a small space and it will, when released, snap back to full size without damage. The first little sprig is coiled up inside the hollow mango pit. As the magician erects the tent, he breaks the thin shell, and the sprig "grows" from the ground.

All the other growth stages are secreted in various pockets of the cloak and are planted into the earth each time the magician rearranges the tent. The prayer recitals merely serve to build suspense and to strengthen the illusion of a growing process.

But the *pièce de résistance* of all *jadoo* art has always been the Indian rope trick, which has become the focal point of an entire mystique as well as of some furious controversy. The rope trick represents the ultimate peak of conjuring craft. Nevertheless, there are quite a number of Western Orientalists willing to swear that the stunt is legendary and has never been performed at all. As proof they relate that when the Prince of Wales (later King George V) visited India in 1902, he offered the fabulous fee of £10,000 (then about $50,000) to anyone who would perform the trick. There were no takers. The same negative result was achieved by the American magician Howard Thurston who offered $1,000.

The trick is claimed to be more than 700 years old. The first European to mention the rope trick was Marco Polo, who reported that he witnessed a performance of it at the court of the Mongol ruler Kublai Khan in 1289. Some Indian sources believe that the trick originated in China, and was brought to India by a troupe of Tartar jugglers.

Wherever its birthplace, the great rope trick has become an all-Indian tradition but a tantalizingly elusive one. Almost as soon as the British penetrated India, they began to send home accounts of this "wondrous feat," usually without having witnessed it. The controversy was born there and then, and is still going strong. Even now you can buy a pretty hectic argument in any gathering place of old Poona hands by merely mentioning the rope trick.

Of the several versions of the spectacle, the most spectacular goes as follows:

CHARMING SNAKES   An Indian demonstrates his art before a crowd of villagers. The expanded hoods of the cobras indicate that they are disturbed.

The magician takes a piece of rope about 40 feet long and throws it into the air. Two, three, four times it flops back to the ground as any rope would. But the fifth—or tenth—time it remains absolutely rigid, rearing high above the heads of the spectators while the magician gestures at it from below.

Then the magician calls his apprentice, a small boy, and orders him to climb up the rope. The boy is unwilling and pleads that he is tired. The magician, angry at this insubordination, seizes a stick and chases the lad up the rope. From above, the boy lets fly with some juicy insults.

Infuriated, his master pulls out a huge dagger, shakes his fist at the culprit, and shins up the rope after him. At the top, the magican lays hold of the boy. There's a flurry of struggling confusion, punctuated by horrible screams. A bloody child's arm comes hurtling down; then a leg; then another arm; then another leg; and finally, the boy's severed head.

The magician comes down, waving his blood-stained blade. His assistants, weeping and terrified, gather up the boy's limbs and place them in a box. The magician checks the contents carefully to make sure nothing is missing, and calls out, "His left leg—where is his left leg, you scoundrels?" They find it somewhere on the ground and come running with it.

Then the magician slams the lid of the box shut, closes his eyes, murmurs a long incantation, and gives the box a hearty kick. Whereupon, the lid flies open, and out climbs the boy, grinning widely and in excellent shape, which he proves immediately by running around the audience collecting baksheesh.

The rope trick is rather strong meat, for both your stomach and your sense of rationality. Not surprisingly, it has provided a field day for the disciples of the all-done-with-hypnotism school. But it has been proved absolutely impossible to hypnotize a single individual against his will, and certainly not a gabbling, jostling, street crowd. Mass hypnosis is a myth and is to be differentiated from mass suggestion, an entirely different matter only too easily accomplished, as every policeman who has ever interrogated a group of witnesses of an accident can testify.

But even if the magician were able to cast a hypnotic spell over his audience, he would certainly refrain from doing so. A person who has been hypnotized has no recollection of anything he has seen or done while in that state; and would be unlikely to hand out baksheesh for something he could not remember seeing.

When the rewards for doing the rope trick were offered, the offerers stipulated that the act should be performed under certain controlled conditions. And under those conditions, the stunt could not be performed—hence the absence of takers.

For, as the term indicates, the rope trick is a trick. It needs a prepared setting, a boy both very small and well trained, at least four other

HUMAN PIN CUSHION   A southern Indian Tamil chants prayers while an arched framework of arrows is fastened through his skin. Only the flesh is pierced; muscles and arteries are carefully avoided. The ordeal, though painful, is harmless. Indian authorities frown on such exhibitions, discouraging them in areas where Western tourists are likely to be shocked.

*BED OF NAILS   An Indian fakir re-
clines on a board studded with pointed steel.*

assistants, and a magician of outstanding skill and agility.

The initial prerequisite for the act is its location. It has to be staged either in a built-up area or on a hilly landscape. Before the audience gathers, a thin but strong wire is stretched overhead between two high points, rooftops or hilltops. The trick is always performed at dusk and always accompanied by the lighting of bonfires. Ostensibly the fires serve to attract attention, but their real purpose is to add an uneven flicker to the already dim light, rendering the wire, high above the ground, quite invisible.

The magician's 40-foot rope has tiny grappling hooks concealed at one end. He throws it up until the hooks catch the wire, making the rope appear to stand, whereas it actually hangs. The illusion is helped considerably by the attention of the audience being focused on the vertical rope, being unaware of the horizontal supporting wire.

When the magician pursues his apprentice aloft, he is wearing a voluminous cloak. Concealed underneath it are the dismembered portions of a freshly slaughtered monkey whose hair has been shaved off. Strapped to the magician's body is a kind of leather harness. He catches the boy at the very top of the rope, a locale only hazily visible to the spectators. He and the boy struggle; the boy screams; and the magician drops the bloody monkey limbs, thereby causing the audience to look at the ground. During this diversion, the boy quickly climbs into the harness, clinging to his master like a baby, and is carried down hidden beneath the cloak.

When the monkey portions are piled into the box, the magician checks to see if everything is there, keeping the open lid between himself and the spectators. Covered by the lid, the boy climbs out of the harness and into the box. A minute later, the flabbergasted onlookers see the youngster emerge unscathed. The magician gestures again, his assistants cut the wire, and the rope collapses. The great trick is accomplished.

Most Western observers can see no appreciable distinction between a fakir slumbering on a bed of nails and a *samp-wallah* working his cobra. But in fact these two belong to entirely different social categories. The habit of lumping them together is responsible for much of our confusion about *jadoo*.

The snake charmers and tree growers are professional entertainers, akin to the Arab gulli-gulli man with his multiplying chickens and the garden variety of stage magician with his top hat full of rabbits. These men perform tricks and lay no claim to be doing anything else. But the fakir or sadhu does not purport to "entertain." By reclining on a nail-studded board or by making a human pincushion of himself or by dragging around crockery attached to hooks embedded in his flesh, he is performing a religious act which demonstrates the sadhu's dominance of his spirit over his body.

There are an estimated four million sadhus and fakirs in India today, each one considered a sacred being by his group of followers, which may range in number from half a dozen to hundreds of thousands. These holy men represent living symbols of the Hindu creed that denies the importance of pain and pleasure and elevates the spirit above every-

BURIED HOLY MAN   *An Indian Sadhu is buried up to his neck in the sand alongside the River Ganges in Benares. He collects alms from passers-by. This sight is still quite common in India's sacred city, although total burial has been banned by the government.*

BURIED ALIVE   On the outskirts of New Delhi, as his disciples look on, Hindu holy man, Ramdasji Girnari, stands in his nail-studded coffin before being buried alive for 24 hours. The 64-cubic-foot coffin was then covered with brick and mortar. Girnari avowed he was doing penance "for the welfare of the people." His disciples claim that on three different occasions Girnari had been buried alive for 13 days.

thing mundane. The more predominant the spiritual concentration, the less the concern about physical discomfort. The sadhu proves his credo by inflicting torture on himself of which the bed of nails is merely a minor demonstration.

The government of India takes a rather dim view of these practices. Over the past 20 years, the government has banned the most blatant of these exercises. You no longer see holy men ambling about the streets stark naked, with steel slivers sticking from their cheeks, arms, and backs, or parading about with heavy wooden balls hooked from their nipples. It is also against the law.to let oneself be buried, unless demonstrably dead beforehand.

Nevertheless the self-mortification goes on, though not where such sights are likely to upset lady tourists. The physical torture persists because this is the way most sadhus earn their living. The more outrageously he treats his body, the more bountiful the gifts of his disciples. There are, of course, thousands of hermits, who meditate, fast, and suffer in the solitude of mountain peaks or forests; but the majority of holy men seem to prefer an audience which bestows alms, admiration, and occasionally, even political power.

It is almost impossible to distinguish the religious stoic from him who suffers for the sake of attracting alms. The stoicism in either case is equal, because the lacerations are real enough—real, though not quite as horrifying as they appear to the uninitiated.

If you press your hand down on a single nail sticking from a board, the result will be a nasty puncture. Do the same on a board closely studded with nails and you would not get a scratch. Provided they are dense enough, the nails will offer an almost solid surface. This is the principle of the fakir's nail bed, which is as closely studded as a hairbrush, and therefore allows him to stretch out on it with some discomfort but with no injury.

The practice of driving pins and nails through portions of the anatomy is also not nearly so agonizing and dangerous as it looks—provided one knows which portions to choose. The fakirs push pins only through flesh, carefully avoiding muscles and arteries. The insertion doesn't hurt much more than a doctor's hypodermic needle; it's the *idea* we find horrifying. Once one gets over the revulsion, it becomes a relatively easy matter to shove hatpins through thighs, cheeks, nostrils, tongue, and eyelids. The pain is considerably less than that inflicted by a dentist's drill.

MORTIFYING THE FLESH One of India's four million fakirs is *demonstrating his indifference to pain by piercing his cheeks and tongue with steel pins. The pain is actually much less than one would assume.*

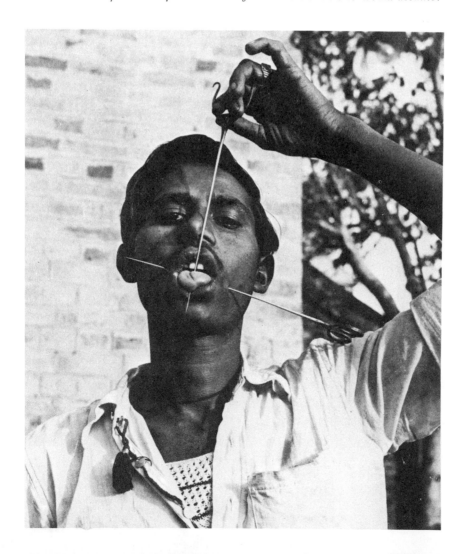

Exhibitions of similar feats were once fairly common at rural American carnival shows, until increased audience sophistication and squeamishness rendered such stunts unpopular. The performer, who might wear Hindu garb, would sew a button to his chest or run pins through the loose skin of his forearm as a preliminary to a fire-eating act. There is no trickery involved; such a performance hurts all right, but not so badly as an empty stomach. With sterilized needles, the act is considerably less risky than prizefighting.

What the rustic performers couldn't parallel was the fakir's feat of body control, although several Westerners—notably the late Harry Houdini have managed incredible performances. The secret behind even the most astonishing of these feats is the mind-over-matter formula. Human willpower is capable of exerting much greater influence over physical functions than we used to believe possible. Since the recent spate of yoga literature, the Western world has become more familiar with this fact, but we still have only an inkling of the extent to which it is true.

A fakir, willing to forego a normal life and by concentrating for years on his brain-body relationship to the exclusion of everything else, can achieve control that appears miraculous. He is able to regulate the blinking of his eyelids, develop dexterity in his toes equal to that of his fingers, able to tense or relax almost any muscle at will. A more advanced practitioner can swallow his tongue, slow down or speed up his pulse beat, contract certain muscles that will cause his blood circulation to come almost to a standstill.

Several years ago, three Indian yogis underwent tests prepared by the University of Michigan Medical School. Each of the three could reduce his heartbeat until it became inaudible through a stethoscope, though the beat still registered on an electrocardiograph. Fifty years earlier, medical science would have pronounced these men dead.

Indian folklore abounds with stories of sadhus who let themselves be buried for ten and even 50 years. When such a holy one was disinterred, he was found to be not only alive but minus a beard. Allegedly, that man was able to suspend hair growth along with all other bodily functions. In the twenties and thirties, American magazines and newspaper supplements regularly printed these yarns, usually with lurid illustrations but omitted to mention that educated Indians regarded the stories in roughly the same light as we regard the tale of Rip Van Winkle.

It is true that until the practice was outlawed in 1955, fakirs had themselves buried alive in droves but not under what could, by any stretch of the term, be called "controlled conditions." The phoney would crawl out of his tomb through a previously dug tunnel, and crawl back in time to be properly unearthed. So many of the sincere were dug up dead that the government authorities issued a ban on the practice.

Harry Houdini, the great American myth mangler, once staged a burial act of his own under circumstances that allowed no trickery of any kind. He had himself locked in a watertight metal casket that was lowered to the bottom of the swimming pool of New York's Shelton Hotel. There the casket remained, clearly visible to hundreds of spectators, for one hour and 28 minutes before Houdini pulled the signal cord. He came out feeling faint and nauseous but otherwise unharmed, and he was soon able to give an account of his experience.

Houdini had mastered the art of breath control as thoroughly as any Hindu practitioner. He found it quite unnecessary to go into a trance. By remaining perfectly still and keeping his respiration down to a minimum, Houdini performed a feat most doctors would have considered impossible. Later, the magician conducted several other experiments in the same casket. He found that even breathing normally, there was sufficient oxygen in the container to last a man for 20 minutes under water, provided the subject didn't move. Houdini, in fact, could duplicate almost any fakir feat without the preliminary trance, for which he professed only contempt. But even the great Houdini never attempted what is possibly the most astonishing *jadoo* display of all—fire walking.

Strictly speaking, fire walking does not come under the heading of Oriental magic. Fire walking is an amazingly widespread cult, practiced in North Africa, Japan, Fiji, and Madagascar, as well as India. There is no unifying motive. Only in India is fire walking regarded as a religious rite, elsewhere people regard it as a form of entertainment with only the slightest of mystical overtones. The only feature shared by all fire walkers is the complete mystery that surrounds the art. Of all the world's

exotic puzzlement, fire walking remains the most baffling.

In 1959, I was privileged to watch a fire walking ceremony on Bora Bora, one of the Society Islands in the South Pacific. Bora Bora lies about 150 miles from Tahiti. The event was announced several days beforehand, like a circus performance. People gathered from every part of the little isle in what was decidedly a family picnic atmosphere. No trace of pagan ritualism here, both spectators and participants were church-going Roman Catholics.

JAPANESE FIREWALKING   Shinto priests walk over blazing logs during the religious ceremony of "Hi-Wattarou," part of the ritualistic worship of the Sun Goddess Amotarasu.

By the time I arrived, the firepit, called the *umu* by the Polynesians, was going full blast. It was 40 feet long and about half as wide. I couldn't estimate the depth because the heat near the edge was almost unbearable, a heat generated by large rocks that had been lying on a bed of burning logs and charcoal for the past 48 hours. Now the rocks were glowing red-hot, making the air above the pit shimmer with the kind of heat waves you see around a blast furnace. The native attendants near the pit were smeared from head to foot with coconut oil.

Aside from several hundred islanders, there were a dozen American and Australian tourists, three French naval officers from the Papeete station, and one solitary policeman. Several of us tried to stand at the edge of the trench long enough to get a good look, but the glow was enough to singe our eyeballs. In spite of our sunglasses, the blowtorch effect on our faces became agonizing within seconds. The attendants obliged us by dropping a few colored rags into the pit. There was a momentary flicker of flame, and in a trice the rags powderized.

At three o'clock sharp, the fire walkers appeared. There were eight of them, all handsome athletic young Tahitians, looking like figures straight off a travel poster. Their arrival was quite unceremonious. They mingled with the tourists, answered questions in broken French, and grinned boyishly when we inspected their feet for possible protective coatings. Their soles were hard and tough, but no more so than those of anyone who is accustomed to going barefoot.

Then a patter of drums sounded, and the eight men formed a single line and picked up palm branches. They began to sing one of the melodious island chants and, eyes straight ahead, marched toward the pit. At the edge, the leader halted for a moment, gazed at the glowing rocks, and then struck the ground in front of him with his branch.

Then he walked into the trench, just as calmly as he might step into a wading pool. The haze of heat blurred his figure, and I tensed myself for a scream of agony and the sizzle of burning flesh. But he kept going, stepping gingerly over the uneven rocks, but nevertheless striding along with the nonchalance of a kid fording a shallow stream. Halfway through the length of the pit, he raised his palm branch as a signal. One by one, the other seven men followed him, walking with the same concentrated stride and the same lack of discomfort and hesitation.

They filed out at the other end of the pit, rested for a few moments, then resumed their single file formation for the return trip. This time they followed close behind their leader, and they seemed to progress a little faster.

Each of the walks across the fiery pit was accompanied by the tapping of drums which beat steadily until the last of the walkers had completed his appointed round.

PAKASTANI FIREWALKER   In Karachi, this Moslem worshiper
marches through a bed of glowing coals fanned by attendants. During
the Islamic month of Moharrum, many members of the Shia sect will
walk through the searing coals to commemorate the Prophet Moham-
med's grandson, Hussain, who was martyred in the burning desert of
Karbala, 13 centuries ago.

When the performance was over, the fire walkers were immediately
surrounded by tourists, who touched the Polynesians nervously as if
to assure themselves that they had not witnessed phantoms. The eight
men were breathing deeply after their exertion. I noticed that their

bodies were drenched in sweat. The heavy perspiration dripped down to their loincloths. The soles of their feet were black with charcoal, yet the skin underneath the charcoal was quite unscathed. A couple of men had developed a few little blisters around their ankles—the kind one gets when one burns one's fingers on a lighted match. But no more than this. As a matter of fact, their feet felt cooler to me than the rest of their bodies.

Later, I asked the policeman whether he had seen many of these ceremonies. He said, yes, about eight or nine. And all exactly like the one we had witnessed? Yes.

FIREWALKING IN SINGAPORE
In the courtyard of a Hindu Temple in
the heart of Singapore, this once-a-year
ceremony is attended by Hindus and
Tamils, and also by Western visitors. It
takes several hours for the faggots to burn
to glowing embers. The red-hot coals are
then spread to form a rectangle. The coals
are stirred by attendants with long poles
who, because of the heat, are continually
doused with cold water by sub-attendants.

"How do you think it's done?" I queried.

He gave the most Gallic of shrugs. "Who knows, monsieur? They just do it."

This laconic answer pretty well sums up our knowledge on this subject. There is no doubt that fire walking began as a religious rite, back in the unrecorded past. But no one has even ventured an intelligent guess as to why the same ritual was adopted by people who live as far apart as Bengal and Hawaii, and by people who worship such diverse deities.

Unlike other cultists, fire walkers have never shown reluctance to

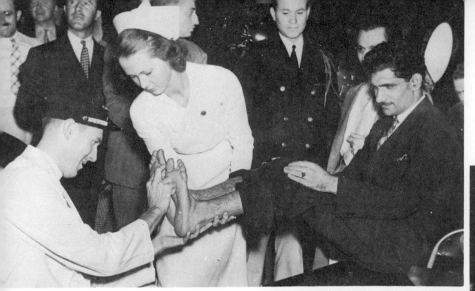

MEDICAL EXAMINATION
Prior to his fiery stroll, the feet of
Kuda Bux are examined in
Rockefeller Center by Dr. E.
Spire and a trained nurse.

FIREWALKING IN NEW YORK   At Rockefeller Center on August 2, 1935, in a stunt promoted by Robert Ripley of "Believe-it-or-not" fame, Kuda Bux walks over a 20-foot long trench of red-hot coals. After negotiating but half the distance, the Kashmiri had to leap out of the coals; but even the ten-foot stroll should have been enough to inflict crippling burns.

FINAL INSPECTION   After walking halfway through the 20-foot long trench of glowing coals, Kuda Bux holds up his feet for examination. His soles revealed no burns nor blisters.

FIREWALKING IN CEYLON   This photograph, taken by science writer Arthur C.
Clarke, shows a ceremony held at the Ceylonese coastal village of Udappuwa. A pile of
glowing embers is banked into a mass about 12 feet long and two inches deep. Nearly all
of the several hundred participants walked or danced across the glowing firebed. The
procession was accompanied by an ear-splitting symphony of shouting and drum beating.
The walkers, who sank into the flickering embers up to their ankles, seemed close to a
state of hysteria. None of them showed signs of acute pain.

have their ceremony observed, filmed, and investigated. Some few in-
quiring scientists have actually participated in these rites. Several
emerged from the ordeal with nary a blister; others were hideously

burned at the first step. How do they account for the discrepancy in the results? None were the wiser for their experience.

Shorn of ritualistic trimmings, fire walking acts have been performed both in Britain and the United States; attending physicians took the temperature and minutely inspected the skins of the participants before and after their walk. Their doctors found that after the walk, the condition of the participants was the same as that of an individual just emerged from an overheated room—much healthy perspiration, slightly increased heart action, but not a scorch mark in sight.

It seems almost a joke at the expense of Western curiosity that the least secretive of pagan rituals should also prove to be the most baffling. For as to those who walk on flames, we can add nothing to the bewilderment of the Carthaginians who first chronicled the spectacle when Rome was still a cluster of hovels and the world was barely middle-aged.

MAGICIAN STROMBOLI   During the 30th Annual Convention of the British Ring of the International Brotherhood of Magicians, Mr. Stromboli walks over a bed of glowing charcoal, demonstrating the "China-Shiki," a Shinto purification ceremony. The Englishman remained unscathed.

The Jinx Ship

She was christened *Amazon*. She was listed as British when she was built at Spencers Island, Nova Scotia, in 1861. No one except the keenest of nautical buffs would have recognized her by the name of *Amazon*, for the ship had a second label and flag when she became the classic ocean enigma, 11 years after her launching. Her registry was then American; her name, the *Mary Celeste*.

On the afternoon of December 4, 1872, the British brigantine *Dei Gratia*, out of New York and bound for Gibraltar, had reached a point about 600 miles from the Portuguese coast when her lookout reported a sail. It turned out to be another brigantine.

The stranger was under short canvas in the brisk northerly wind, yawing heavily while lurching along at a bare two knots. Two of her sheets were missing; the lower foretopsail hung slackly by the corners.

On the *Dei Gratia*, Captain Morehouse and First Mate Oliver Deveau raised their telescopes.

"Why, it's the *Mary Celeste*," exclaimed Morehouse, "and by the looks of it, she's in trouble."

"Seems to be no one at the wheel," said the mate. "Nobody on deck at all. But I don't see any distress signal."

The two ships had now approached within hailing range. Captain Morehouse broke out his speaking trumpet.

"*Celeste* ahoy!" he bellowed. "Can you hear me?"

There was no reply. Just the creaking and flapping of plank and canvas. Morehouse roared again and again, but nothing stirred on the other ship. Only the swish of the waves as the *Celeste* wallowed on,

THE BRIGANTINE "DEI GRATIA" **This is a** *contemporary Italian painting by Giuseppe Coli.*

stumbling unevenly, like a blind horse. The captain saw that she was on the starboard tack, but that the jib sail was set to port. To experienced windjammer eyes, this meant only one thing: the ship was out of control, her crew either incapacitated or dead.

Morehouse turned to his first mate. "Mr. Deveau, take two men and board her. Find out what's amiss."

A few minutes later, Deveau and a seaman named Wright were standing on the deck of the *Mary Celeste*. They shouted, stamped their feet, shouted again. No answer . . . only the soft groaning of wood and rope. The wheel stood unattended, spinning idly as the waves slapped at the rudder. The silence was uncanny.

The two men went below and peered into the hold. They searched the galley, the deck cabins, and the forecastle. There wasn't a soul on board. The *Mary Celeste* was a drifter.

But she was a drifter in amazingly good condition. One of Deveau's first acts was to sound the pumps to make sure he hadn't boarded a sinking vessel. There were 40 inches of water in the hold, which meant nothing on a wooden ship. Otherwise, the brig was as tight as a bell, the pumps in prime condition, the rigging neglected but intact, wheel undamaged, not a crack in the planks.

The cargo, consisting of 1,700 casks of undrinkable commercial alcohol, was solidly stowed and in place, though one of the containers had been opened. The only clue to the missing crew was something that *wasn't* there—the lifeboat. The *Celeste,* as Deveau remembered, had carried a yawl lashed to the main hatch. Now the spot was empty. A piece of railing parallel to it had been removed, apparently in order to launch the craft.

The crew, it seemed, had left the ship in the yawl, but they must have left in a feverish hurry. For in the forecastle, the crew had left their sea chests containing their personal possessions, their clothing, oilskins, heavy boots and most significantly their pipes and tobacco, articles sailors do not abandon unless in fear of death.

In the captain's cabin stood the ship's strongbox safely locked, and the skipper's clock. There were also a few pieces of women's jewelry, a valuable Italian sword, and the logbook. The last entry was dated November 24, and simply recorded the *Celeste's* position, "about 110 miles due west of the island of Santa Maria in the Azores."

But everything about the vessel's evacuation spelled hurry—hurry —hurry. The captain's bed was unmade; a scrap of paper with an unfinished calculation was lying on the table; loose charts rolled on the floor. A bottle of medicine stood opened, with the cork and spoon lying alongside, as if whoever was about to take it had rushed out in mid-act. In the deck cabins, the skylight stood wide open; and consequently, rain and heavy seas had soaked the bedding, clothing and shoes and formed large pools on the floorboards.

By way of contrast, all of the cabin's six windows were boarded up with canvas and planks, apparently against heavy seas. Incongruously there was a small phial of sewing-machine oil standing on the table, flanked by a neat array of reels of colored cotton, and some thimbles. Somebody had been preparing to do some sewing when whatever calamity befell the ship interrupted her.

But what calamity? Mate Deveau could find nothing—absolutely nothing—wrong with the vessel. The water below had come in through the open skylight, not through a leak. The pumps worked smoothly and had the water out in a short space of time. There was plenty of food and drinking water in store. Even the missing mainstay sail was found lying on the forward house. Only the foresail and upper foretopsail had been blown from the yards, another indication that the brig had experienced some rough weather.

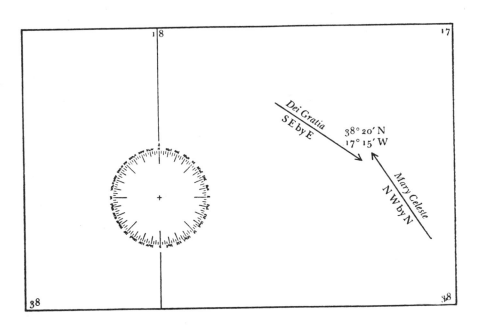

THE "DEI GRATIA" MEETS THE "MARY CELESTE"   This *diagram was first published in the* Mary Celeste: The Odyssey of an Abandoned Ship *by Charles Edey Fay. It shows the relative position of the "Mary Celeste" and the "Dei Gratia" at the time of their meeting on November 15, 1872.*

CAPTAIN BENJAMIN SPOONER BRIGGS   The captain of the "Mary Celeste" was born in Wareham, Massachusetts on April 24, 1835, the second of five sons of a seafaring family. Like four of his brothers, Briggs became a master mariner when quite young. When, at 38, he took command of the "Mary Celeste" in the fall of 1872, he had already captained the schooner "Forest King," the bark "Arthur," and the brigantine "Sea Foam."

Captain Morehouse shook his head over his mate's report, but he saw his opportunity. Leaving Deveau and two seamen on board the *Mary Celeste*, he ordered them to follow the *Dei Gratia* into Gibraltar. He would claim the derelict as a salvage prize, his good right—even his duty—but still a very handsome stroke of luck for himself and his company.

The journey to Gibraltar proved a test of the drifter's seaworthiness. The ships struck foul weather that separated them. But the *Celeste* gave her skeleton crew no trouble whatever. She arrived at the British stronghold on December 13, 1872, just 24 hours after Morehouse.

The moment she dropped anchor, the vessel was "attached"—meaning impounded—by the marshal of the Vice-Admiralty Court, prior to the hearing of the salvage claim. And almost immediately, the official atmosphere grew distinctly chilly.

THE "DEI GRATIA" SIGHTS "MARY CELESTE"
This painting by Gordon A. Johnson was commissioned in
1965 by the Atlantic Mutual Insurance Company, the in-
surers of the "Mary Celeste."

According to international maritime law, salvagers acquire a lien on property they recover through their efforts. In most cases, a salvaged vessel is a partial or complete wreck, left as a dead loss by the original crew. Here, however, the craft in question was an eminently seaworthy ship, whose cargo alone was valued at around $30,000. Why, then, had it been abandoned?

The British naval authorities sent two divers down to inspect the *Celeste* below the waterline. They detailed one shipwright, two carpenters, three Royal Navy captains, the local shipping surveyor and a timber expert to go through every rib and beam of the vessel in search of some flaw that might have caused her evacuation. They found nothing except signs of normal wear and tear. If anything, the *Mary Celeste* was in better all-round condition than the majority of small cargo craft plying the North Atlantic.

And yet, as the skipper, mate, and the entire crew of the *Dei Gratia* asserted in unison, they had come upon this amply-provisioned brigantine drifting unmanned in mid-ocean. Odd—very, *very* odd!

Now there came upon the scene Her Majesty's Advocate-General and Proctor for the Queen in her office of Admiralty, and Attorney-General for Gibraltar, one Solly Flood. Mr. Flood was an excitable little man of unsquelchable pomposity, towering bathos, and considerable shrewdness. He was also a painstaking investigator, a legal bloodhound of the stripe who would rather see ten innocent men hanged than a single guilty one escape. Mr. Flood convinced himself that he was dealing with a case of piracy and multiple murder.

Foul play *must* have taken place. How else could the crew of the *Dei Gratia* have gained possession of a perfectly sound ship? And in order to substantiate his notion, Mr. Flood was ready, if not to move mountains, then at least to juggle the evidence.

He ascertained the fact that the two ships had lain in New York harbor at the same time before their departures. He also discovered—and this struck him as particularly suspicious—that the two skippers knew each other well and had had dinner together before leaving New York. "Captain Morehouse, therefore, was familiar with the strength of the crew as well as the value of the *Mary Celeste's* cargo," he proclaimed, his tone hinting that this unremarkable fact somehow indicated piratical intent.

Then, during the proceedings before the Admiralty Court, Solly Flood unrolled the strands from which he hoped to twist a rope for the necks of the *Dei Gratia* crew.

There was, the Advocate-General asserted, a deep cut in the starboard rail of the ship, a notch such as must have been inflicted by the blow of a sharp instrument. Had Mr. Deveau noticed that? The mate replied that he hadn't. The relevant piece of railing was brought into court.

There was a brown spot on the deck near the cut, Mr. Flood went on, a spot which *might* have been blood. Did Mr. Deveau, by any chance, have the deck scraped?

"I didn't notice any blood on deck," said the mate. "And we never washed or scraped the deck of the *Mary Celeste*. We didn't have the time. But the sea washed over the deck."

"Salt water," Mr. Flood announced ominously, "contains chloric acid which dissolves blood particles."

Having driven home this point, the Advocate-General proceeded. Had Mr. Deveau seen the Italian sword aboard the *Mary Celeste?*

"Yes, I found that sword under the captain's berth," the mate replied. "I looked at it by drawing it from its sheath. Then I put it back where I found it, or somewhere near. There was nothing remarkable about it. It seemed rusty."

"That sword," Mr. Flood thundered, "has been cleaned with lemon, which covered it with citrate of iron. Therefore, another substance was put there to disguise the original marks of blood which were once there!"

Having found no blood stains on either the deck or the sword blade, the legal eagle was trying to make a case out of an assumption that bloodstains *might* have once been on the deck and the sword.

But these were merely random shots. Flood's broadsides were still to come. He seized on the last entry in the derelict's log, which placed her off Santa Maria Island on November 24, heading northeast. According to their statements, the crew of the *Dei Gratia* had sighted the *Celeste* ten days later, about 550 miles farther on than Santa Maria, and the *Celeste* was still heading northeast. How, Mr. Flood asked, was it possible for an unmanned ship with a loose wheel and the wind blowing

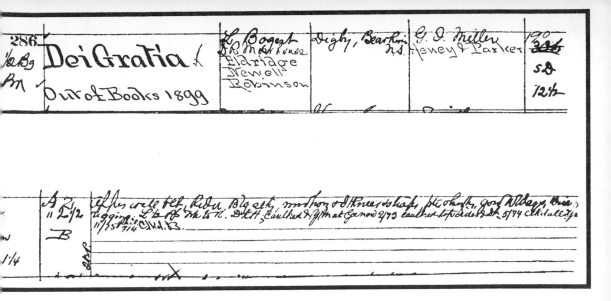

steadily from the north to have maintained her course over such a time and distance? The implication was clear: the *Dei Gratia* must have met and boarded the *Celeste* much earlier than they said they had.

Mate Deveau was quite unable to clear up that point. All he could do was surmise that the drifter might have changed directions several times in the meanwhile. He grew even more uncomfortable when the Advocate-General inquired whether he had kept the salvaged ship's log up to date from the time he sailed her, as required by law.

"Yes, I kept the log after I got on board," said the mate hesitantly, "—that is to say, I wrote it out by memory after we got into Gibraltar."

"My own theory," thundered Solly Flood, "is that the crew got at the alcohol, and in the fury of drunkenness murdered the master, his wife and child and the chief mate; that they then damaged the bows of the vessel with the view of giving it the appearance of having struck on the rocks, so as to induce the master of any vessel which might pick them up, if they saw her at some distance, to think her not worth attempting to save; and that they did, some time between the 25th November and the 5th December, escape on board some vessel bound for some North or South American port of the West Indies."

Before a jury of landlubbers, Mr. Flood might have boxed the *Dei Gratia's* crew into a corner. Luckily for them, he was performing before a naval court and judge. For all their pettifogging slowness, these gold-braided seadogs knew more about windjammers than did the Advocate-

ALBERT G. RICHARDSON
The First Mate was listed as 28 years of age when he signed aboard the "Mary Celeste" on November 4, 1872, in New York. A seaman of considerable experience, he had previously sailed under Captain Briggs, who held him in high regard.

General, enough to realize that the points he had so elaborately made weren't worth a pinch of snuff.

The deep cut in the starboard railing could have been made by any sailor hacking a rope. The cleaning job on the sword blade had, in all probability, been done by the skipper of the *Celeste* himself. If the weapon had really shown bloodstains, the man who wished to eliminate such evidence would have simply thrown it overboard.

The sailing feat of the unmanned brig had an equally simple explanation. Mr. Flood had assumed that the last entry in the log meant that the *Mary Celeste* must have been abandoned the same day. Actually, many small merchant vessels did not make daily log entries, the court pointed out, frequently missing three or four days unless something of importance occurred. The evacuation of the *Celeste*, therefore, could have happened much later than November 24, which would reduce the span of her unmanned run.

The court also concluded that the cargo alcohol was quite undrinkable. If the men had quaffed the stuff, they would have been rolling around in convulsions instead of murdering their officers.

Finally, the court refused to attach any sinister motives to the fact that Deveau had written up the log of the salvage prize in retrospect. Having only two men with which to work a vessel that normally required seven and, being unfamiliar with the ship, Deveau could hardly have had time for much paperwork en route.

The naval authorities were fairly prompt in clearing Morehouse and his men of any suspicion. But they spent months trying to formulate an official explanation for what had happened to the *Celeste*. They drove her American owner into a roaring fury with their demands for more detailed information about the ship, her crew, her skipper, her history and himself, grilling him to the stage where he barked: "I'm a Yankee with some English blood, but if I knew where it was, I'd open a vein and let the damned stuff out!"

They queried every port within reach for news of possible survivors. They solicited the opinions of American marine brokers, Canadian ship builders, and British naval experts. They consulted meteorologists, zoologists, and criminologists. They questioned London's venerable Lloyd's Corporation for cases of precedence. But their efforts produced no satisfactory answer—in fact, no answer at all. When, in March 1873, the court finally handed down its judgment, it did so without expressing an opinion—the first time in its existence it had ever refrained from offering one. The decision awarded 1,700 pounds (about $8,300) to the *Dei Gratia*, roughly one-fifth of the combined value of the salvaged ship and her cargo.

The *Mary Celeste* was handed back to her Yankee owner. She got a new captain, and a new crew, and she sailed on to Genoa where she discharged her cargo—perfectly intact but three-and-a-half months late. Over her loomed an invisible but everpresent question mark that cast a shadow nobody has ever been able to lift—what had happened to the

Mary Celeste on that stretch of water between the Azores and the coast of Portugal?

It would be just as pertinent to ask what had been happening to her from the moment her keel touched saltwater. For if ever a ship carried a jinx, it was the *Mary Celeste*, née *Amazon*, and she carried that curse up to the moment of her death.

There is a universal sailors' superstition about "ships born unlucky," and such a hoodoo has certainly applied to particular ships. One thinks of the *Great Eastern*, of England's *Hood*, and of Nazi Germany's *Tirpitz*. And surely a jinx haunted the *Celeste* without letup from the day of her baptism on.

She began life as a British brigantine in Nova Scotia, Canada, an all-wood 282-tonner, 103 feet long, 25 feet across the beam, with very comfortable deck houses. She was registered as the *Amazon*. Forty-eight hours later, her skipper died. On her maiden voyage, she ran into a fishing weir off the coast of Maine, which put a severe gash in her hull. While still under repair, fire broke out amidship. This cost her second captain his job. It was under her third commander that she crossed the Atlantic for the first time—and promptly collided with another vessel in the Straits of Dover. Repaired once again—and with yet a fourth skipper—she returned to Canada. There, in November 1867, she ran aground on Cape Breton Island and became a wreck.

At this point, the history of her ownership grows somewhat murky. She was salvaged by either a Mr. Haines or an Alexander McBean—accounts differ—but either or both of these gentlemen went bankrupt almost immediately, and the hulk passed into the possession of one John Beatty of New York, who, in his turn, sold the *Amazon* to another New York ship owner, James H. Winchester.

In the process, the ship acquired a different name and nationality as well as a new structure. For reasons unknown, Winchester rechristened her the *Mary Celeste*. Now, she flew the Stars and Stripes instead of the Red Ensign, had a brand-new copper-lined bottom, and an extended deck cabin. Her underwriters, the Atlantic Mutual Insurance Company, passed her as "well built and seaworthy." But there were any number of seamen who refused to sail on her. An unlucky maiden voyage AND a change of name was a combination almost as ill-starred as the shooting of an albatross.

The ship's fifth master was also part-owner. Captain Benjamin Spooner Briggs, from Marion, Massachusetts was as straight-laced a puritanical gentleman as ever left New England. He stood in striking contrast to the hard-swearing, semi-literate Winchester. At 38, Briggs was a stern-featured, slightly stuffy man of few words, who placed a

THE MARY CELESTE—A SEA MYSTERY

As found abandoned in mid-Atlantic in December 1872. Atlantic Mutual is the only surviving American insurance company which had any insurance on that venture.

DRAWN FROM RUDOLPH RUZICKA'S WOOD ENGRAVING FOR CHARLES EDEY FAY'S BOOK, "THE MARY CELESTE"—PUBLISHED BY THE PEABODY MUSEUM OF SALEM, MASSACHUSETTS.

A WOOD ENGRAVING BY RUDOLPH RIZICKA   The "Mary Celeste," built of sturdy Nova Scotian maple, birch, and beech, was originally 99.3 feet long, 25.5 feet wide, 11.7 feet deep and weighed 198.42 tons when she slid down the ways. She was originally christened the "Amazon." The wooden-shelled twin-masted brigantine was "carvel-built," which meant that her planks met flush at the seams. In 1872, just before her fateful journey, the ship, renamed the "Mary Celeste," underwent substantial changes in construction. Her one deck was increased to two; her length increased to 103 feet.

harmonium on board the vessel, read a Bible chapter aloud every eve-, ning, and said "durn" when he meant "damn."

Captain Briggs took along his wife Sarah Elizabeth, and their baby daughter, by no means an unusual act in those days of long voyages. As first and second mates, he had two Yankees, Albert G. Richardson and Dane Andrew Gilling. New Yorker Albert Head came as sea cook. The four seamen—Goodschad, Lorenzen, Martens, and Volkert—were of German birth. It was a good, solid ship's company, every one a man of spotless reputation, and morally at least, several cuts above the average windjammer crew.

Early in November, 1872, the *Mary Celeste* lay at Pier 44 in New York's East River where she was being loaded with a cargo of commer-

CONJECTURAL COURSE OF THE "MARY CELESTE"   This drawing projects the possible course taken by the unmanned "Mary Celeste" from her last noted position (A), east northeast of St. Mary's Island, as entered in the ship's log, 8 a.m. on November 25, 1872. It is likely that after meeting adverse winds after a continued easterly sailing, her heading was reversed (B), bringing her to the west northwesterly tack she held when sighted by the "Dei Gratia."

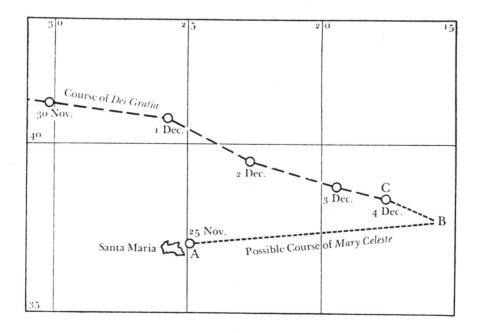

cial alcohol destined for Genoa, Italy. Nearby, lay the brigantine *Dei Gratia,* taking on a mixed cargo for Gibraltar. Her skipper, David Reed Morehouse, was an old friend of Captain Briggs. Their wives knew each other, too. Two nights before his departure, Briggs dined with his fellow-captain at the Astor House and they wished each other fair winds. They were never to meet again.

Briggs seemed happy about his crew. "They are all good and willing fellows," he remarked, "but I have yet to find out how smart they are."

With his vessel in fine sailing trim, the bewhiskered, pious, teetotalling captain embarked from New York on November 5. Because of severe headwinds, he anchored off Staten Island for two days, and then set out into the North Atlantic.

The *Dei Gratia* left on November 11. Twenty-three days later, the two ships met in mid-ocean, an encounter that scriptwriters have been embellishing ever since.

After she was found unmanned, interest in what had happened to the *Celeste* grew only gradually. Brief notice was taken at the time of the proceedings before the Gibraltar Admiralty Court. It was over the years that the story gained in bulk, developing an avalanche of books, articles, poems, radio dramas, films, and television features. For the *Celeste* turned into a universal guessing game. A few dramatic touches were added, of course: her tables were set with uneaten food; an all-revealing page was missing from the log book; Briggs was a religious maniac; his crew were professional cutthroats.

In 1884, Conan Doyle wrote a blood-drenched little romance called "J. Habakuk Jephson's Statement" relating the fate of the "Márie (sic) Celeste." Unbeknown to contemporaries, she had carried an exceedingly ambitious colored passenger named Septiminus Goring who proceeded to slaughter every soul on board in order to seize the ship and with it establish his own black empire in Africa. Doyle at least disguised his brainchild as semi-fiction. Those who followed his path unblushingly proclaimed theirs as revelations.

Around 1900, came a spate of "monster-from-the-depths" accounts. Some of these tales recounted how the brigantine had been attacked by

Register entry for the ship *Mary Celeste* (No. 156), formerly the *Amazon* of Parrsboro, Nova Scotia, built May 1861.

a kraken, a devil fish or giant squid, which picked up the crew rather like a gourmet picks snails from their shells, reaching its tentacles through the portholes until the last human morsel had gone. After which, it presumably swallowed the yawl by mistake.

In 1926, the Englishman Adam Bushey suggested that the *Celeste* had been "de-materialized" en route. If one follows Bushey's logic, the people who sailed on the *Celeste* remained, well——de-materialized—— while the ship itself returned to its solid form.

Charles Fort—the world's foremost interpreter of unsubstantiated newspaper clippings—hinted that the missing crew and passengers could have been whisked away by what he termed a "selective force," a force that left the ship itself untouched. He didn't say where the people had been whisked *to*, but then Fort rarely concerned himself with trivialities.

In 1955, UFO expert Professor Jessup came up with the unchallengable hypothesis that the company was snatched away by a Flying Saucer. Since UFOs have been accused of purloining anything from Texan cows to lady realtors, there is no reason why they shouldn't have indulged in a spot of marine kidnapping, too.

Although nothing was actually ever heard again from any known member of the ship's company, there was a steady surfacing of *Mary Celeste* survivors whose names, somehow, had been left out of the ship's

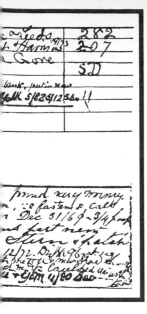

RECORD OF THE "MARY CELESTE"   *Here is an entry made by the Atlantic Mutual Insurance Company. The record includes the names of the ship's master, Benjamin S. Briggs, and her owner, J. H. Winchester. The vessel's original name, "Amazon," is noted, as well as the date of her original launching at Parrsboro, Nova Scotia, in May of 1861.*

register. They popped up in all localities, with stories that ranged from the ridiculous to the imbecilic.

In 1913, the *Strand Magazine* of London, published the adventures of one such survivor, yclept Abel Fosdyk. Mr. Fosdyk had it that the crew and passengers were drowned while watching a swimming race around the ship between the captain and the mate. For this purpose, they had built a platform under the bow (hence the scratches) which collapsed under their combined weight. All perished except the author, who saved himself on a raft.

Only one unprovable yet feasible solution has ever been advanced —unprovable because no witnesses are available. This one theory takes into account all of the verified circumstances.

According to the evidence, three salient facts emerge: 1) The ship was abandoned in great haste; 2) Those who abandoned ship, did so in the ship's yawl; 3) The abandonment took place under responsible guidance, since the chronometer, the sextant, the navigation books, and the ship's papers were missing and in all probability had been taken along.

Since the vessel had sustained no structural damage, the cause of her evacuation was not something that *had* happened, but something that seemed *about* to happen. The only danger potential at the time was her cargo.

Captain Briggs had never carried crude alcohol before, and was likely unfamiliar with its chemical reactions. He had come from wintry New York to the much warmer region of the Azores; and the barrels—severely shaken by stormy weather—might have exuded vapors. One of the barrels, it will be remembered, had been opened—probably in the course of a cargo inspection. If this inspection had taken place with a naked light, there might have been something of a slight explosion—too slight to inflict damage—but loud enough to convince the skipper that the whole cargo was about to blow sky high.

The presence on board of his wife and baby daughter may have raised Captain Briggs' fear to panic level, and he precipitously ordered all hands into the lifeboat.

In all likelihood, the captain intended to stick close enough to his ship to get back on, if no further explosion occurred. But for safety's sake, he couldn't linger *too* close. Then—with a gust of wind—came tragedy! The *Mary Celeste* sailed away from the little craft.

The rest is easily imagined—the men rowing with the strength of despair—the distance increasing inexorably—finally exhaustion—and the ship gliding out of sight.

There was no land closer than three or four hundred miles, and during the next few days, a single wave could have swamped the yawl.

This theory was first offered by James Winchester, the ship's owner at the time. This hypothesis was later expanded by several authors, but somehow has never found general acceptance. Mutineers, pirates, ocean monsters, unknown forces and man-snatching Saucers, were so-o-o-o much more exciting.

Winchester got rid of the ship as soon as she arrived back in New York, some say at a dead loss. But this seems improbable from what we know of Winchester. The man who took the real loss was her unlucky purchaser, for the jinx that lurked in the *Celeste's* very timbers, remained as potent as ever.

The new owner loaded the *Celeste* with a cargo of lumber and despatched her to Montevideo. En route, in a storm, she lost her entire deck cargo and a good part of her rigging, a loss severe enough to knock any profit out of the journey. On the return trip, carrying a load of

horses and mules, most of the living cargo died in the hold; and a few days later, her new skipper followed suit.

From then on, the *Celeste* changed hands so fast and frequently that it becomes almost impossible to keep track of who owned her and when. Ships in those days of lax safety regulations were kept in service until they literally fell apart, and ownership was frequently split among 20 or more part-owners. This seems to have been the fate of the aging *Mary Celeste*—lurching up and down the American coastline, shedding spars, sails, and sailors, scraping on sandbanks, catching fire—but still holding together, still running sweet if well handled, still piling on mishap after mishap.

Then, in 1884, she fell into the hands of a grizzled sea shark named Gilman C. Parker, another Massachusetts man, but not of the teetotalling kind. For most of his 61 years, Captain Parker had dabbled in every brand of nautical skulduggery, except outright piracy. Now he and a group of dryland buccaneers hatched a scheme to wring a fat profit out of the notoriously unprofitable *Celeste*. They loaded her with a cargo of

THE "MARY CELESTE" MUSEUM   In New York City, at 45
Wall Street, a small museum dedicated to the mystery of the "Mary
Celeste" is maintained by the Atlantic Mutual Insurance Company.
The "Mary Celeste" Room simulates an underwriter's office of bygone
days. Among the memorabilia is a 35-inch model of the ship, authentic in every detail. A lap desk, which originally belonged to the ship's
master, stands exactly as it appeared when the vessel was boarded
by the crew of the "Dei Gratia."

junk, worth but a few hundred dollars, but registered the cargo as high-
class merchandise and managed to insure the ship for $27,000. Then
Captain Parker took the *Celeste* on her death ride to the Caribbean.

In the Haitian Gulf of Gonave lies a coral reef named Rochelois
Bank that looks like a row of teeth which were especially designed to
tear wooden ships to shreds. Parker set course for that reef and he ordered his helmsman to stay on it. The brigantine ground into the razor-
like coral, and with the waves crashing around her, began to settle.

There was no imminent danger, for the ship stuck high and dry. The crew had ample time to row the cargo ashore. When everything sellable had been salvaged, Parker ordered kerosene sprinkled over the deck, and he then lit the torch. Under the hot sun, the *Celeste* turned into a roaring pyre. That evening nothing remained of her save her charred ribs.

Back in Boston, Parker and associates filed their claim. The insurance companies, however, smelled a herd of rats, and dispatched their detectives to quiz the crew. The sailors talked; the investigators took notes. In due time, Captain Parker and three of his partners faced a federal court in Boston on a charge of barratry—a hanging crime in those days.

But it was the jury which was hung instead of the defendants. The four conspirators walked out of the court scot-free, but they couldn't collect their claim, and the notoriety killed their credit. Eight months later, Parker died in disrepute and poverty. One of his associates was consigned to a lunatic asylum; another committed suicide. Within a year, the two companies involved in the swindle went bankrupt.

Even after her immolation, the most famous bad luck ship in history affected all connected with her.

The ABC of ESP

In October, 1956, *Newsweek* magazine startled its readers with the following announcement:

> *A serious psychological research project being conducted for the Joint Chiefs of Staff is a study of the possible use of extrasensory perception. Those in on it are looking into the possibilities of using ESP not only to read the minds of Soviet leaders but to influence their thinking by long-range thought control.*

In January, 1961, a Russian science weekly proudly reported:

> *Professor Leonid L. Vasiliev, lecturer at the Leningrad University's Institute of Psychic Research, has successfully concluded one of the most impressive parapsychological experiments of our time. Under his supervision, the "inductor" I. F. Tomachevski, stationed in Sevastopol, concentrated on "thinking to sleep" a young woman subject kept under observation in Leningrad. Over a distance of 1,700 kilometers the subject was telepathically put to sleep twice in one afternoon and again the following morning.*

Read together, these news releases conjure up a vision of future cold war tactics—a team of American psychics trying to influence the minds of Soviet political chiefs, while the American leaders struggle against a barrage of slumber suggestions projected from Moscow by squads of iron-willed Russian inductors.

Since the 1956 *Newsweek* announcement, nothing more has been heard of the American study project; and Professor Vasiliev died in 1966, apparently without making further progress with long-distance sleep inducement. But the fact that statements of this kind are published in all seriousness on both sides of the Iron Curtain shows to what extent the concept of ESP has gained recognition.

The abbreviation stands for extrasensory perception which covers a wide range of phenomena. ESP of another's thoughts is called telepathy; ESP of distant events is clairvoyance; and ESP of future events is precognition. Related to these are such practices as mediumship, psychometry, and even dowsing (the alleged ability to locate underground water or minerals through the movements of a pointer held in the hand of the gifted individual). The varied manifestations of ESP have long puzzled researchers and have delighted the crackpots; but then, the spontaneous forms of natural phenomena have historically been unpredictable and seemingly mysterious at first. However, we shall deal here with the more commonly studied types of ESP, telepathy, or thought transmission, and clairvoyance.

Unknown to most people, telepathy has been for years a subject of

LEONID L. VASILIEV   Professor at Leningrad University's Institute of Psychic Research is noted for his experiments in thought transference.

JOSEPH BANKS RHINE   The world's greatest living authority on extrasensory perception, Dr. Rhine is professor at Duke University in North Carolina.

serious study; but not until 1927, at Duke, did an uninterrupted program of laboratory study finally get underway.

As a random phenomenon, it is as old as mankind and as common as hayfever. There is hardly an adult who has not had some direct or secondhand experience with mental telepathy. The Roman chronicler and gourmet, Appius Mannus, complained about having to listen to "pointless and witless" telepathic anecdotes at table in 270 B.C.; he would find as many sympathizers now as he undoubtedly had then. Most of us have sat and suffered while Aunt Agatha related how that very morning she had a thought that she simply must ring Marge and how at that very moment the phone rang and it *was* Marge, who had the same idea at the very same instant, my dear, and wasn't it amazing, and there must be something to this telepathy business after all. Full stop.

Much of the early work with telepathy attempted to record and fathom the para-normal functions of certain allegedly gifted individuals; since most such people were professional mediums, the experiments were, for the most part, psychic demonstrations, rather than rigidly objective laboratory tests.

The first man who consciously set out to isolate and identify the phenomenon itself rather than its exponents was Dr. (later Professor) Joseph Banks Rhine of Duke University. Rhine was the pathbreaker in the field of parapsychology; his most famous experiments were concluded more than 30 years ago. Since then, much progress and confirmation have been added to Rhine's basic findings. Not the least of Rhine's accomplishments was that he made the letters "ESP" an international concept.

Originally a preministerial student, Pennsylvania-born, Rhine was a plant physiologist by training. He became curious about the claims of spiritualism in the early twenties through the lectures of Sir Arthur Conan Doyle. Doyle was a fine writer and a brilliant lecturer, but so agog with enthusiasm for things psychic that he virtually abandoned his critical faculties and became an eager prey to any medium. Rhine, although vastly impressed by Sir Arthur's theme, was considerably less so by his methods. Rhine developed the idea of using the strict and uncompromising test procedures of the naturalist for the study of the supranatural. He got his opportunity when, in 1928, he joined the psychology department of Duke University and began the testing for ESP which eventually led to the establishment of the Parapsychology Laboratory at Duke. Since 1965, this organization has been located as an independent institute across from the campus.

In 1933, Rhine met Hubert Pearce, a divinity student who believed he possessed ESP. To test Pearce's perception, Rhine devised a classically simple and apparently fraudproof and foolproof system. With some minor improvements, this system is still being used in extrasensory experiments throughout the world. The equipment consists of a pack of cards, 25 to the pack. Each card is marked with one of five symbols: a circle, a set of wavy lines, a cross, a star, or a square.

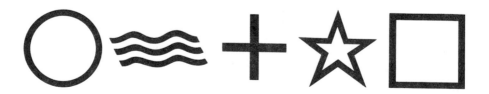

HUBERT PEARCE   Divinity student who is alleged to have possessed ESP, guessing a card drawn by Dr. Pratt in another building.

In one series of tests conducted by J. G. Pratt, a graduate student in psychology who was working directly under Rhine's supervision, Pearce sat in another building 100 yards away. Pratt shuffled the cards. At intervals of one minute, he drew one card from the top of the deck. Simultaneously, Pearce recorded his guess as to what symbol had been drawn. After the men had gone through two decks, Pratt turned his cards face up, and made notes of the sequence in which the symbols had occurred.

Pratt and Pearce played 37 sets or 74 decks, a total of 1,850 cards. According to Rhine's mathematical calculations, if only sheer chance were operative, Pearce should have guessed about one-fifth of the symbols correctly. Instead of the mathematically expected 370 correct guesses, Pearce scored 558 correct answers. The odds against this hap-

J. G. PRATT   The doctor is conducting an experiment in ESP with Hubert Pearce who is seated in the Duke University library, 100 yards away.

pening by chance alone are greater than 10^{22} to 1. This is an astronomical number of 22 digits.

Painstakingly, Rhine and Pratt checked these data again and again. The results were quite the same. A cross-check yielded further assurance that Pearce's success was only on those particular cards which Pratt was holding at the time of Pearce's guesses.

In this experiment, Pratt did not look at the cards until after Pearce had made all his guesses for that day. Thus Pearce demonstrated that it was not necessary for anyone to help him by "sending" the message to him.

After thousands of runs with slightly fluctuating but similar results, Rhine believed he had effectively ruled out chance as a factor. The only alternative was the existence of ESP—now, for the first time, proved by mathematical formula.

In 1934, Rhine published his first book under the title of *Extra-Sensory Perception*. This and his subsequent work, *New Frontiers of the Mind*, created a sensation in psychological circles—possibly a much greater sensation than he had either intended or expected. His statistics were checked by R. A. Fisher, one of the world's top experts in probability calculus, and were found to be accurate. As news of the experiments at Duke University percolated into other scientific spheres, the news had the effect of an earthquake on fundamental tenets of thinking. Arthur Koestler described the impact on Professor Hans Reichenbach, then professor of philosophy at the University of California. Reichenbach, a leading mathematical logician, was the proponent of a materialist philosophy. When told of Fisher's verification of Rhine's statistics, Reichenbach went pale and said, "If that is true, it is terrible, terrible! It would mean that I would have to scrap everything and start from the beginning!" In other words, the proved existence of ESP meant that Reichenbach's philosophy had a basic flaw and would have to be rebuilt on changed premises.

DUKE UNIVERSITY   *The seat of Dr. Rhine's experiments in parapsychology is located in Durham, North Carolina.*

Almost immediately, critics arose to challenge Rhine's findings. They said that the pattern of his tests contained faults that rendered the results open to doubt. To start with, most of the participants in the Duke experiments had been openminded to the possibility of psychic phenomena. When the same tests were conducted elsewhere with skeptical subjects, the results often failed to rise above the level of normal probability. Thus, the experiments, the critics alleged, defied a basic law of scientific research—the law of reliability—which states that experiments conducted under the same circumstances and with the same materials must produce the same results.

Rhine answered this charge by explaining that the attitude of the experimenters could have a marked influence on the attitude of the subjects, and hence on the outcome of the tests, in other words, that ESP is not a strong trait in those who do not believe in ESP.

Rhine was also accused of having published only a small portion of the total number of tests he had made—only those portions which bore out his theories. This charge, if true, would overthrow the basis of statistical probability on which Rhine's thesis rested. According to Rhine, the charge was not valid.

Another charge was that Rhine had carefully selected his assistants from students who had shown exceptional luck during preliminary trial runs. As H. L. Mencken, then America's foremost literary critic, phrased it, "In plain language, Professor Rhine segregates all those persons who, in guessing the cards, enjoy noteworthy runs of luck, and then adduces those noteworthy runs of luck as proof that they must possess mysterious powers."

Rhine countered this accusation by stating that he had most certainly selected Pearce, not on a basis of luck, but because he had recognized Pearce's particular extrasensory gifts. In oft-repeated tests taking nearly two years, Pearce proved that he *had* the gift of ESP.

When the subjects at Duke showed a decline in the scoring rates, Rhine insisted that the decline was due to "loss of original curiosity and initial enthusiasm." His critics claimed that it was merely the law of chance asserting itself.

Rhine was as intrigued as his opponents by the instability of Pearce's perception. He noted that the divinity student's ESP dropped sharply when he had been studying too hard or was in bad health. His ESP power also diminished after he had received a worry-provoking letter from home. Pearce's psychic sense seemed to depend on a whole range of physical and emotional factors, including momentary irritability and absentmindedness.

In the course of several million test runs with Pearce and other subjects, Rhine concluded that the "psi" (for psychic) trait was neither stable nor permanent. It was, in fact, "the most variable ability on record," liable to come and go, grow or shrink, and sometimes fade out altogether, never to return. A subject might score astonishingly high in 50 runs, only to drop below the average in the 51st. However, in spite of his critics, Rhine was generally credited with having achieved a major breakthrough. For no matter how indifferent his scoring became later on, Pearce at one stage of his life had demonstrated extraordinary extrasensory abilities. What he had demonstrated, other gifted subjects would confirm. And this turned out to be the case.

Not until the summer of 1960 was this claim seriously challenged. The challenger was C. E. M. Hansel, professor of psychology at the University of Wales. Hitherto it had been taken for granted that, however debatable mathematically, Rhine's experiments had been free of fraud. This was partly because of Rhine's undoubted personal integrity, but chiefly because of the seemingly airtight testing method he had devised.

Now Professor Hansel put the test to a test. He visited Duke University and persuaded a man who had a connection with Rhine's laboratory to let him take over Pearce's role. Hansel was to sit in an office down the corridor a few yards away from the room in which the cards were drawn. At the conclusion of the run, the visitor came up with the fantastic score of 22 out of 25 correct guesses. Hansel revealed how it had been achieved. He had simply left his office, climbed a chair outside the room, and peeked through a crack at the top of the door while the drawn cards were being tabulated. He had then gone back to his office and had written down his "guesses."

The point Hansel would like to make was not whether Pearce or any of his successors had cheated—but that they *could* have cheated. This meant that even if Rhine had succeeded in eliminating the element of chance from his experiments, the unusual results might have been achieved by fraud as well as by ESP. It is only fair to note, however, that Hansel had tricked a person who was not, like Pratt, a trained scientific researcher, but in fact had no scientific training and had never published a scientific report. Moreover, Rhine was not on the scene watching, as he had been in the series of tests with Pratt.

Certainly the field of psychic phenomena as a whole is a difficult one to control; but there is little rigged evidence in any field in university research, and this is especially so with mature scientists who devote their lives to pioneer investigations. Closer examination would have indicated to Hansel, as it has to others, that the possibility of fraud in this particular Duke experiment as in the majority of others was highly unlikely.

But the question of fraud is best dismissed by independent confirmation. The work at Duke stood by itself, unsupported, for only a very short time. All the main points of Rhine's work were borne out by the work of others in research centers throughout the world, as the reports of the last 30 years in the *Journal of Parapsychology* will indicate.

However, despite all the controversy, the existence of some form of psi ability seems reasonable to accept. The phenomenon is too universal, too frequent, too generally observable to be casually dismissed. The man riding a bus and thinking of a certain tune which his neighbor promptly commences to whistle; the woman suddenly worried about her sister who at the same moment is injured in a car smash; the child in school answering a question before the teacher has asked it—all these experiences, major and minute, seem to add up to the existence of some intangible, not accounted for by our scientific knowledge.

In October, 1937, Sir Hubert Wilkins of England and Harold Sherman of the United States decided to make use of a fairly unusual opportunity to test the extent of this intangible. Their experiment is the most dramatic case history of telepathic communication ever recorded.

In September, 1937, the Russian airman, Sigismund Lewanevsky, disappeared while trying to fly from the Soviet Union to Alaska via the

SIR GEORGE HUBERT WILKINS
The Australian-born explorer
and aviator earned knighthood
through his pioneering flights over
the polar regions.

North Pole. Sir Hubert—a world-famous explorer-aviator, the first man to fly over the North Pole, and a participant in five Arctic and Antarctic expeditions—offered to conduct a one-plane search for the missing pilot. Sherman, a writer, was a casual acquaintance of Sir Hubert. He shared with the Englishman an intense interest in anything pertaining to telepathy. Neither Wilkins nor Sherman trusted the radio equipment then in use. Sherman therefore suggested that Wilkins try to report on the progress of his search by thought transmission—an idea that Sir Hubert accepted enthusiastically.

They arranged that Wilkins would concentrate on sending psychic messages for three half-hour periods each week, from 11:30 P.M. to midnight Eastern Standard Time every Monday, Tuesday, and Thursday. During the same periods, Sherman would concentrate on receiving those messages.

Two of Wilkins' New York friends agreed to sit with Sherman, in turns. Sherman undertook to mail immediately any impressions he received from Wilkins to Dr. Gardner Murphy, a member of the depart-

*HAROLD M. SHERMAN
The ESP correspondent was
co-author with Sir Hubert
Wilkins, the arctic explorer, of
a book entitled "Thoughts
Through Space" which de-
tailed their notable experience.*

ment of psychology at Columbia University. Wilkins was to be kept
informed of the progress of the experiment by Reginald Iverson, one of
the operators of the short-wave radio station owned by the *New York
Times.*

Because the experiment was to serve a practical purpose, they arranged that in case Sir Hubert was forced to land anywhere and that if
his radio gear was damaged, he would concentrate on figures which
would indicate his longitude and latitude. If Wilkins had an accident,
he would focus on the color red; if he were injured, he would concentrate on the color black; if unhurt, on white.

Wilkins' search lasted from October 1937 to March 1938, through
some of the worst weather ever encountered by polar flyers. The radio
equipment of the Wilkins party was almost inactivated by a series of
electric storms. The New York short-wave station managed to make
contact with the plane only 14 times during the five months. Wilkins
did not succeed in finding the Soviet aviator, but he established a telepathy record that has never been matched or explained.

The timing arrangement did not work too well, because Wilkins
was frequently otherwise occupied during the periods he had planned
to concentrate on transmitting. Instead, he made a point of focusing his
thoughts whenever anything noteworthy occurred, and every time he
did so, he made an entry in his diary.

When Wilkins returned to New York, he compared his entries with

Sherman's records, and with the duplicates of those records dispatched to Dr. Murphy at Columbia. The results were phenomenal.

On November 11, 1937, the explorer's plane was forced down by a snow storm at Regina, Saskatchewan. The local dignitaries arranged an impromptu reception in Sir Hubert's honor, a formal affair that he had to attend in a borrowed dress suit. The suit was too small for him, and the event, thronged with army and police officers and their gowned ladies, was something of an ordeal. Sherman's notes on the same evening read, "You are in company of men in military attire—some women—evening dress—social occasion—important people present—you appear to be in evening dress yourself."

Four weeks later, Sir Hubert's seaplane landed in a fjord at Point Barrow. The party watched as an Eskimo shack on the shore burned to the ground because, amid all the ice, there was no water available to quench the blaze. That evening Sherman had recorded, "I seem to see a crackling fire in the darkness—I get a definite fire impression, as though a house were burning. You can see it from your location on the ice. Quite a crowd gathered around it. Many people running toward the flames. Bitter cold."

On March 14, 1938, Wilkins got into mechanical difficulties because he was late in switching fuel from one tank to another. He had to pump furiously, with the motor coughing and spluttering and threatening to conk out. According to his own statement, "The trouble only lasted for a few minutes, but it occupied my mind much of the day."

Some 3,000 miles away Sherman noted, "I seem to see you manipulating a hand pump of some sort in flight. One engine is emitting spouts of black smoke—uneven choked sound—as though carburetor trouble."

Sherman recorded such incidents as Wilkins' lecturing, chalk in hand, to a class of Eskimo children. He noted Sir Hubert's worry about dangerous ice formations on the wings, and he gave the plane's location at the time as 86-115. Wilkins had indeed concentrated on his exact whereabouts at that moment, because he might have had to try a forced landing. The figures that Wilkins "sent" New York and which Sherman "received" from the Arctic were within 45 miles of the explorer's own estimate!

Once Sherman wrote that he could see Wilkins dropping a wreath over a town. This was incorrect, insofar as it never happened. But Sir Hubert had *considered* dropping a wreath over Regina as a gesture of thanks for its hospitality; he had not done so for fear of hitting someone.

After a fruitless search during which he covered 45,000 miles, Wilkins returned to New York. He and Sherman unfolded the story of their unparalleled telepathic feat in their book *Thoughts through Space.* What they had accomplished was almost incredible. Yet they had the evidence in Sir Hubert's diary, in Sherman's duplicated notes, in the testimony of Dr. Murphy, and in the postmarks that proved that all the reports had been mailed to Dr. Murphy *while Wilkins was still flying in the Far North.*

It is true that Sherman had also written a great many inaccurate impressions which he believed he was receiving from the aircraft. But in Sir Hubert's words, "Too many of Sherman's notes were approximately correct and synchronized with the very day of the occurrences to have been guesswork."

Although it made fascinating reading, their experiment was not, of course, proof in the scientific sense. By laboratory standards, the project had been uncontrolled, meaning that the possibility existed that the whole thing was an elaborate plot arranged among the three main participants. But this possibility was not seriously advanced by anyone, for the international reputations of these men virtually ruled out such a hoax, all the principals publicly swore affidavits attesting to the accuracy of their stated procedures.

None of the three men claimed to understand the manner in which the thoughts of the flyer had reached the mind of the writer. Somehow, the great intangible had worked for *them;* there was no assurance that it would ever do so again or that ESP would work similarly for others.

This last point was exactly what scientists could not—and still cannot—accept. Granted the existence of telepathy, it has to occur through some set of procedures. Labeling the process "ESP" or "psi" still does not explain it. Granted that some humans have a sixth sense—we know a little about how the other five senses work—at least how the sense organs are stimulated—why can we not understand how the sixth one operates?

The *process* of ESP is now a major concern of Dr. Rhine and is being investigated. What are the best conditions for ESP, and who has it? Concerning the latter, there are countless reports (albeit mainly unsubstantiated) of a twin sensing his sibling's death even though the two were hundreds of miles apart, or of a twin intuitively sensing that his sibling was rescued from a perilous situation, or of twins dreaming identical dreams the same night.

Whatever their factual basis, these accounts did suggest that twins might prove to be favorable test candidates for ESP. In 1965, two ophthalmologists, Thomas Duane and Thomas Behrendt, conducted a series of tests on identical twins at the Jefferson Medical College in Philadelphia. The original idea had been to learn whether twins showed a similar pattern in their brain waves. But in two of the sixteen pairs selected for the test, the doctors made a startling discovery. Whenever one twin closed his eyes—an act that produces alpha waves—the electroencephalograph of the other twin, who was several feet away in a separate room, showed the same wave pattern.

These observations supported a speculation long held by some parapsychologists that telepathy might be a sort of "mental radio," based on as yet unidentified brain waves that can be transmitted from one person to another over considerable—perhaps unlimited—distances. Some evidence for this theory was found by the Soviet researcher Vasiliev during his long-range sleep-inducing experiments mentioned earlier. While trying to isolate the transmitting factor, Vasiliev discovered the presence of hitherto unknown electromagnetic waves that he presumed might be the activating force behind every form of mental telepathy. Vasiliev immediately tested his theory. He placed his subject, a 23-year-old Leningrad girl, inside a chamber lined with lead plating, a metal that electromagnetic forces cannot penetrate. Then the sleep inductor attempted transmission. The girl promptly dozed off, proving that whatever was reaching her did so through the lead walls, and were not electromagnetic waves. Vasiliev was obliged to admit, "My electromagnetic hypothesis is erroneous."

The Russian was merely one of scores of psi researchers who have tried in vain to locate some kind of brain waves that might substantiate the "mental radio" theory. A number of researchers have even claimed to have discovered such waves, have given them fancy names, have constructed elaborate apparatus to regulate these waves, and have sold or rented their machines' to the gullible. The activating force of ESP remains unknown, and ESP remains uncontrollable and uninducible.

The mind readers who perform on stage or television invariably use tricks; they do not pretend to be anything more than entertainers. In the most primitive form of these acts, "assistants" are planted in the audience; on a slightly higher level, there is an intermediary who uses a silent and almost invisible system of code signals to inform the telepathist of whatever has been said or handed to him.

"Pencil reading," which enables a performer to read whatever a member of the audience writes on a piece of paper, is a variation of the mind-reading act. The pencil used is always very large so that the writing motions are clearly discernible. Pencil reading can be learned as easily as mirror writing, and forms part of the training of most intelligence agents. But all this legerdemain is unconnected with ESP.

SHUFFLING BOX   *This apparatus was used by Dr. J. B. Rhine in his ESP experiments.*

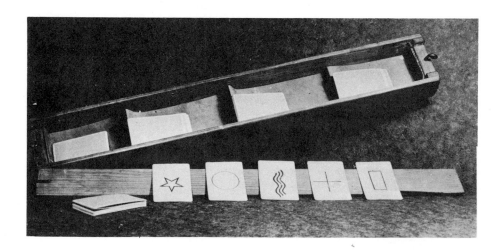

PARAPSYCHOLOGY LABORATORY   *Between 1935 and 1965, Dr. J. B. Rhine's ESP experiments were conducted on the upper floor of this building.*

It is sometimes pointed out that Dr. Rhine has never been able to repeat the remarkable success ratio of his early test runs, and that as he gradually imposed more rigid controls on his subjects, their performance levels sank.

Rhine replies that there was no such connection; scores declined under the very same conditions. "We got those high scores by the hard work of encouraging subjects to give maximal effort. No one, however, can keep that up forever. Others have done the same for a time—usually at the start when zeal is high."

He adds: "By learning better how to handle test-subjects, we can likely get top level scoring again eventually, and do so with less effort."

The evidence that ESP exists has now grown to be overwhelming. Ranging in impact from the Wilkins-Sherman experiment to the constant stream of telepathic experiences reported daily, ESP remains a scientific unknown, a most baffling phenomenon in this baffling world.

THE WILKINS-SHERMAN TELEPATHIC CORRESPONDENCE   *Here are fac-*
similes of four representative pages which appear in "Thoughts Through Space," the book
which reports the Wilkins-Sherman ESP communications.

WILKINS-SHERMAN TELEPATHIC TESTS

SHERMAN   WILKINS

SHERMAN	WILKINS
Some one of crew seems to have hurt left leg during work on plane— someone else has skinned hand or finger . . .	Dyne had hands spotted with frost "burns" which blister or else the skin is pulled right off when the hand is pulled away after being frozen to any metal.
See great clouds of smoke or vapor about plane and hear uneven coughs of motors . . .	With a wood stove going inside the "tent" over the motor, there are always clouds of steam and smoke on cold days.
Use made of part of damaged engine—see someone tinkering with it—removing some parts . . .	Some parts of old engine fitted to the new.
You have some wine with several friends who welcome you back Aklavik . . .	They have had some liquor that I brought with me. I didn't have any.
Your cold, which you mentioned in your letter to me, has given you a little trouble—in your head and throat . . .	Cold really bad.
You brought back to Aklavik several boxes of cigars, cartons of cigarettes . . .	One box of one hundred cigars for Wilson.
Seems as though Dyne wanted you bring him something special or some member of crew requested you to get some article—can't make out what it was . . .	Kenyon wanted receiver radio.
Someone has had toothache—sore condition mouth . . .	*I had tooth filled evening before I left Edmonton. Was still tender and jumped each time I trod heavily.*
Think you would like to get some word through to Iversen if you could reach him before Thursday— wonder if this thought in your mind tonight as you think of me? . . .	*Sent word to Iversen.*

In ESP work, conditions of reception are different. The conscious mind tries its best to be of aid. It over-impresses the subconscious with its responsibility in "pulling through" an exact impression of a certain symbol. This over-anxiety brings about a reaction on the nervous system, which seems to center in the solar plexus.

If the sender, with every good intention, is not sending with sufficient "emotionalized force"—for want of a better way to describe it—then it is like trying to pick up a weak broadcasting station with one's receiving set. Either you have to secure a more powerful set—or find some way of increasing the receiving power of the set you have—or the power of the sending station must be increased, to permit good reception.

Sometimes I find my body and mind becoming too tense, almost a subconscious realization that impressions from outside are too faint to grasp . . . my own system seems to try to "step up" its sensitized power . . . This either results in "unintended forcing," which colors impressions . . . or if I am able to "make contact," I cannot hold it long because of an indescribable nervous exhaustion.

Any individual who is doubtful of body changes or reactions during telepathic attempts at receiving thoughts—particularly when the mind is trained down to the point of picking up specific test impressions, should subject himself to a series of experiments.

I believe, as in all things, that continued practice brings greater mastery over all elements. A runner is more easily exhausted and is shorter of wind in the first weeks of training.

A human, learning to use the power of telepathy, long dormant in the mind of average man, is somewhat in the position of a person calling upon unused muscles, and inviting or compelling them to respond.

The mind itself seems to know no fatigue. It is only the

instrument of the mind—the human body—that has difficulty in making the adjustment required.

Tonight, with no ESP test, my mind "went out" with a surge of human interest, to discover the present plans and experiences of Sir Hubert Wilkins, and the following is an exact transcription of my impressions:

SHERMAN	WILKINS
Real action scheduled for tomorrow 400 to 600 mile flight in offing over mountains . . .	Correct. 1300 miles.
Investigating rumor reported by natives or Eskimos that an airplane motor was heard the day Levanevsky and companions came down— this motor over mountain regions— I feel tonight that this basis for your search this locality— Have wondered consciously why you would make flight this region—this seems to come to me as answer . . .	Correct.
Several flights, planned, shortly following one another—to cover mountain territory . . .	Correct.
If Russian plane wreckage sighted, you would mark location on map— and make trek by land to reach scene . . .	Correct.
Believe cloudy weather over mountain passes holding up flight— You can't go too far in such weather—if you took off, you'd have to turn back . . .	Correct. Wind drifting snow.
There seems to be a certain mountain peak or elevation you intend	

SHERMAN	WILKINS
to circle—in vicinity of which you believe Russians might be, if anywhere in this locality . . .	South of Barter Island.
Liquor—in that connection—seem to sense commercial interest—like some firm wanting endorsement— you considering if they will offer you enough money . . .	Correct. Hiram Walker. Didn't offer enough money.
I feel necessity for exercise of greater caution your part these next several weeks—have not experienced this feeling at any time before in many sittings I have had— deeply hope nothing may happen to force you down on any of your flights— Suggest you check oil and gas feed lines leading into engines as possible source of trouble.	*Oil pressure on new propeller gave trouble next day!*

TEST 58

March 3, 1938.   11:30-12:00 P.M.

The Strath-Gordons drove my wife and me home from the Open Forum meeting of the Psychic Research Society tonight, and came up for a visit; but I excused myself at the appointed time, and went into my study.

I felt much like a radio operator tonight who hears his "call letters" coming in. I could seem to sense Wilkins' thought in my direction.

An exact transcription of my impressions is as follows:

SHERMAN	WILKINS
I had recorded my impressions on Monday and Tuesday of your taking off for search flight on	

376

The Restless Coffins of
Christ Church

Oistin's Bay, on the south coast of the West Indian island of Barbados, looks like a setting from a Caribbean travel poster. Its tourist fame, however, is not based on waving palms and coral sands. Here, in the graveyard of Christ Church, lies one of the great riddles of the last century.

The graveyard is nothing but one massive overgrown vault, built partly above and partly below ground. Today, it stands completely empty; and this emptiness represents its secret. For the vault could not be used for its original purpose, as a quiet, dignified resting chamber for the dead.

In the church records, the tomb is referred to as the Chase Vault, though others than members of the Chase family were interred therein. Such a burial shell would cost a small fortune today, and was considered very expensive 170 years ago. Constructed of huge blocks of coral stone firmly cemented together, the vault was sunk two feet into the hard limestone ground. The roof, arched on the inside, appears flat above ground. The interior is 12 feet long by six-and-one-half feet wide. The entrance, set in one side, was closed by a large, weighty slab of blue marble, which gave the structure the air of a fortress and an aura of Egyptian impenetrability.

Nothing except her name is known about the first person buried here. She was a Mrs. Thomasina Goddard; her coffin was placed in the vault in July 1807. In 1808, followed the coffin of little Mary Anna

Chase, who died of obscure causes at age two. Then, on July 6, 1812, came Dorcas Chase, an older sister of Mary Anna, whose death caused some whispering. It was bruited about that the girl had been driven to despair by her tyrannical father and that she killed herself by refusing all food. Whatever the strength of this rumor, her funeral passed without incident.

Four weeks later, the tomb had to be opened again to receive the body of the head of the Chase family, The Honorable Thomas Chase, who was, by all accounts, one of the most hated men on the island. And as the lamplight illuminated the chamber, it became clear that something had happened. *The coffins were not in their original positions.* That of the Chase infant had been hurled head downward into the opposite corner, while the coffin of Mrs. Goddard was lying on its side against the wall.

The white members of the burial party were indignant about this desecration which they automatically blamed on the colored graveyard laborers. The Negroes appeared much more disturbed—though for a different reason. The coffins were reverently put back in order; that of Thomas Chase was added to the row, and the vault was shut up again.

Another four years passed. Then, on September 25, 1816, the somber marble slab at the entrance to the sepulchre was hoisted aside to admit another child. Master Samuel Brewster Ames was dead at 11 months. As the accompanying group of mourners entered the chamber, they stared and stood aghast. Desecrators had been at work again! The four coffins lay tumbled around in wild disorder.

Immediate reaction was pure rage. No one doubted that this was the handiwork of black ghouls. The previous April, Barbados had been the scene of one of the many abortive slave risings that periodically drenched the West Indies in blood. The rebellion had been crushed, as most of them were. This desecration of the dead was clearly an act of revenge.

But after the first angry hubbub subsided, the facts began to appear considerably less obvious. The vault had only one entrance, and the marble slab guarding it was found to have been firmly in place. The cement around the edges of the entrance was as hard as rock.

Then there was the matter of the coffins themselves. That of Mrs. Goddard was a flimsy wooden affair, easy to shift around. But the coffin of The Honorable Mr. Chase was tremendously heavy. It was constructed of an inner shell of wood; the outer container was made of lead. With Chase inside that box—a giant of a man, who weighed about 240 pounds—it had taken all of eight persons to shift the coffin into place. Now it lay on its side, several feet to the left of where it had been placed. How had the vandals—at least eight of them—entered the tomb and done their work unnoticed?

The black slaves, who did all the heavy work at burials, were far more upset than their masters. Only sharp commands kept them near the vault and made them pick up the coffins and place them, once again, in dignified order. This time the marble slab was replaced with especial care.

The next burial took place the following November, only 52 days later. The dead man was Samuel Brewster, father of the boy already lying in the vault. He had been bludgeoned to death by his slaves during the April revolt, and he had temporarily been buried elsewhere. Now, as the procession neared the Chase Vault, the funeral group was followed by a flock of the curious. Word of the weird findings had spread.

On this occasion, the marble slab seemed definitely untouched; it took considerable effort to move. But as the first thread of light fell into the awesome chamber, those nearest could see that *it had happened again.*

The coffins were scattered. Mrs. Goddard's wooden shell had disintegrated, whether from natural causes or through rough handling was impossible to determine. The other four—all made of lead—had been shuffled like a deck of cards.

This time the Reverend Thomas Orderson, Rector of Christ Church, a magistrate and two other men conducted a thorough search of the vault. They tested the walls and the domed roof for moisture and they found the interior completely dry. They scanned the floor for cracks and found it solid. There was nothing they could do except to supervise the work of stacking the coffins, once again, in the prescribed order.

The slaves were in a state of abject terror. Although Barbados Ne-

THE CHASE VAULT   This is a photograph of the tomb of the "Restless Coffins" as it looks today—148 years after the last casket was removed. The vault is located on the grounds of Christ Church, seven miles from Bridgetown, capital of Barbados.

groes were less steeped in Voodoo than their fellows on Haiti, they were convinced the vault was cursed. Evil powers in that chamber could strike at whoever entered. Only the more immediate fear of their masters could keep them at work. Once again, the slab went over the entrance, and the tomb was left in darkness and silence.

Within weeks, all of Barbados and all of the British West Indies had learned about the happenings at Christ Church. Throngs of sightseers flocked to the graveyard, then crowded around the vault and angered the Reverend Orderson with questions he couldn't answer.

White Barbadians quite blatantly waited for the next funeral, asking friends and relatives in the area "to be sure and let us know in good time." Several captains sailed their vessels into Oistin's Bay on the off-chance that the vault might be opened while they were there. On the other hand, the colored population couldn't stay far enough away from the site. Even hardened graveyard attendants gave the tomb a wide berth and always worked near it in pairs—never alone.

The curious had to wait almost three years before the next installment unfolded. On July 17, 1819, the wooden coffin of Mrs. Thomazina Clarke was made ready for its resting place in that restless chamber. There was no doubt about the importance of the occasion. Although Mrs. Clarke had been of little consequence while alive, her remains were followed by the Governor of Barbados, Lord Combermere, his aides-de-camp, the commander of the garrison, and by most of the island clergy, and by hundreds of spectators.

The Negroes had to work long and hard to shift the marble slab away from the entrance to that tomb. The cement holding the door in place was solid and untouched: something from the inside seemed to resist, something heavy and inert. When the slab was finally shifted, it was clear what it was: The coffin of the late Mr. Chase was rammed solidly against the doorway, almost six feet away from the spot where it had been placed!

The other coffins were scattered. Those of the children, which had been placed on top of the larger ones, were now lying on the stone floor. Only Mrs. Goddard's wooden box stood where it had been positioned.

This was the most bewildering detail. The Goddard container had been found badly splintered on the previous opening of the vault. The wooden planks of the coffin were coming apart and had to be tied together with wire. The coffin, therefore, had been leaned against the rear wall of the vault, away from the others. Yet this, the flimsiest and the most precariously placed, was the only coffin that hadn't moved.

For a long time, the burial party stood in silence; astonishment took over; no one could believe his eyes. Then the murmurs of those outside the vault, shoving and elbowing to get a closer look, drifted into the chamber. His Excellency, the Governor, remembered his position, and the dignity that had to be preserved. He went into action.

Lord Combermere was an old cavalry trooper, an up-and-at-'em soldier who had led four saber charges against the French during Wellington's Spanish campaigns, and had his scars to show for it. He took a lot of frightening. Now he assigned each man in the party a specific task. They went over the floor, the walls, the ceiling foot by foot, searching for the slightest crack that might indicate a hidden entrance or a tunnel. They minutely scanned the sealed coffins to see whether anyone had attempted to pry them open.

All lines of investigations drew blanks. There was absolutely no other way of entering the chamber, save through the front. The lids of the boxes were firmly closed as ever they could be, with nary a mark nor a splinter to indicate a breaking attempt. The vault was dry. It was apparently airtight.

DRAWINGS OF THE RESTLESS COFFINS   *These two sketches made by the Honorable Nathan Lucas, an eyewitness of the strange events on Barbados Island, show the change in position of the coffins, before and after the disturbance.*

SKETCHES OF THE CHASE VAULT.

From the manuscript of the Hon. Nathan Lucas.

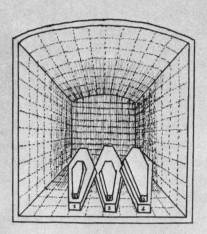

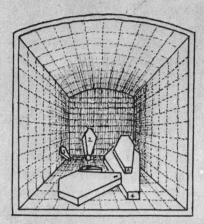

Situation of the Coffins when the Vault
was closed July 7th., 1819
in the presence of the Reverend
Thomas H. Orderson.

Situation of the Coffins on April 18th,
1820, when the Vault was reopened
in the presence of the Rt. Honble. Lord
Combermere, R.B. Clarke, Esq., .
Rowland Cotton and Honble. N .
Lucas

July 6th, 1812.	Dorcas Chase; leaden coffin, No. 1.
August 9th, 1812.	Honble Thomas Chase; leaden coffin, No. 2.
September 25th, 1816.	S.B. Ames; infant; leaden coffin, No. 3.
November 17th, 1816.	Samuel Brewster, shot in the Insurrection, April 15th; his remains removed to the Vault, November 17th; leaden coffin, No. 4.
February 22nd, 1818 [?1808].	A.M. Chase; infant; leaden coffin, No. 5.
July 7th, 1819.	Thomasina Clarke; wooden coffin, No. 6

Certified,

T.H. ORDERSON, D.D.,

Rector of the Parish of Christ Church.

On the side of No. 4 there were the remains of an old
wooden coffin tied up between the wall and the coffin, and these
were found in their original situation when the vault was opened
in 1820.

T.H. ORDERSON.

The coffins had been moved
twice before their last inspection.

T.H.O.

For the fourth and final time, the coffins were hoisted back in line, the three large leaden ones placed on the ground, those of the two small children and the wooden one of Thomazina Clarke placed on top of the larger ones.

Then the Governor personally supervised the sprinkling of a thick layer of soft white beach sand on the floor—sand that would show telltale footprints of anyone who entered the vault. The marble slab was hoisted in place and cemented shut. As a last safeguard, Lord Combermere and his aide and his secretary, and two other men made several impressions into the wet cement with their private seals. Whoever tampered with the door from now on would *have* to break those imprints.

In the months that followed, Christ Church became the object of a pilgrimage. Much to the Reverend Orderson's annoyance, people from every part of the West Indies were constantly knocking at his door for information, and spent hours gaping in morbid fascination at the silent stone bulk. They came in groups and in family parties from as far off as Jamaica. In the words of the parish clerk, their behavior was marked by "nothing of Christian decorum and little of common courtesy. They appeared to regard that portion of hallowed ground as no better than a bull pit or puppet show, but with the advantage that it did not cost them a farthing."

The Negro slaves were the exception. They were in terror of the place, and didn't dare to even mention it. Visitors soon discovered that it was useless to ask any slave for directions to the vault. They pretended never to have heard of it; even promise of money failed to elicit an answer.

The matter of the Chase Vault preyed on the mind of the Governor. The subject frequently cropped up in his conversations, particularly with the men who had helped him seal the tomb.

On the afternoon of April 18, 1820, almost the entire party was gathered at Lord Combermere's residence. Talk, once again, centered around the tomb. It was now more than eight months since the last interment, and His Excellency was frankly bursting to know if anything had happened "down there." One of the advantages of being a colonial Governor in those days was that you could scratch your personal itches.

Combermere suggested that they visit the tomb at once.

The party set out. Apart from the Governor, there was Major Finch, his secretary, and three members of his staff named Nathan Lucas, Rowland Cotton, and Bowcher Clarke. On the way, they picked up two masons to take care of the manual labor, and also Rector Orderson, to lend the investigation some spiritual solemnity.

One glance was sufficient to show that none of the half dozen seals at the entrance had been disturbed. The cement around the marble slab was granite hard. The masons chipped away silently. None of the officials spoke.

Then the massive marble was lifted aside, and the tomb lay open. Slowly the men filed in, their eyes growing accustomed to the dimness, their lungs breathing the cold, musty air.

The vault was in chaos! Some of the coffins had been turned upside down, including the tremendously heavy one belonging to Thomas Chase. A child's coffin was now lying on top of the steps that led down to the chamber. Once again, the only coffin to remain undisturbed was the wire-tied bundle of planks that housed the remains of Mrs. Goddard. It was leaning against the wall where it had been left.

The white layer of sand still covered the ground. There were no footprints, no marks of any kind to be seen.

Lord Combermere once again went through the motions of having the tomb examined. According to Nathan Lucas's account:

"I examined the walls, the arch, and every part of the vault, and found every part old and similar; and a mason in my presence struck every part of the bottom with his hammer, and all was solid..."

Other men raked through the vicinity of the vault above ground, hoping to find some indication of tunneling. They found nothing. The tomb was to all intents and purposes airtight; the entrance, sealed. And yet some force had entered that could upset a lead coffin it had taken eight strong men to lift.

At this point, the Governor gave up. He ordered the vault to be evacuated, the coffins to be buried elsewhere. The tomb has been empty and open ever since.

In trying to answer the riddle of the Chase Vault, we are handicapped by our lack of information about the people interred in that sepulchre. The Reverend Orderson was the Rector of Christ Church during the entire period. Although he kept a detailed record of the events, he did not reveal why so many outsiders were buried in the Chase Vault, nor who they were. In most cases, he didn't even state the cause of death.

We know from other sources that The Honorable Thomas Chase had an evil reputation as a slave-driver and a family bully.

There is no way of telling whether the rest were as hated as Chase— if hatred it was that motivated the vandalism against their coffins. Robbery can be discarded. All the people concerned were Anglicans, and were buried without valuables. If it was a human agency that shifted the coffins, those hands could just as well have forced them open. Yet all the lids remained in place.

But it seems extremely unlikely that the disturbances were caused by any human agency.

Three possible natural causes have been advanced to account for the disturbances: earthquakes, escaping gases, floodwater. None of these, however, make much sense.

The West Indies is, to be quite sure, a volcanic region, and small tremors do occur with great frequency. But never has there been an earthquake which would affect but one particular patch of ground— 12 feet by six feet—and remain unnoticed everywhere else. It would be even more absurd to assume such a freak tremor would strike the same patch five times in a row, affecting only the contents of the tomb while leaving the ground, walls, and roof unmarked.

As to flooding, water from somewhere might have entered the vault, shifted the contents, and subsided before the next inspection. Even lead coffins will float, provided they are airtight. But this theory, too, must collapse after full consideration.

To start with, such a quantity of water would have been noticeable in the surrounding area. The Governor's party considered the possibility of flooding and they searched diligently for signs of it, both inside the tomb and around it. But in Lucas's words: "There was no vestige of water to be discovered in the vault, nor any marks where it had been..."

SIR STAPLETON COTTON The First Viscount Combermere was Governor of Barbados from 1817 to 1820. The Viscount had been one of Wellington's most resourceful cavalry commanders.

The most telling refutation to the flood surmise is the fact that Mrs. Goddard's coffin, which consisted of mere slabs of wood, would have floated easier than the leaden containers. Yet that coffin was the only one that consistently stayed in place.

Which exhausts all the causes that might be termed "natural." Leaving the field free for the supernatural ones. Therefore, enter the spiritualists:

Three or four researchers with strong psychic leanings—the most famous being Sir Arthur Conan Doyle—became intrigued by the enigma, and attempted their own particular interpretations. All of the psychically oriented put their finger on one fact that doesn't seem to have occurred to any of the people involved: the tomb became "restless" only after the burial of a suicide. No disturbance of any kind had been reported prior to the interment of Dorcas Chase.

It was one thing, however, to point out this undeniable truth; quite another, to draw conclusions from it. How this could account for the shuffling of the coffins was still unexplained.

Conan Doyle tried to be a little more illuminating, but in a fashion that would have set Sherlock Holmes' teeth on edge. In what was probably the silliest magazine article he ever wrote, Sir Arthur declared that the turmoil was due to a substance called "effluvia." The effluvia was brought into the vault by the Negro slaves carrying the coffins. Now effluvium, in the dictionary sense, means simply exhalation. But Doyle, in a delightfully nebulous way, has the effluvia combine with certain unnamed "forces" inside the sealed vault. The combination then becomes a combustive force which proceeds to toss around the contents of the tomb. The genesis of this force was facilitated, according to Sir Arthur, by the presence of "unused vitality" which he claimed lingers wherever life has been cut short by suicide or murder.

Sir Arthur was modest enough to call this a "provisional theory." The great pipe-smoking sleuth he created would undoubtedly have called it something else.

The main difficulty in working out a feasible solution lies in the nature of the evidence. The Reverend Orderson's original records were either lost in the hurricane that destroyed Christ Church in 1831, or in the fire that gutted the rebuilt edifice in 1935. Later researchers could only deal with copies of the records, or copies of the copies. Once such a narrative becomes third-hand, many essential details may be lost.

The accounts penned by members of the Governor's staff were preserved; but these eyewitnesses were present only at two of the five vault openings. As to the other three, they merely stated what they *heard*. These gaps may not make any appreciable difference in the case, but the holes render the evidence incomplete.

A strikingly similar series of events occurred on another island, on a different portion of the globe, 24 years later. The island was then called Osel, but has since been named Saaremaa. Osel formed part of the Imperial Russian province of Estonia, now known as the Estonian Soviet Socialist Republic. The town we are concerned with was then named Ahrensburg but has since been rechristened Kuresaare. The inhabitants of Osel are Lutheran Balts, quite unrelated to the Slavic Russians.

During the July of 1844, several visitors to the cemetery of Ahrensburg found that their horses grew panicky when left tied to the rails which enclosed the graveyard. On at least six occasions, the tethered animals went crazy with fear, rearing and kicking to get free, and one actually died in its frantic efforts.

The hitching rails were along the road which lead from the town to the cemetery. Facing the highway were three private chapels and vaults belonging to the nobility. Among them was the imposing tomb of the Buxhoewden family, an ancient clan of barons.

On July 24, one of the Buxhoewdens was to be interred. The oaken coffin stood in the chapel, and was to be transferred to the vault. When the door of the burial chamber was unlocked, the mourners were greeted by a weird sight. All but three of the coffins inside the family vault had been dragged from their iron stands and had been piled up in the middle of the sepulchre.

After replacing the coffins, the family complained to the Consistory, an ecclesiastical court, presided over by the Baron de Guldenstubbé. The members of the court consisted of the Lutheran bishop, the town mayor, a physician, two craft guild laymen, and a secretary. The Consistory concluded that the cemetery had been visited by ghouls and it took immediate action. The court placed guards in the vicinity and added two more locks to the vault entrance, which had both inner and outer doors, each heavily barred.

Three days later, the court inspected the vault. The guards—soldiers of the island garrison—reported no disturbances. Both the new and the old locks on both doors were intact. Yet inside the tomb, all was a shambles. Every coffin, save the same untouched three, had been hauled down from their stands, two had been overturned and had been left lying on their sides.

An official investigation followed, with Baron de Guldenstubbé and the bishop questioning every graveyard worker and many of the visitors. The soldiers searched the vault for a hidden passage; a wide area around the situs was scrutinized for signs of tunneling. No other entrance was found. Nor did a close examination of the locks reveal any tampering.

The Consistory then ordered two of the displaced coffins opened but found inside them only human remains in various stages of decomposition. The vault was checked for traces of moisture, but was found to be perfectly dry. Finally, workmen ripped up the entire flooring of the tomb and searched through the foundations of the chapel above . . . Nothing!

As a precaution, all the door locks were changed once again, the floor of the vault sprinkled with fine wood-ashes, and the doors sealed with both the seals of the municipality and those of the Buxhoewden family. Still another layer of ashes, several inches deep, was scattered over the steps leading from the chapel to the vault. The guards were now drawn in a ring immediately around the site of the tomb.

The Consistory waited only three days before conducting a check-up. The vault was opened and found to be in a state of chaos. The coffins were scattered, overturned, standing on end. The lid of one had sprung open; two others had been jammed into a corner like two bits of fire-wood.

As before, the same three containers remained untouched. And the coating of ashes presented a smooth, undisturbed surface!

The court admitted defeat. The coffins were removed and buried in a different part of the cemetery. The family vault of the Buxhoewdens was left empty. Strange that the last member of the Buxhoewden clan interred in that tomb before the trouble started was a young man who was said to have shot himself.

The above account was first published by the American diplomat-scholar Robert Dale Owen, who had heard it from the son and daughter of Baron de Guldenstubbé in Paris in 1859—which makes the story third-hand and places the recital 15 years after the event—certainly not the most reliable form of chronicling. Subsequent efforts by representatives of the British Society for Psychical Research failed to uncover any documentary evidence. But the older inhabitants of Osel remembered the story well, and the empty vault was there for anyone to see.

Just what caused those two sumptuous family tombs to be abandoned is something no one has fathomed. As the Reverend Samuel Wesley once remarked, "Wit, I fancy may find an interpretation; but wisdom, none."

THE

JOURNAL

OF THE

BARBADOS MUSEUM

AND

HISTORICAL SOCIETY

VOL. XII.   MAY, 1945.   No. 3.

PRICE 4/-

PUBLISHED BY THE BARBADOS MUSEUM AND HISTORICAL SOCIETY
ST ANN'S GARRISON, BARBADOS, B.W.I.

THE JOURNAL OF THE BARBADOS MUSEUM AND HISTORY SOCIETY   Here is the cover of Vol. XII, No. 3, of the Journal which contains an account of the Barbados mystery. The excerpts which follow are facsimile pages from Vol. XII and Vol. XIII, and together give a detailed account of the baffling events.

He was Snatched away from us
the 14th of May Anno Dom 1724
in the 34th year of his Age:
And died Lamented by all who knew him.
In Honour to his Memory His truly sorrowful
Widow has erected this Tomb.

In this vault the leaden coffins having been found displaced several times, it became matter of curiosity and inquiry; and being at Elridge's Plantation next the Church in company with the Right Honble Lord Combermere on a visit to the proprietor, Robert Boucher Clarke Esqr., on the 18th of April 1820, it became a subject of conversation at noon when the negroes were coming from the field: we took eight or ten of the men directly with us to the Church Yard to open the Vault and sent off for the Rector, the Rev. Dr. Thomas H. Orderson, who very soon arrived. His Lordship, myself, Robert Boucher Clarke and Rowland Cotton Esqrs. were present during the whole time.

On our arrival at the vault every outward appearance was perfect: not a blade of grass or stone touched; indeed collusion or deception was impossible; for neither ourselves nor the negroes knew anythng of the matter; for the subject was hardly started in conversation before we set out for inspection and the Church Yard cannot exceed half a mile from Eldridge's.

The annexed drawing with the references was made for me at the instance of the Doctor, copied from one sketched on the spot by the Honble Major Finck who very soon joined our party at the vault. The followng particulars were obligingly supplied by the Doctor.

I was present from beginning to end and no illusion or deception could have been practised.

PARISH OF CHRIST CHURCH

There is a Vault, which by the inscription on the tomb belongs to the Elliot family in which vault no person had been buried for many years. In July 1807, application was made to the Rector to permit the remains of Mrs. Thomasin Goddard to be interred in the vault; and when it was opened for her reception it was quite empty without the smallest appearance of any person having been buried there. Mrs. Goddard was buried July 31, 1807. February the 22nd 1808—Mary Ann Maria Chase, infant daughter of the Honble Thomas Chase was buried in the same vault in a *leaden coffin*. When the vault was opened for the reception of the infant, the coffin of Mrs. Goddard was in its proper place. July the 6th 1812, Dorcas Chase, daughter of the honble Thomas Chase was buried in the same Vault; and the two other coffins were in their proper places. August 9th, 1812 the H o n b l e Thomas Chase was buried in the same vault. Upon the vault being opened for his reception, the two *leaden* coffins were evidently removed from the situation in which they had been placed; particularly the infant's which had been thrown from the north east corner of the vault where it had been placed to the opposite angle. The coffin was nearly upright in the corner, but the head was down to the ground. September the 25th, 1816, Samuel Brewster Ames, an infant, was buried; and the *leaden* coffins, when the vault was opened, were removed from their proper places, and were in much disorder. November 17th. 1816, the body of Samuel Brewster (who had been murdered in the Insurrection of slaves on the 15th of April preceding and who had been previously buried in the Parish of St. Philip), was removed, and interred in the vault. Great confusion and disorder were discovered among the *leaden* coffins. July 7th, 1819, Thomasina Clarke was [P·332] buried in the same vault; and upon its being opened, much confusion was again discovered among the *leaden* coffins. N.B., When Miss Clarke was buried, the coffin of Mrs. Goddard had fallen to pieces and was tied up in a small bundle between Miss Clarke's coffin and the wall; and on April 20th, 1820 the bundle was *in situ*.

N.B. At each time that the vault was opened the coffins were replaced in their proper situations and the mouth of the vault was regularly closed and cemented by masons in the presence of the Rector and some other persons.

On the 7th of July 1819 private marks had been made at the mouth of the vault in the mason work; and on the 18th of April 1820 the vault was opened at the request of Lord Combermere, in the presence of His Lordship, the Honble Nathan Lucas, Robert Boucher Clarke and Rowland Cotton Esqrs :

The two annexed drawings represent the situation of the coffins; No. 1, as they were left on the 7th of July 1819; and No. 2, the situation they were found in the 18th of April 1820.

Ann Maria Chase
Dorcas Chase
Honble Thomas Chase
S. B. Ames
    &
S. Brewster } Were in *leaden* coffins.

Mrs. Goddard and
} were in wooden coffins.
Miss Th. Clarke

Since the 18th of April 1820 all the coffins have been removed from the vault at the desire of Mrs. Chase and have been buried in a grave; and the [P·333] vault still continues open. The vault is dug in the ground about two feet in the lime rock; and the descent into it is covered with a large block of blue Devonshire Marble which will take some hours to be removed and replaced again in its proper situation. It will take at least four able men to remove the stone.

Certified March 26th, 1824.

          T. H. ORDERSON D.D,, Rector,

For the Honble Nathan Lucas.

AN UNSOLVED BARBADOS MYSTERY.

By SIR ALGERNON ASPINALL

ON a slight eminence above Oistin's, the small town on the south coast of Barbados where the Royalist Commissioners after stubborn resistance signed the Articles of Capitulation of the island at "Ye Mermaid's Inn" in 1652, stands the parish church of Christ Church. It replaces one destroyed by fire on the 2nd of March, 1935, whose only claim to notice was that it was built in 1837 on the lines of a ship, having been designed by a naval officer, Captain Senhouse, R.N.

The graveyard surrounding the church is, however, a centre of interest to visitors—especially those of a psychical turn of mind —for between the years 1811 and 1821 a vault there was the scene of remarkable manifestations of evil, the causes of which have never been discovered, though many people have been inclined to attribute them to poltergeists or other supernatural agencies. Repeatedly when the vault was opened for a burial the coffins deposited in it were found to be in a state of confusion.

After the death of the last eye-witness of these discoveries the "Barbados Coffin Story" as it was called came to be regarded in time as a legend, there being no tangible evidence that it was founded on fact; but Mr. Forster Alleyne, an old friend of the writer, was convinced that it was true, and was determined to prove it. He had heard the tale from his father; his brother-in-law, Mr. Andrew Lang drew his attention to reports of similar disturbances among coffins in the public cemetery at Arensburg on the island of Oesel in the Baltic in 1844, as related by Mr. S. R. Vale Owen in his "Footfalls on the Boundary of Another World;" these too were unconfirmed. They were said to have been the subject of a report deposited in the Consistory; but the Society of Psychical Research doubted its existence and the owner of the Arensburg vault had no knowledge whatever of the story. A paper on the Barbados mystery read by Mr. Lang before the members of the Folk-lore Society was received "very sceptically by the President" and was indeed "treated with scant interest." Undeterred by the negative result of his researches so far, Mr. Alleyne next inspected the Register of Burials at Christ Church. In it he found the names of the occupants of the vault during the period concerned and the dates of their interment duly certified by the Rector, the Rev. Thomas H. Orderson, with, however, "absolutely no comment" nor "the smallest hint that anything extraordinary had taken place." The accounts of the Parochial Treasurer afforded no clue; nor did the files of contemporary newspapers. It is curious that Isaac W. Orderson, the Rector's brother, should have made no mention of the mystery in his volume on "Social and Domestic Scenes and Incidents in Barbados in Days of Yore," published in 1842.*

Mr. Alleyne was almost in despair when, by a lucky chance, he came across the manuscript journals of the Hon. Nathan Lucas, a member of the Legislative Council of Barbados, who had been spoken of as having been one of a company present when the vault was opened in the presence of the Governor in 1820. They consist of a number of manuscript volumes containing copies of old records, notes of Archaeological and topographical interest and narratives of outstanding occurrences in Barbados within his memory. Some of the volumes had passed into the possession of Mr. Edward T. Racker, proprietor and editor of the *Barbados Agricultural Reporter,* who gladly made them available.†
Mr. Alleyne read the journals eagerly and to his intense satisfaction found that they not only covered the years in which the mysterious events at Christ Church were believed to have taken place, but actually contained a first-hand contemporary account of what happened. "This," wrote Mr. Alleyne in a letter to the writer, "is an absolutely authentic document; it is in the handwriting of Mr. Nathan Lucas, who was himself an eye-witness, and is attested by the Rev. Thomas Orderson, D.D." Mr. Alleyne's patience was rewarded. There was no longer any doubt that the disturbances among the coffins were not imaginary but very real.

Here is the gist of Mr. Lucas's narrative based on his personal experience and the information given to him by Dr. Orderson, with some additional notes by Mr. Alleyne.

It appears that the vault at Christ Church was originally an appurtenance to Adam's Castle Estate, the property of the family of Waldron, from which it passed to the Elliots. It is situated at the west end of the churchyard and is partly below and partly above the level of the surrounding ground. The lower portion is hewn out of limestone, coral rock, which forms the core of Barbados, while the upper is constructed of blocks of the same material cemented together so firmly that in appearance it is one solid mass. The entrance was closed by a double brick wall "from top to bottom, an inner and an outer, not united," and the few steps leading down to it were covered by "a large block of blue Devonshire marble." On the tombstone, since removed, was recorded the interment of the "Honble. James Elliot, Esq." (sic) who died on the 14th of May, 1724, "son of the Honble. Richard Elliot, Esq.", and husband of "Elizabeth, the daughter of the Honble. Thomas Waldron, Esq."*

---

* Creoleana, or Social and Domestic Scenes and incidents in Barbados in the days of Yore. London's Saunders and Ottley 1842.

† The volumes are now in the Public Library in Bridgetown.

* Members of the Legislative Council in those days while granted the honorary title of "Honourable" evidently retained the style of "Esquire" as well.

The Hoodoo Sea

At two o'clock on the afternoon of Wednesday, December 5, 1945, five Avenger torpedo bombers roared down the runways of the U.S. Naval Air Station at Fort Lauderdale, Florida. They rose smoothly into the radiant sky, assembled in formation, and swung out eastward over the Atlantic. And this was the last any living soul ever saw of them!

The flight they left on was a routine patrol, old hat to all of the pilots, scheduled to take about two hours. That flight was destined to become the darkest riddle in the annals of aviation—a *Mary Celeste* of the airways—but with an explanation that was minus even the logical guesswork offered in the famous case of the marine derelict.

The five planes carried a total of 14 men. Their fuel tanks, engines, instruments, and self-inflating life rafts had been checked before takeoff. The patrol flight was to take them on a triangular course, first east, then due north, then back to base. The Weather Bureau reported good flying conditions over the area they were to cover.

At 3:45 p.m., well on schedule, the control tower at Fort Lauderdale established radio contact with the flight leader. But instead of asking for landing instructions as expected, the commander's voice sounded both vague and worried:

"Cannot see land . . . We seem to be off course . . ."

The base tower crackled back: "What is your position?"

A few moments of silence. Then, "We are not sure where we are . . . Repeat: Cannot see land . . ."

At this point, contact was temporarily broken off. About ten minutes later, the flight came in again; at least the tower operators could hear the bomber crews talking to each other. The fliers seemed utterly confused, continually asking directions in tones of ominous panic. They sounded more like a bunch of boy scouts lost in the woods than experienced airmen flying in clear weather.

Shortly after four o'clock, the astonished base operators heard the patrol leader hand over his command to another pilot, without any apparent reason.

Twenty minutes later, the new commander spoke to the control tower. His voice came in abrupt jerks, like that of a man desperately trying to suppress hysteria: "We can't tell where we are . . . Everything is . . . can't make out anything . . . We think we may be about 225 miles northeast of base . . ."

He broke off; and for a few moments the only sounds were incoherent mumbles. Then again: "Looks like we are . . ."

Then complete, final silence.

At Fort Lauderdale, they sounded the emergency alarm and the station's smoothly efficient rescue apparatus swung into action. Within minutes, a large Martin Mariner flying boat took off and headed in the direction last indicated by the bombers. The Martin had a specially reinforced hull, enabling it to make sea landings in rough conditions. It carried a crew of 13 and full rescue equipment.

Approximately ten minutes later, the control tower lost radio contact with the flying boat *and never established it again!* The last communication had been a routine position check without an inkling of trouble. But as dusk approached, it became obvious to the flabbergasted men at the base that they had lost the rescuer as well as the flight it was supposed to rescue.

Before the sun went down, Coast Guard vessels from Miami took up a search; while overhead, a dozen naval aircraft scouted the area. They found a calm sea, a clear evening sky, middling winds of around 40 miles per hour—nothing else. Not a flare, not an oil slick, not one piece of floating wreckage.

The search continued all night. It was reinforced with the first light of dawn. The aircraft carrier *Solomons* joined in, together with 21 additional vessels. Some 260 U.S. planes scoured the ocean from above,

GRUMMAN AVENGERS   *A formation of five torpedo bombers, same as those shown here, made up the "Lost Patrol"—the most mysterious disappearance in the history of American aviation.*

aided by 30 Royal Air Force machines from British bases in the Bahamas. Fifteen land parties—soldiers, Marines and civilian volunteers—systematically worked up and down the Florida beaches, looking for bodies, or bits of debris, or anything that might constitute a clue.

Gradually the search was extended beyond the Atlantic into the Gulf of Mexico, covering almost a quarter of a million square miles. Hundreds of volunteers swelled the parties operating on land, nosing through swamps and through isolated patches of forest in jeeps, on horseback, and on foot. It was one of the greatest sweeps ever conducted in America, engaging enough men, ships, and aircraft to launch a fair-sized invasion. The total result was zero! Not a speck, not a screw, not even a button was found that came from the missing planes.

MARTIN MARINER FLYING BOAT   *A machine of this type followed the "Lost Patrol" into oblivion.*

After five days, the searchers abandoned their efforts, leaving a Naval Board of Inquiry with the task of explaining a jigsaw puzzle without a single fitting piece.

Had the five Avengers experienced engine trouble or fuel shortage, they would have reported such facts to the base operators. No, the only concern of the pilots was location. But even if, through some incomprehensible mishap, the compasses on all five planes had somehow gone awry, even that should not have created a grave problem. For the sun was clearly visible in the sky, and the pilots needed no other guidance to steer westward and reach their base.

Whatever had happened to the lost patrol offered no lead to the fate of the Martin Mariner. The flying boat was certainly not lost when it last communicated with the control tower; the huge plane simply faded into oblivion without an inkling of trouble.

But had all six aircraft for some undiscoverable reason crashed into the sea, why was there no debris? The Avengers were equipped with life rafts and flares; the Martin, with special rescue gear. All of the 27 men on board had received extensive training in ditching procedures. Why, in spite of tranquil water and clear sky, could no one locate a single raft, or life jacket, or parachute, or even a floating body? No matter how the machines might have disintegrated in mid-air, some pieces would have bobbed around on the surface of the sea; and, of course, there would be the inevitable oil patches.

The experts on the Board studied the riddle from every conceivable angle. A gigantic question mark remained. Their report summed up the investigation by saying: "*We were not able to even make a good guess as to what happened.*"

Nothing to date has illuminated the mystery. The fate of the missing planes remains as dark as ever.

What we have gained since is different perspective. We have come to realize that the "Lost Patrol" is just one chapter in a long series of similar happenings. Viewed separately, each of these occurrences is merely a baffling disappearance; taken as a whole, these happenings conjure up the frightening vision of an ocean patch in which—at irregular intervals —ships and aircraft vanish without trace.

The portion of sea involved can be imagined as a rough square whose northern limits stretch between Bermuda and the Virginia coast, its southern boundary formed by the islands of Cuba, Hispaniola, and Puerto Rico. And as far as researchers have been able to tally, some 60 ships and airplanes have sailed or flown into that void and have been swallowed up.

The earliest link in the chain dates back to 1866. In March of that year, the Swedish bark *Lotta,* out of Goteborg and bound for Havana, vanished somewhere off the north coast of Haiti. Two years later, the same fate befell the Spanish merchantman *Viego.*

In January 1880, the British training frigate *Atalanta* left Bermuda for England and was never seen again; with her, vanished a crew of 250 cadets and sailors. In 1884, it was the turn of the Italian schooner *Miramon,* which was bound for New Orleans but ended up in limbo.

In those days of "wooden ships and iron men," such disappearances were by no means rare, but in each case, the searchers were puzzled by the complete absence of the flotsam that usually marks a shipwreck.

The first missing ship to cause a real stir was the U.S. Naval collier *Cyclops.* Built in 1910, and, at the time, considered the last word in marine construction, the *Cyclops* displaced 19,500 tons. Her special superstructure enabled her to deliver coal to other vessels at sea. The giant collier frequently accompanied American warships abroad. When she visited Kiel in 1911, she was inspected by German naval engineers who pronounced her an "outstanding ship." On March 4, 1918, she sailed from Barbados of the British West Indies, for Norfolk, Virginia. Her crew consisted of 221 men, and she carried 57 passengers, as well as a valuable cargo of manganese ore. The *Cyclops* was due in Norfolk on March 13. She never arrived.

On April 14, the Navy Department announced that she was missing. On August 30, the Navy officially announced her as lost. In the intervening period, one of the most intensive sea searches ever staged failed to locate so much as a splinter of the missing vessel.

At the time, the Naval authorities assumed that the *Cyclops* had fallen victim to a prowling German submarine. Even that assumption left a host of unanswered questions. The collier carried full wircless

U.S.S. "CYCLOPS"   The disappearance of this somewhat grotesque looking, but entirely seaworthy, collier in 1918 is one of the most baffling mysteries in Navy annals.

equipment and lifeboats. Even a sudden torpedo attack would have allowed for time to radio an S.O.S. and to lower at least some of her boats. But these theoretical objections turned out to be nought, for after the war, the records of the Imperial Admiralty revealed that there were no U-boats anywhere near the area between March and April, 1918.

The *Cyclops* could have struck a floating mine. But no mines had been sighted near her course. Assuming that a solitary mine was involved, the ship still would have had time to use her wireless and launch her lifeboats. Moreover, a mine explosion invariably leaves wreckage, and such floating evidence would have been spotted in the wide search that followed.

The longer the mystery remained unsolved, the more fanciful the theories spun to unravel it. Probably the most startling hypothesis was that the *Cyclops'* commander, Lt.-Commander Warley, was a German by birth, whose name had originally been Wichman. This man had sold his home in Norfolk before leaving on his last journey. Herr Wichman had steered the *Cyclops* into a neutral port and had handed her cargo over to agents of his Fatherland or the traitor had sailed the ship right into Germany.

This particular brain bubble hardly deserves to be pricked. Regardless of his origin, Warley had an American crew who would have objected to such a procedure. The ocean in which he sailed was alive with Allied shipping; every neutral port was under observation. Apart from being some 4,500 miles away, Germany, at the time, was tightly blockaded.

A more plausible explanation was based on the fact that the collier had an unusually high superstructure. A sudden shifting of her cargo said some, had caused the boat to turn turtle and go to the bottom within minutes—a fate that had actually befallen the British battleship *Captain*.

But the Naval Board of Inquiry didn't go along with that theory either. The collier had shown her seaworthiness through seven years of rugged service. It would have taken extremely rough weather to cause her cargo to slide so badly; and during the period in question, the winds had been light to moderate.

So the fate of the *Cyclops* remains a blank in the annals of the U.S. Navy. It was not until almost 40 years later that investigators began to add up the awesome number of similar blanks and scratch their heads at the sum total.

Taking just a few examples: the American freighter *Cotopaxi* vanished in January, 1925, while en route from Charleston, S.C., to Havana, Cuba. Fourteen months later, the cargo tramp *Sudoffco*, out of Port Newark and bound for Puerto Rico, went the same ghostly way. In October, 1931, the Norwegian *Stavenger*, carrying a crew of 43, seems to have evaporated somewhere south of Cat Islands in the Bahamas. In June, 1950, the U.S. freighter *Sandra* sailed from Savannah, Georgia, was last seen off St. Augustine, Florida, and then never seen again.

All these vessels varied greatly in age, tonnage, cargo, and equipment. The only similarity among them was the manner of their disappearance. Although all carried radios, none sounded a distress call. Not one of these ships had encountered severe storm conditions. In spite of wide search sweeps, nothing associated with any of them was ever found. The case of the *Cyclops* was repeated over and over again.

However, one of the most recent vanishing acts *did* leave a trace— if a solitary floating life jacket can be called that. That jacket belonged to the *Marine Sulphur Queen,* a modern tanker which left the port of Beaumont, Texas, on the morning of February 2, 1963. She was bound for Norfolk, Virginia. Her final radio message was received a day later, and placed the ship near Key West in the Straits of Florida—a routine call. Then a curtain of silence fell.

Three days later, on February 6, Coast Guard planes and cutters launched an extensive search which yielded all of one life jacket bobbing on a calm sea about 40 miles southwest of the tanker's last known position. *One life jacket!* Otherwise the pattern of oblivion remained unbroken. No drifting boats, no oil spots, not a sign of the 39 men who had sailed on the missing ship.

The absence of bodies is perhaps the most baffling aspects of these disappearances. In any case of shipwreck, though sharks and barracudas might take a heavy toll of floating corpses, nevertheless at least some bodies are washed up on the nearby beaches. This has been true, for the most part, when ships have been wrecked in the South Pacific Ocean or in the Indian Ocean, two bodies of water which are much more shark-infested than the Caribbean. Furthermore, since almost all the ships lost in the American Zone vanished in sight of land, the absence of corpses renders these occurrences even more striking.

Casting around for parallels, investigators—particularly those connected with marine insurance—came upon another patch of water, fogged in a similar aura of mystery. The so-called "Devil's Sea" is that small portion of the Pacific which lies between Iwo Jima and Marcus Island somewhat southeast of Japan. A region of underwater volcanoes, that stretch of sea has long had an evil reputation among Japanese seafarers.

S.S. "MARINE SULPHUR QUEEN"   *Before her disappearance at sea in February, 1963, this 523-foot vessel of 15,260 gross tons, had been converted to carry molten sulphur. The tanker left Beaumont, Texas, bound for Norfolk, Virginia, with a crew of 39 men.*

ROUTE OF THE "MARINE SULPHUR QUEEN"   *The cross indicates the spot where a Navy plane reported sighting some debris which, however, turned out not to have been part of the vanished tanker.*

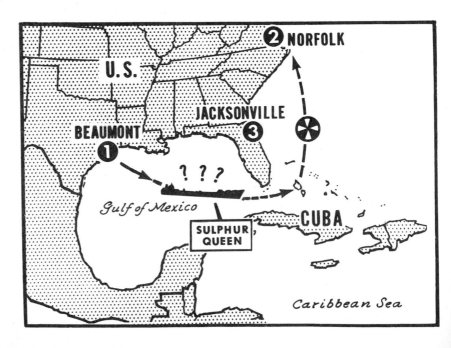

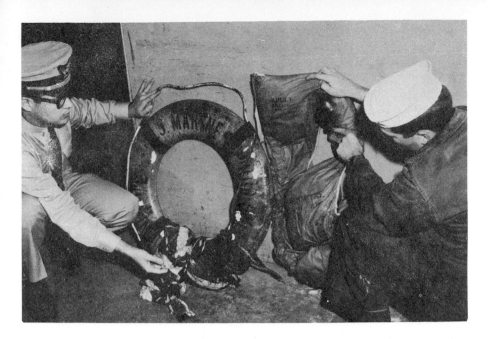

U. S. COAST GUARD EXAMINATION *Personnel in Miami examine a life ring and a life jacket of the missing "Marine Sulphur Queen." The objects, tied together with a man's shirt, were picked up by a Coast Guard helicopter, seven miles southeast of Key Biscayne.*

CIVIL GUARD BOARD OF INQUIRY *In session in New York, this Committee unsuccessfully attempts to shed some light on the disappearance of the "Marine Sulphur Queen." In the background sits Mrs. Adam Martin whose husband sailed as an engineer on the converted tanker. Mrs. Martin attended all sessions in the vain hope of learning something about her husband's fate.*

Hostile demons and ocean monsters were blamed for whatever happened there that could not otherwise be accounted for.

Stories of sudden shipwrecks in fair weather and reports of unaccountable disappearance date back more than a century. Until quite recently, the Japanese maritime authorities paid little attention to these tales. After all, only small fishing craft of doubtful stability were involved.

But between 1950 and 1954, no fewer than nine ships vanished in the "Devil's Sea"—a staggering number by modern safety standards. And these craft were not fishing smacks; rather fair-sized coastal freighters with good engines and radio equipment. Only one of them sent out an S.O.S. call. Intensive air-sea searches which frequently involved American planes, found bits of floating debris from two of the missing ships. But *no lifeboats, no survivors, no bodies!*

Early in 1955, with every sign of alarm, the Japanese government instituted a survey of weather and water conditions in the area. Apart from discovering a new volcano, the survey wound up with only one dramatic result: one of the research vessels itself disappeared, together with her crew of 15 sailors and scientists! Since that fearful day, the naval authorities have declared the "Devil's Sea" to be a danger zone. No one has been able to pinpoint exactly what constitutes the danger.

There seems to be a definite parallel between that particular patch of the Pacific and the stretch of North Atlantic off the southeast coast of America. The American sector, however, is unique as a sky trap—it is a region that swallows airplanes as well as ships.

The furor raised by the "Lost Patrol" had barely died down when three large civil airliners—one American and two British—whisked out of sight swiftly, silently, without a trace, leaving no hint of what force or dimension had betrayed them.

The *Star Tiger* and the *Star Ariel* were four-engined Tudors, both bound for Kingston, Jamica, via Kindley Field, Bermuda. Both sister ships vanished during what—according to their radio reports—were smooth flights in perfect weather.

At 10:30 on the night of January 29, 1948, the *Star Tiger*, with 29

COAST GUARD REPORT   This is the first page of the Marine Board Investigation which was convened to discover the truth about the disappearance of the S.S. "Marine Sulphur Queen."

ADDRESS REPLY TO:
COMMANDANT
U.S. COAST GUARD
HEADQUARTERS
WASHINGTON 25, D.C.

·MVI-3
5943/MARINE SULPHUR
QUEEN a-8 Bd

17 MAR 1964

Commandant's Action

on

Marine Board of Investigation; disappearance of
the SS MARINE SULPHUR QUEEN at sea on or about
4 February 1963 with the presumed loss of all
persons on board

1. The record of the Marine Board of Investigation convened to investigate subject casualty together with the findings of fact, conclusions and
recommendations has been reviewed.

2. The SS MARINE SULPHUR QUEEN, a T2-SE-Al type tank vessel of U. S.
Registry, converted to carry molten sulphur, departed Beaumont, Texas,
with a full cargo of 15,260 tons on the afternoon of 2 February 1963
enroute Norfolk, Va. The ship and crew of 39 men disappeared. The
vessel was last heard from at 0125 EST on 4 February 1963.

3. The ship's conversion in 1960 to a molten sulphur carrier necessitated
the removal of all transverse bulkheads in way of the original centerline
tanks and modification of the internal structure to accommodate one continuous independent tank 306 ft. long, 30 ft. 6 in. wide and 33 ft. high,
which was internally divided by transverse bulkheads into four cargo tanks
of about equal size. The external surfaces of this long independent tank
were insulated with a fibrous glass material 6" thick on the top of the
tank and 4 in. thick on other surfaces. A void surrounded the tank which
allowed a space about 3 ft. 6 in. between the bottom of the tank and the
bottom plating of the ship, 2 ft. between the sides of the tank and the
original wing tank longitudinal bulkheads, and 3 ft. between the top of
the tank and the weather deck. A watertight bulkhead was installed at
frame 59 which divided the void into two spaces. The forward space contained cargo tanks one and two and the after space contained cargo tanks
three and four. A partial or diaphragm bulkhead which did not extend to
the top or bottom of the void was installed where the first and second
cargo tanks were divided at frame 65 and where the third and fourth cargo
tanks were divided at frame 53. Near its midpoint the tank was welded
to its supporting structures at frame 59, and provision was made to permit

people on board, gave its position as 400 miles northeast of Bermuda. Talking to the control tower, the pilot commented on a favorable tail wind and the excellent performance of his engines. His final words were: "Arriving on schedule."

After that, not another sound.

Almost exactly a year later, on the morning of January 17, 1949, the *Star Ariel,* carrying 20 passengers and crew, took off from Bermuda and roared into a clear tropical sky. At 8:20, 35 minutes after becoming airborne, the pilot radioed back his first and only message, a report of fine weather, ending with: "All's well." Then he faded out for keeps.

The two airliners disappeared within about 600 miles of each other; both were in the general area of Bermuda.

The search machinery set in motion was vast. Looking for the *Ariel,* were two U.S. fleet carriers, half a dozen destroyers, Coast Guard cutters and aircraft, and a score of civilian aircraft.

The search parties found nothing—not a sliver that could by any stretch of the imagination have come from the Tudors. It was as if the airliners had blown into fine dust in mid-sky—as if an aerial trapdoor had closed behind them—as if they had never existed.

In London, the Brabazon Committee (named after its chairman, Lord Brabazon) sat nonplussed over the same clueless conundrum that had confronted the American Naval Inquiry Board in the case of the "Lost Patrol." The possibility of a bomb explosion on board the airliners could be ruled out: such an explosion would have produced quantities of scattered wreckage.

For some reason, both aircraft must suddenly, and without the slightest warning, have dived straight into the sea and sunk to the bottom. Moreover, the ships must have remained sufficiently intact to keep *all of their contents* confined in their hulls—technically an almost impossible assumption.

The Committee conducted a series of experiments with exact replicas of the vanished planes. These experiments merely solidified the puzzle: there seemed to be no way an aircraft of such size could crash into water without leaving bits and pieces scattered on the surface.

Yet even if we grant that there was a sudden crash, the cause of such a sudden crash proves equally bewildering. Some members of the Committee advanced a theory according to which quantities of methol bromide had accidentally been circulated in the pressurization system, thus rendering the pilots unconscious before they could radio a distress call. But while there may have been a remote chance of this having occurred in one plane, it seems beyond coincidence that this same mishap would have repeated itself in another. And if one were to credit this coincidence, would such an accident have happened *simultaneously to all the five Avenger Torpedoes lost on December 5, 1945 without a trace.*

Like their American predecessors, the British investigators pondered long, hard and intelligently and came up with precisely nothing.

Meanwhile, during the Committee's deliberations, still a third aircraft disappeared. A chartered DC-3, flown by Captain R. Linquist, took off from San Juan, Puerto Rico, on the night of December 28, 1948. On board were 33 holidaymakers who had spent Christmas in Puerto Rico and were now returning to Florida. The weather was idyllic; the night sky ablaze with stars; a gentle tail wind helped push the big plane along its thousand-mile journey.

In spite of the late hour, the passengers were still bubbling with holiday spirits, and the crew found the mood contagious. According to the captain's radio reports, everyone aboard was singing Christmas carols.

Shortly after 4:00 a.m., the plane radioed its position as 50 miles south of Miami, well within sight of land. Linquist asked for landing instructions. Instructions were given to him. But nobody knows whether or not he received them—for the captain's routine request was the last sound ever heard from the aircraft. Something happened up there, something nobody has yet been able to fathom, and the plane never landed.

With the first light of dawn, a search began. Some 50 Navy and Coast Guard vessels criss-crossed the pinpointed area; while overhead, several dozen aircraft scrutinized the clear blue Atlantic in ever-widening sweeps.

If any search operation was ever made under ideal conditions, this was it. The last position of the DC-3 had placed the airship over coastal waters so shallow that large objects could be clearly sighted on the bottom from the search planes. There were no disturbing winds, no rough seas to disperse oil slicks. Neither life rafts nor corpses nor debris was discovered. Once again searchers drew a bewildering blank.

In retrospect, the pattern of these disappearances may seem obvious, but that there was a pattern did not suggest itself at the time to the investigators. Technical specialists are considerably more reluctant than journalists to see a grand design in what may just be a chain of coincidents. It took many more such coincidents before anyone voiced the suspicion that there just might be something wrong *with the area* in which these mysterious disappearances occurred.

In the five years following the *Ariel* riddle, at least half a dozen military and civilian aircraft went the same mysterious way. In October, 1954, a giant Navy Super-Constellation vanished in fair weather with passengers aboard. During 1956, there were four more unaccountable disappearances, which included a Navy patrol bomber and a Marine Skyraider.

The pattern was monotonously alike: good flying conditions, normal radio contact, and then—oblivion!

Followed by intensive searches which failed to find a thing.

Since then, odd bits of wreckage have been sighted, though none could be positively identified as belonging to the missing planes.

One aircraft, a British York, sent out an S.O.S. before vanishing north of Jamaica; but neither the few scraps of flotsam nor the brief distress call yielded a clue as to the cause of the crash.

In January, 1962, a somewhat lengthier last message was received from a U.S. Air Force tanker en route from Virginia to the Azores. Fifteen minutes after takeoff, the control tower at Langley Air Force Base caught a series of almost incoherent signals which seemed to indicate some direction difficulty. Then a void swallowed the tanker. A six-day search failed to find a trace of the vessel.

Three months later, still another baffling distress call was picked up at Nassau in the Bahamas. The S.O.S. came from a private twin-engined plane approaching the airfield from the direction of Great Abaco Island, due north. With the morning sun beaming in an almost cloudless sky, the pilot acted as if he were flying through dense fog. He kept calling for directions, but he couldn't give his own position. After several urgent exchanges, radio contact broke off. Parts of one wing were later found floating about 20 miles from the shore. Which merely added to the bewilderment, for even if the ship's instruments had gone haywire, the island itself should nevertheless have been clearly visible to the pilot, and would have given him his position.

In August, 1963, the same trap caught two U.S. Stratojet tankers which had taken off together from Homestead Air Force Base in Florida. The four-engined planes maintained radio contact with the base and with each other until they reached a position 300 miles west of Bermuda. Then nothing further was ever heard from either of them.

But this time search vessels did find wreckage that could be identified as having come from the tankers. The findings ruled out a midair collision, since the debris was discovered about 150 miles apart. Here were two new, recently checked aircraft, flown by veteran pilots. Though they must have gone down separately, so sudden were the disasters that neither pilot had time to send a single distress call to the other. If such a call had been sent, the receiving pilot would have relayed the S.O.S. to shore, unless, of course, he too was similarly overwhelmed *at that exact point of time* by a like disaster. The Air Force investigators could merely shake their heads.

There were other disappearances: an American super-fortress south of Bermuda . . . a British army transport near the Virgin Islands . . . two U.S. Navy patrol planes south of Florida . . . a Dominican charter aircraft over the Windward Passage. All of them without a distress call, under fair skies, and without leaving a visible trace.

Unlike their Japanese counterparts, American and British authorities have never officially admitted the existence of a "Devil's Sea" in the North Atlantic. Nor are they ever likely to proclaim the area a "Danger Zone." But privately, both marine and aviation experts have confessed that they *may* be facing a phenomenon of environment rather than a chain of technical mishaps.

The exact nature of this phenomenon is at present as unknown to us as, say, the power of radium was to the alchemists of the 15th century. We can't even be certain whether a link exists between vanishing ships and vanishing aircraft. Except that all these craft were crowded into the same narrow geographical confines.

In the Caribbean, we can safely dismiss the possibility of under-water volcanic activity which might in some way account for the loss of ships in the Japanese sea. Nor do we have to spend much time refuting the hare-brained theory of a marine monster who can drag a 19,000-ton vessel to the bottom. But there are other ocean perils about which our knowledge, even in this day of science, is astonishingly hazy.

Some scientists have advanced the theory of the freak sea, a single mountainous wave of fantastic proportions that has been known to en-gulf large ships. Rising up to 100 feet or more, such a saltwater Everest can catch a vessel square on the beam, can cause a well-secured cargo to slide, thus rolling the craft over within less than a minute. In such an accident, there would be no time to radio nor to launch a lifeboat.

Such a wave accounted for the ore freighter *Mormackite,* which went down off Cape Henry, Virginia, in 1954. According to the 11 lucky survivors, the ship was struck on the beam and simply kept going over before it went to the bottom, tossed like a tin boat in a bathtub. If it hadn't been for those 11 who were hurled clear of the vessel and later rescued by another ship, the *Mormackite* would have joined the ghost fleet of missing craft, for but a few seconds earlier, she had been sailing along peacefully.

The old titan, the *Lusitania,* and the modern giant, the *Michelangelo,* each had parts of their navigation bridges smashed by gargan-tuan rollers—and each of those bridges were 75 feet above the water line! Waves of such incredible size would cause a smaller ship to heel over more than 60 degrees, and there are few types of cargo that would remain secured through that kind of list.

Marine experts do not know what causes these freak seas. Such a wave seems to rise singly from the heart of a storm, which otherwise produces no crest higher than 50 feet. Guesses vary. Some think that powerful ocean currents cause the freak occurrence; others, that a twister inside the storm area is responsible.

But here's the rub: it takes a storm to produce a freak sea, and in

SURVIVORS FROM THE "MORMACKITE"   On deck of a United States
destroyer, these 11 survivors of the lost freighter are given emergency treatment.

COAST GUARD BOARD OF INQUIRY   This committee conducts a hearing
on the sinking of the "Mormackite."

all the baffling disappearances we have listed, the weather had been fair to middling, which more or less disqualifies the monster wave as a possible cause.

In any case, waves cannot be blamed for missing airplanes. And with aircraft too, we find that almost monotonously fine weather conditions prevailed at the crucial times. This fact would rule out the hypothesis that powerful winds might have driven the planes far off course.

The aerial equivalent of the freak sea is something airmen call a "turbulence," and about which we know just as much or as little. According to aviation theory, a turbulence is an immensely powerful current of rising air in a cumulo-nimbus cloud, a current so powerful that it can actually flip jetliners on their backs or disintegrate them within seconds. As stated already, the cause is still obscure. But pilots have learned that a turbulence almost always occurs inside cumulo-nimbus clouds. Pilots will, therefore, give such cloud formations a wide berth whenever feasible.

We might assume that for some reason the North Atlantic zone in question produces an unusual number of these turbulences, and that these air disturbances were responsible for the many missing aircraft. But this theory won't stand up.

A plane, literally torn to pieces in midair, will scatter wreckage and bodies over a wide surface area. In the majority of cases of lost aircraft, there has been a total absence of telltale evidence.

What is even more significant is that in not a single instance did the radio calls of the lost airplane mention anything at all about air currents or report rough flying conditions. The trouble always seemed to stem *from direction or location.*

Could there be forces at work in certain regions of the world which somehow interfere with the human sense of orientation? Is the area where the five Avengers and the Mariner were lost such a region? Our only answer to this question has to be a shrug.

Through the ages there have always been certain areas which the people of the day endowed with supernatural attributes. Even today, it is alleged that there are several such odd spots on earth where normal physical laws do not apply. Perhaps the most famous of such loci is the

"Oregon Vortex," one of that state's major tourist attractions. Situated 30 miles from Grant's Pass, the vortex—which measures roughly 125 feet in diameter— constitutes, according to its promoters, an electro-magnetic phenomenon.

Within the "Oregon Vortex," there stands a hut, dubbed "The House of Mystery." Its owner, John Lister says, "Nowhere in the area does the visitor stand upright. Inevitably one assumes a posture that inclines toward magnetic north, beginning with a minimum of divergence from normal at the edge of the area, and increasing to an acute angle as "The House of Mystery" is entered. So gradually is this latter stage reached that visitors seldom realize the phenomenon until the seemingly impossible posture of the guide or their friends brings a realization of their own tilting."

Suspended from the roof of "The House of Mystery" hangs a heavy steel ball, but that ball presumably doesn't hang straight down. It would seem to lean inward, pulled toward the center of the hut by some weird gravitational shift. It is claimed that a person who enters the hut will feel the odd pull quite distinctly; it is further alleged that the power which is exerted will force one to lean over at a ten-degree angle. Viewers have alleged that a rubber ball, placed on the floor here, will roll uphill. Cigarette smoke here, it is said, performs a stronge sort of whirling dance, as if stirred by spiraling air currents.

However avidly these miracles are asserted by the promoters of "The House of Mystery" and by visitors to the site, scientific opinion holds that there is nothing in the so-called "Vortex" that is indeed a bafflement. "The House of Mystery" is nothing more nor less than a house of illusion, and does *not* defy any of the set laws of nature.

Herbert B. Nichols, formerly natural science editor of the *Christian Science Monitor,* effectively deflated the "Vortex." He had visited the spot armed with a carpenter's level, a light meter and a plumb bob, and his report explained that in this locality all was right with the world. No, the laws of nature were not awry—only the impressions of the visitors who were victims of optical illusion.

In 1951, a goodly portion of the populace of Britain was excited by the reports of a "Mystery Mile," a two and a quarter mile stretch of road

OREGON VORTEX   On the right there is a picture of the mystery house with a crowd lined up before it awaiting admission. The other pictures taken by visitors would seem to indicate that the force of gravity has gone beserk. The angles produced by the camera are quite illusionary and the weird results are but optical illusions. Natural forces in the so-called Oregon Vortex follow recognized scientific laws.

between the towns of Cobham and Esher, in southern England. Motorists passing over that well-traveled piece of highway began to complain
that they were being shot at by a sniper. As evidence, drivers showed
windshields punctured by what certainly looked like bullet holes. However, no slugs could be found inside the cars, nor was there a second hole
by which the bullet could have passed out of the car. Police carefully
went over the road, which was flanked on both sides by flat, open fields
which offered no hiding place for a marksman. Yet the incidents continued. Sometimes they occurred at night; sometimes, in broad daylight.
That the "shots" might have been fired from another vehicle was a theory
that did not hold up when it was proven that the stricken car was the
only one on the road at the time. The sizes of the holes in the windshields
varied sharply: some were of bullet dimensions, and other breaks were
as large as a man's palm. But two features apparently remained consis-
tent; only the windshield was affected, and no form of projectile was
discovered inside the automobile. Such were the facts that the local
citizenry attested to again and again, and such were the facts that were
publicized repeatedly by the local press.

On a clear afternoon in May, 1952, one William Decker, a London
insurance agent, was on his way to a client in Portsmouth, when he drove
over the "Mystery Mile" at 1:30 P.M.

"I had the road to myself, and was doing about 50 miles per hour,"
he later told police. "Nothing on either side except open fields. Suddenly
there was a bright flash in front of my eyes; then a sound like a gunshot,
and something crashed against my windscreen. I stopped the car. There
was a hole in the glass about the size of my fist, and a lot of splinters on
my chest and lap. I looked all around, but there wasn't a soul as far as I
could see."

As the "attacks" continued through 1952 and 1953, the police began
to patrol the road in unmarked cars. On different occasions, two of the
disguised radio cars had their windshields shattered; in each instance the
detective was incapable of locating the cause. The police, however did
put their finger on an important detail.

Motorists had always reported hearing "shots." But this turned out
to be an illusion. Invariably there was a bright flash, but the "shot" was

merely the impact of something striking the glass. The sensation was rather like being fired on by a gun equipped with a silencer; the only sound was the busting of the windshield.

Gradually, the police abandoned the idea of a mystery sniper. The size of the holes varied too much. Lab experts testified that while some of the punctures could conceivably have been inflicted by bullets, others looked more like rocks or pebbles. Yet no trace of any such objects could be discovered.

At this point national guesswork got under way. Thousands of people sent to the newspapers their theories about the "Mystery Mile." Radio programs were agog with the matter; so were television panels. Some suggested invisible bullets fired for experimental purposes by agents of Soviet Russia. Others dreamed up a glass-shattering ray operated by a deranged scientist. Still others postulated that swarms of tiny meteorites, for good reasons of their own, chose to gambol on that particular stretch of highway. However, neither the police nor the scientists managed to come up with even a feasible explanation. Luckily for the tranquility of British motorists, the attacks began to peter off in 1955, and they have finally ceased altogether.

Was this then an area in which the known laws of nature did not operate? Dozens of journalists throughout England either believed that this was the case, or else, writing with mock sincerity, made capital out of the story. But it is noteworthy that that bulwark of conservatism, *The Times* of London has written me to say, "The Mystery Mile story is not worth proceeding with. Proper investigations show that the rate of breakage was no greater than on other comparable main roads, and the publicity was due to a live and enterprising journalist in the area."

However, despite the fact that the so-called "Vortex" in Oregon and the so-called "Mystery Mile" in England have both been effectually debunked, it is nevertheless quite logical to believe that there may exist other areas which, *in fact*, do operate in a manner which does not accord with our present beliefs about physical science. Did the lost airplanes and lost ships encounter phenomena unknown to today's science? Do the laws of nature still contain a few paragraphs not covered in our textbooks?

REPORTS IN "THE TIMES" OF LONDON   In its issue of January 31, 1948, the authoritative London "Times" carries a story, reporting the loss of the aircraft "Star Tiger." Seven months later, in its issue of September 29, 1948, "The Times," evaluating the report of the Board of Inquiry which had conducted the investigation of the lost "Star Tiger," stated: "It may truly be said that no more baffling problem has ever been presented for investigation." The final paragraph of "The Times" comment was: "In the complete absence of any reliable evidence as to either the nature or the cause of the disaster to 'Star Tiger,' the court has not been able to do more than suggest possibilities, none of which reaches the level even of probability."

JANUARY 31   1948

31 MISSING IN AIR LINER

NOW "PRESUMED LOST"

ALL-DAY SEARCH OFF BERMUDA

The British South American Airways Tudor IV aircraft Star Tiger, reported missing yesterday, with 25 passengers and a crew of six on board, on its way to Bermuda, is now presumed lost, according to a Ministry of Civil Aviation statement issued last night.

The aircraft, which was due at Hamilton, Bermuda, at 6 o'clock yesterday morning—it left the Azores on Thursday afternoon—last reported its position in a routine wireless message as 380 miles north-east of Bermuda.

FROM OUR CORRESPONDENT

BERMUDA, JAN. 30

Seventeen aircraft were searching a wide area of the Atlantic to-day for traces of the Star Tiger. The air liner's last radio message was a routine report at 11.15 p.m. giving her position as 440 miles north-east of Bermuda. No distress signals were sent, nor was there any hint of trouble.

The first search machine left at 3.15 this morning. A coordinated search was conducted by the United States naval operating base at Bermuda, with the help of civilian aircraft. Rescue and search units from Newfoundland and along the Atlantic coast also cooperated, and the search will continue until wreckage or survivors are sighted.

Fifteen hours after the search started no trace had been found, and it was reported that the weather was squally and visibility " low."

INQUIRY ORDERED

The Ministry of Civil Aviation announced last night that a public inquiry would be held into the presumed loss of the airliner. A preliminary investigation into the cause of the accident had already been undertaken.

SEPTEMBER 29

MYSTERY OF THE STAR TIGER

———◆———

LOSS UNEXPLAINED

The fate of the Star Tiger, the British South American Airways liner that disappeared in flight between the Azores and Bermuda on January 30 this year, must remain an unsolved mystery. Such is the verdict of the court appointed by the Minister of Civil Aviation to investigate the accident. Its report was published yesterday as a White Paper (Cmd. 7517, Stationery Office, 2s.).

"It may truly be said that no more baffling problem has ever been presented for investigation," the final paragraph of the report reads. "In the complete absence of any reliable evidence as to either the nature or the cause of the disaster to Star Tiger the court has not been able to do more than suggest possibilities, none of which reaches the level even of probability. Into all activities which involve the cooperation of man and machine two elements enter of very diverse character. There is the incalculable element of the human equation dependent upon imperfectly known factors; and there is the mechanical element subject to quite different laws. A breakdown may occur in either separately or in both in conjunction. Or some external cause may overwhelm both man and machine. What happened in this case will never be known."

Lord Macmillan was appointed to hold the inquiry, and Professor A. A. Hall and Captain J. W. G. James sat with him as assessors.

FLIGHT OF 1,960 MILES

At 3.34 p.m. on January 29 the Star Tiger left the airport of Santa Maria in the Azores for Bermuda on the third stage of a flight from London to Havana. She had a crew of six and carried 25 passengers, one of whom was Air Marshal Sir Arthur Coningham. The distance from the Azores to Bermuda is 1,960 nautical miles across the open Atlantic, and the route is one of the longest in operation for passenger and commercial flights. At 3.15 next morning the Star Tiger asked the Bermuda wireless station for a bearing, which was sent about one minute later and immediately acknowledged by the aircraft. The acknowledgment was the last message received from the Star Tiger, which was then about 340 nautical miles from Bermuda, and to this day nothing is known of what became of her, her passengers, and her crew.

Analysing possible causes of the accident, the report says there is good reason to suppose that no distress message was sent from the Star Tiger. There would appear to be no grounds for supposing that she fell into the sea through having been deprived of her radio, having failed to find her destination, and having exhausted her fuel.

Turning to the possibility of a catastrophic or a rapidly developing accident, the following causes of occurrences of that character can, the report states, on the evidence available, be eliminated: Constructional defects, meteorological hazards, errors of altimetry, and mechanical failure of engines.

Under the first of these heads it observes:— "There are no grounds for supposing that in the design of the Tudor IV aeroplane, or in the manufacture of the particular Tudor IV aeroplane Star Tiger, there were technical errors or omissions, judged against a standard of agreed good practice."

Possibilities which cannot with reasonable certainty be eliminated are then examined Though it cannot be shown with certainty on the evidence that fire did not occur, it is nevertheless most improbable. The possibility of a disastrous mechanical disruption of any part of the power plant is, again, most remote.

FLIGHT PREPARATIONS

The more important points to which the criticisms of the court are directed are set out in the following summary of recommendations:—

The programme for the training of crews should be more comprehensive, and in particular pilots ought to have adequate experience of airports to which passenger-carrying flights are planned.

Instructions to pilots should contain specific directions about actions to be taken in the event of having to alight on the sea.

Adequacy of fuel reserves should receive special attention on this route.

Provision should be made for adequate resting facilities for the crew on so exacting a route, and in particular there should be either a 12-hour stop at the Azores or two radio officers should be carried who could relieve each other.

Greater care should be taken in the preparation of flight plans.

Strict compliance with the provisions of maintenance schedules is desirable.

The organization at Bermuda should be overhauled to ensure that there is constant attendance of officials at all appropriate hours, that the regulations as to maintaining contact with aircraft are observed, and that all signals are promptly dealt with.

A B.S.A.A. spokesman said last night:— "All the matters included in the report have already been dealt with by the corporation. Most of them were put into effect before the inquiry opened. In some cases the action taken has gone beyond the recommendations of the court."

REPORTS IN "THE TIMES" OF
LONDON   Just about a year
after the mysterious loss of the aircraft the "Star Tiger," "The Times"
of London reports in its issue of
January 18, 1949 and in its issue of
January 21, 1949 that a similar aircraft, the "Star Ariel," has been lost
in the same general location, under
similar circumstances. "The Times"
points out that the court of investigation appointed by the Ministry of
Civil Aviation drew a blank in its
investigation of the "Star Tiger"
loss. "What happened will never be
known," says "The Times," "and the
aircraft's fate must remain an unsolved mystery."

JANUARY 18 1949

29 IN MISSING AIR-LINER

STAR ARIEL OVERDUE FROM BERMUDA

From Our Correspondent

BERMUDA, JAN. 17

A British South American Airways airliner on its way from Bermuda to Kingston, Jamaica, is missing over the Atlantic.
It left Bermuda at 8 o'clock this morning.
The pilot is Captain J. C. McPhee.

The aircraft was on a regular flight
from London Airport to Jamaica, and
Bermuda was the last stop on the journey.

The following statement was issued in
London early this morning:—

" B.S.A.A. regrets to announce that the
corporation's aircraft Star Ariel, which left
London for Santiago, Chile, on Saturday, is
overdue on passage between Bermuda and
Kingston, Jamaica. The aircraft, which left
Bermuda at about 1230 G.M.T. yesterday
(Monday) and was due at Kingston at 1802
hours G.M.T., was carrying, so far as is
known at present, 22 passengers and a crew
of seven.

" The last message received rom the aircraft was dispatched about an hour after
leaving Bermuda. Air-sea rescue operations
are in progress."

Five British passengers for Kingston and
two for Santiago boarded the machine at
London airport.

MIAMI, Jan. 17.—An air rescue aircraft from
Findley Field, Bermuda, searched the area
over which the Star Ariel was travelling
without finding any trace of it.

New York coastguard officials said that
rescue machines from Salem, Massachusetts,
Brooklyn, New York, and Elizabeth City,
North Carolina, would go to Bermuda to-night
to join searchers to-morrow.—*Reuter.*

** Thirty-one people—six crew and 25
passengers—lost their lives when the Tudor IV
Star Tiger disappeared between the Azores and
Bermuda in January, 1948. All Tudor IV aircraft were then grounded for reliability trials
and did not return to the Bermuda run for 11
weeks.

A court of investigation appointed by the
Ministry of Civil Aviation said in its report:
" What happened will never be known and
the aircraft's fate must remain an unsolved
mystery."

LOSS OF STAR ARIEL

RIDDLE UNSOLVED BY INQUIRY

DELAY IN SIGNALS

From Our Aeronautical Correspondent

The reason for the disappearance of the British South American Airways Corporation's Tudor IV air-liner Star Ariel on January 17 last while on a flight from Bermuda to Jamaica has not been explained by the inquiry. The report by the Chief Inspector of Accidents, Air Commodore Vernon Brown, which is published to-day (M.C.A.P. 78, H.M. Stationery Office, 3s. net), states: "Through lack of evidence due to no wreckage having been found the cause of the accident is unknown."

The Star Ariel, which carried 13 passengers and a crew of seven, was lost almost exactly a year after a sister aircraft, the Star Tiger, had disappeared in much the same area in equally mysterious circumstances, with 31 people, including Air Marshal Sir Arthur Coningham, on board. These two losses led to the withdrawal of the Tudor 1Vs for carrying passengers, and they have not been employed for this purpose by the corporation since, though they have operated successfully on the Berlin air-lift and elsewhere.

In his report on the Star Ariel, Air Commodore Brown states that there was no evidence of defect in, or failure of, any part of the aircraft or its equipment before the aircraft's departure from Bermuda. The all-up weight and the centre of gravity were within the prescribed limits; a daily inspection had been carried out; sufficient fuel was carried for the flight; the pilot was experienced on the route; the radio officer was very experienced and dependable and above average in being able to effect instrument repairs, and he also was experienced on this crossing; good radio communication had been maintained with the aircraft up to and including receipt of its last message; there were no weather complications, and a study of weather reports gives no reason to believe that the accident was due to meteorological conditions. There was no evidence of sabotage, though the possibility of the planting of an infernal machine cannot, of course, be entirely eliminated.

A GENERAL GUIDE

The chief inspector adds that for the Bermuda-Jamaica route there are no internationally agreed control procedures, except in certain specified areas. Under the existing arrangements the possibility of air-sea rescue delay cannot be ignored should a forced landing be necessary during so long a flight over the sea in an uncontrolled area.

B.S.A.A. operational orders were written for the very purpose of ensuring safe flight in such conditions; nevertheless, they are not entirely applicable to this particular Caribbean route, where there is such an extensive uncontrolled area and where radio conditions often make adequate communication very difficult. Moreover, the orders for the corporation's flight operations officers are issued only as a general guide and must at times have been difficult to interpret and implement by the corporation's staff at both Bermuda and Jamaica.

The report states that representations are being made to Icao (the International Civil Aviation Organization) for the immediate reconsideration of air traffic control and search and rescue procedures in the Caribbean area, and it is understood that arrangements have been made for the reconsideration of the requirements of this region in the near future.

In view of the corporation's orders, Air Commodore Brown states, its operations officer at Bermuda ought to have expected a control acceptance signal from Kingston. Allowing for communication delay, it is considered that he should have initiated inquiries by not later than 4 p.m. The last signal received from the aircraft was in the hands of Kingston control at 2.26 p.m., stating that at 1.42 p.m. frequency was being changed to make contact with Kingston. Thus, 44 minutes had elapsed without the expected communication. By the time the corporation operations officer received this message a further 49 minutes elapsed—that is, one hour 33 minutes from the time of its origin.

THE LAST SIGNAL

Between 4.26 and 5.13 Kingston was in communication with Nassau, and it would, therefore, have been possible for Kingston to obtain from Nassau any information that might have been available there concerning the aircraft. There was no evidence to show that a specific request for information was made before 5.54 p.m. It was not until 5.52 p.m. that B.S.A.A., Kingston, made inquiries from Bermuda about the Star Ariel, having tried at 5.44 to get information from Miami and Nassau.

It was accepted that radio communications were poor during the early part of the afternoon and actually became worse between 4 and 5, but, says the chief inspector, it seems strange that until 4.10 p.m.—that is, until two hours 28 minutes had elapsed since its last signal—no attempt should have been made by the B.S.A.A. staff at Kingston to make a formal inquiry as to whether anything had been heard of the aircraft; nor, it seemed, did Kingston control attempt to establish contact with the aircraft itself until 5.10 p.m. or later to inquire if it had made contact with Nassau or New York or any other station.

The report mentions that the Star Ariel had five emergency exits, carried three large dinghies, one fitted with a radio transmitter, and lifebelts were stowed under the passengers' seats and in the crew compartment.

A Prevalence of Prophets

Man's quest for glimpses of the future is older than recorded history, dating back to the mystery-shrouded civilization of the Sumerians of Mesopotamia around 4000 B.C. Since then, the hope of bridging the gap between today and tomorrow has produced a dizzying variety of rituals, most of which were far more remarkable in their procedure than in the results obtained. There was necromancy, the conjuring up of the spirits of the dead; extispicy, the examination of animal entrails; hepatoscopy, inspection of the liver; acromancy, divination from the air; sycomancy, forecasting through the study of figs; tyromancy, auguring with the aid of mildewed cheeses; and of course, astrology, which tried to predict the fate of earthly bodies through the movements of heavenly ones.

The Chinese sought the future in magic mirrors; the Persians, in magic beakers; the Egyptians, in dreams; the Babylonians and Mayas, in the planets; the Phoenicians, in the throw of dice; the ancient Britons, in treetops; and the American Indians, in the earth. The Romans obeyed prophetic chickens; Australian aborigines interpreted animal bones; Mongolian and Tibetan shamans studied the fire; and assorted African tribes, the spilled blood of sacrificial victims. These methods were no more fanciful than the tea leaf readings of today. All the systems depended on the interpretation of signs and omens, a task that became the preserve of specialists. And whether the signs boded ill or well, these augers, oracles, diviners, or soothsayers soon evolved a jargon designed to render the signs safely unspecific.

We still use the word "Delphic" to denote a particularly ambiguous

PRIESTESS PYTHIA   *An illustration of the famous seeress with her poisonous*
snakes making an augury.

pronouncement—a word that refers to the oracle of the shrine of Apollo at Delphi, hallowed by the ancient Greeks. The prophecies there were uttered—or rather, shrieked—by a hysterical priestess called Pythia, but the interpreting was done by highly sophisticated priests who set a pattern for ambiguous predictions that prophets still copy today.

When Croesus, last king of Lydia, contemplated war against Cyrus of Persia, he consulted the oracle about his prospects. The reply was, "If you attack, a great empire will fall." Croesus believed this to be an indication of victory and promptly marched on the Persians. He suffered devastating defeat, losing most of his army and his entire realm. The unhappy king sent a messenger to Delphi, accusing the oracle of false prophecy, and received the answer, "You did not ask which empire."

Professional augurs lean heavily on the Delphic formula, which consists either of predicting the obvious—if two empire rulers fight each other, *one* of them is pretty certain to lose his empire—or on couching the prediction in a verbal fantasy that leaves the meaning to anyone's imagination. Some splendid samples of the latter technique occur in the Chinese game *I Ching* in which prophecies are delivered in such phrases as "Dragons fight in the meadow. Their blood is black and yellow."

The astrology columns of the newspapers use still another brand of prediction, one that, for accuracy, relies solely on the law of averages. I once ran such a column during the temporary absence of the staff writer and found my complete ignorance of the zodiac to be no handicap. I merely wrote out a bland batch of prognostications, divided them by twelve, and gave each a heading running from Aries to Pisces. Judging by the mail I received, our readers never noticed the difference. Apparently, I achieved about the same ratio of success as our professional horoscope-caster.

The savants of the late 19th century predicted the total disappearance of prophecy as a business within 50 years or so. But their forecasts were issued during an exceptionally progressive and stabilized era. The 40 comfortable years in the Western world that ended with the "guns of August" also constituted the low ebb of soothsaying. The 20th century—

World War I, the jazz age, the Depression, World War II, the Cold War, and the Bomb—enabled augurism to achieve a comeback in public esteem. For the prestige of prophets is closely linked to the social and political atmosphere: the more disturbed and uncertain the present, the greater the urge to peer into the future.

It is no coincidence that the Weimar Republic—that ill-fated period of German democracy that occurred between the departure of the Kaiser and the arrival of the Führer—produced a large and colorful collection of prophets. Erik Jan Hanussen was the first in the chain of politically oriented oracles that stretches right down to the contemporary American scene. Hanussen claimed to be a Danish baron, but his real name was Hermann Steinschneider, and he hailed from a decidedly *petit bourgeois* environment in Prossnitz, Bohemia. He did not, in fact, speak more than a few words of Danish or of any other foreign language. But in the depression-ridden 1930s, Hanussen reached a peak of influence that no man of his calling has achieved in modern times. He became a latter-day Count Cagliostro.

Short, stocky, and handsome in a way, Hanussen had the magnetism of an evangelist combined with the *savoir-faire* of a Riviera hotel manager. He was extraordinarily versatile, displaying equal skill as a hypnotist, telepathist, clairvoyant, and sleight-of-hand magician.

He began as an above-average vaudeville entertainer, but gained national publicity as a "psychic detective" by unmasking an embezzler for one of Berlin's largest banking corporations. How he accomplished this is a moot point—but the culprit broke down and confessed when Hanussen accused him to his face.

As far as publicity was concerned, Hanussen had a golden touch. When a local scandal sheet accused him of hoaxing his audiences, he sued for libel. The trial gave him a wonderful opportunity to introduce as evidence virtually his entire act, and to dazzle the jury, as well as the spectators, with a display of occultism that was the talk of the capital. Hanussen made newspaper headlines. He also won his case.

Late in 1930, Hanussen switched to prophecy. He established a monthly magazine in which he predicted everything from financial developments to political events, scoring a remarkable percentage of

THE ORACLE OF DELPHI   This engraving by Claudius Harper shows the oracle, surrounded by parrots, assistants, magicians and a secretary, pronouncing a prophecy.

bull's-eyes. His *pièce de résistance* was the forecast that one of the
nation's three large joint-stock banks would shortly collapse. Three
weeks later, in July, 1931, the Darmstadt & National closed its doors,
with shattering results for the country's economy and excellent ones for
Hanussen. On July 1, 1932, he oracled that he could see "a river of blood
flowing near Hamburg." On the 17th came the "bloody Sunday of
Altona;" in Hamburg's adjoining twin city, Nazi Storm Troopers clashed
with Communist "Red Front" fighters in a five-hour battle that left 19
dead, 285 wounded, and the gutters literally running with blood.

Hanussen became the lodestar for thousands of people who
dreaded tomorrow more than purgatory; he was the one man who
seemed to know where their lunatic world was headed for. Business
leaders paid him up to the equivalent of $600 for a single private con-
sultation. He kept a huge, white cabin cruiser on the Wannsee Lake—
the ultimate in Berlin status symbols—and he built himself an ostenta-
tious villa in the fashionable suburb of Charlottenburg.

The villa's cubistic front and Shangri-la interior may have seemed
comical, but there was nothing funny about the people Hanussen received there. His visitors included the top names of Germany's financial,
sporting, and entertainment worlds and portions of the capital's social
register. Hanussen's following also included an array of demimonde
figures who combined political and underworld activities with the erotic
tastes and talents of imperial Rome. There was Karl Ernst, the blonde,
good-looking former bellhop and cocaine pusher who now commanded
the Berlin Storm Troopers. There was Edmund Heines, S.A. "Gruppen-
führer," who had served a term in prison for murder. There was the
somewhat more respectable but equally lethal Count von Helldorf, an
aristocratic soldier of fortune who now shared leadership of the local
Brownshirts with Ernst. These men, and a dozen others like them, mingled with Hanussen's elite patrons as well as with the film and theater
starlets who provided additional entertainment.

There is no doubt that Hanussen obtained the data for most of his
prophetic coups from his guests. He had only to keep his ears open and
a few palms greased to get advance tips of what was afoot in Germany.
The same pipeline also fed him gossip concerning the private lives of

PYTHIA PRONOUNCING AN AUGURY   *An artist's conception of the famous seeress of Delphi who, atop a huge tripod entwined with reptiles, is prophesying.*

ERIK JAN HANUSSEN   Taken in 1932 at the peak of the Berlin prophet's fame, this photograph shows him conducting an occult session in his villa. His illuminated cocktail bar was engraved with astrological symbols. Part of his fabulous collection of tropical fish and reptiles are seen in the background.

prominent personalities, who gasped with astonishment when Hanussen revealed to them things they thought no one but themselves could know. To the uninitiated, his divinations appeared little short of miraculous.

Gradually, however, his prognoses took on a distinct Nazi coloring, subtly pushing the cause of the National Socialists. For instance, while ignoring its political significance, he recommended the swastika as an "Indian luck symbol," and indicated that its wearers would be blessed by good fortune. When forecasting election results, he invariably discovered that the planetary conjunction favored Adolf Hitler, thereby persuading multitudes to "vote with the stars." Without ever abandoning his pose as just another worldly mystic, he added an inestimable number of crosses to the Nazi ballots.

A great many rumors and very few facts have leaked out concerning Hanussen's association with the Nazi movement. He was originally introduced to Hitler by Heinrich Hoffmann, the Führer's private photographer, who was also to become the sponsor of Eva Braun. Several German writers have since claimed that Hanussen gave Hitler lessons in public speaking, and that Hanussen's coaching was responsible for the Führer's demonic platform manner. The only basis for this claim seems to have been a definite similarity in their style of oratory and in their tremendous suggestive powers.

There is concrete evidence, though, that Hanussen was heavily subsidized by the National Socialists. The prophet drew large sums of money, earmarked for propaganda purposes, into his own pockets. His precise method of accomplishing this is still unclear, but he seems to have had a private working arrangement with either Karl Ernst or with Helldorf, with one of whom he split the take.

In January, 1933, Hitler became chancellor, with his hands firmly—though not yet completely—on Germany's levers of power. Helldorf was appointed police president of Berlin; Karl Ernst assumed command of all Storm Troop units in the capital; and Hanussen evidently believed that his hour of glory had likewise struck.

Knowing what he did of some of the financial manipulations of the new leaders seemed to give him a strong position. He had but to speak out and they would face a party tribunal. There is no way of knowing exactly what role Hanussen visualized for himself in the setup, but whatever it was, it apparently deluded him into thinking he now bore a charmed existence. For in mid-February he uttered the most momentous—and foolhardy—prophecy of his career. His motivation remains obscure to this day.

During a social gathering at his villa, he suddenly adopted his famous I-hear-inner-voices stance and intoned dramatically, "I see a building, a great building, in our city . . . it is burning . . . flames are roaring high . . . smoke is billowing . . . ah, but out of the blaze there arises a bird . . . a magnificent Phoenix . . . bringing new might . . . new hope . . . from the ashes!"

It was all a bit bewildering until, on February 27, the Reichstag, Germany's parliament, suddenly and mysteriously caught fire. Although there is every reason to believe that the Nazis themselves set the fire, Hitler termed it "an act of Communist terrorism." The blaze enabled the Chancellor to push through an emergency law that gave him powers to suppress all opposition to his regime. Under these circumstances, Hanussen's prophecy became a fatal indiscretion. It provided those who might have feared his blackmail with a valid excuse for murdering him.

On the evening of March 24, Hanussen was leaving the bar-restaurant "Grüner Zweig" when a waiter noticed two men stopping him in the doorway. They accompanied him into the street. This was the last time anyone saw the oracle alive. The following noon, his secretary reported him to the police as missing. Thirteen days later, the body of a well-dressed man was discovered lying in a patch of woodland at Baruth, several miles outside Berlin. The police identified the corpse as Hermann Steinschneider, alias Erik Jan Hanussen. The Berlin homicide department announced that "Investigations are proceeding."

This was the last official statement on Hanussen for 33 years. In January, 1966, an anonymous letter reached the desk of Inspector Alfred Eitner, deputy chief of the political section of the West Berlin police. According to this note, a certain Captain Karl Becker had shot Hanussen in the backseat of a moving car, acting on orders issued by either Ernst or Helldorf. But since the police have not, to date, been able to locate Mr. Becker, the statement remains unproved, leaving the death of Hanussen as mist-clouded as his life.

Hanussen had a female counterpart—not a parallel—in France. Madame Geneviève Tabouis was a unique figure on the prewar Paris scene and, although unsubsidized by anyone, she leaned as strongly toward the radical left as Hanussen had to the right. She ran a column in the daily L'Oeuvre in which she combined politics, society gossip, personal commentary, astrology, and prophecy. She wrote with so much wit and erudition that she attracted thousands of readers who did not share her radical views.

Madame had an inspired knack for picking up the rumors which drifted around the diplomatic and artistic salons in which she moved, selecting the likeliest tidbits, and presenting these as prophecies. Sometimes they materialized; sometimes they didn't. In the first eventuality, she reminded readers frequently of her prognosis; in the latter, she charmed them into forgetting it.

Most of the time it didn't matter much whether she had been right or wrong, but occasionally, her errors came close to sabotaging the very causes she favored. As a sworn foe of Nazi Germany, she took every opportunity to highlight real or imaginary weaknesses in Hitler's war machine. She thus managed to project a dangerously false image of the Wehrmacht's striking power, quite unwittingly helping to lull her compatriots into the false sense of security that, together with the Maginot Line, crumbled in 1940.

In 1936, Madame Tabouis interviewed Marshal Michael Tukha-

SIDEWALK ASTROLOGY   *An Indian seer, reputed to have knowledge of what the movements of the stars connote, advises for a fee just what the future has in store.*

VI

L'AMOVREVX

XX

LE JUGEMENT

VIIII

L'HERMITE

LE·MAT

XIII

XV

LE·DIABLE

TAROT CARDS   *Used for astrological purposes, these French cards depicting lovers, the devil, death, the Day of Judgment, and other such concepts have been used extensively since the 14th century to foretell the future.*

GENEVIEVE TABOUIS   Fulltime
journalist and part-time prophet, Madame
Tabouis was one of the most influential
newspaper women of pre-war France.
She was photographed at her wartime task
of editing the New York-based French
periodical "Pour la Victoire."

chevski, chief of the Red Army general staff, an outstanding military figure. She described his career in her column and quoted him at length on
the need for closer Franco-Soviet defense cooperation. When less than
a year later, on Stalin's orders, Marshal Tukhachevski and eight other
ranking Red Army commanders were placed before a secret court martial, and charged with high treason and executed, the story spread, in
some mysterious fashion, that Madame Tabouis had noticed "an aura of
death" around the marshal's head during their conversation and had, in
fact at the time, predicted his demise. Not a word of this could be found
in her columns of that period, but her disciples swore she had mentioned
just that several times in private gatherings, and within earshot of numerous reliable witnesses. Many witnesses came forward, all eager to
confirm that yes, indeed, she had quite unequivocally stated that the
marshal was not long for this world.

    This technique—by which a prophet's reputation is fortified by what her friends *say* she had said to them—forms the basis for about 99 percent of all soothsaying reputations. In almost every case there exists a gap between the printed and verifiable prediction and the breathtaking prophetic utterance delivered verbally, which numerous reputable witnesses are willing to confirm— *after* the predicted event has occurred.

Mrs. Jeane Dixon, the sibyl of Washington, D.C., is in some respects the exact opposite of Madame Tabouis. She is a most conservative Republican and a devout Roman Catholic, much given to beholding visions inside cathedrals and on top of graves. Politics apart, though, the two ladies show some strikingly similar features.

Like Madame, Jeane Dixon has produced hundreds of predictions— some right, some wrong, a great many unprovable. Her system could be practiced by anyone with access to newspaper files and an ear for cabinet rumors. The required omens can be picked up there just as plainly as Madame picked them up in Parisian gossip parlors.

Mrs. Dixon is the more impulsive of the pair, likely to give predictions in the course of casual conversation. In June, 1966, she spent a day in a New York bookshop, autographing copies of her best-selling autobiography, *A Gift of Prophecy.* A Cuban customer wanted to know

JEANE DIXON   The Washington seeress peers into a crystal ball.

FORTUNE TELLING IN CHINA   *An augur consults his "Sticks of Fate."*

HEPATOSCOPY   The practice of foretelling the future by examining the entrails of chickens was a common Roman ritual. This painting, by E. H. Blashfield, was engraved in Paris in 1877.

what Mrs. Dixon was hearing of Castro and he received the prompt reply, "My vibrations now tell me that he's nowhere around. He's either in China or he's dead." It so happened that Fidel was neither, but that did not prevent the book from selling.

Whereas Madame Tabouis tended to ignore her more blatant boners, Jeane Dixon prefers to explain them. Thus when her forecast that the U. S. would go to war with Red China by 1958 failed to materialize, Mrs. Dixon explained that she had got the right omens but had misinterpreted them. This was undoubtedly true; so had a couple of hundred news commentators. The difference was that *they* didn't claim the gift of prophecy.

Mrs. Dixon's most famous alleged prediction was of the murder of President Kennedy. A 1956 edition of the national Sunday supplement, *Parade*, quoted her as stating that the 1960 Presidential election would be won by a Democrat, "But he will be assassinated or die in office, though not necessarily in his first term." However, before the actual election, Mrs. Dixon reversed her previous pronouncement and predicted a victory for Republican Richard Nixon. After the votes were counted, she explained that Nixon had really won but that the Democrats had "stolen" the election. Since that time, there has not been one printed word to show that Jeane Dixon had foreseen the Dallas tragedy —*printed* word, that is as distinct from a premonition she supposedly *voiced* during a ladies' luncheon at Washington's Mayflower Hotel on the day of the assassination.

And here we find ourselves in the nebulous borderland that divides precognition from the feeling engendered by an intelligent assessment of a situation. On that fateful 22nd of November, 1963, I remember several of my friends—decidedly non-oracular types—announcing similar fears. All they had done was follow the reports about the hate and vituperation voiced by a considerable segment of the Dallas citizenry prior to the President's visit. Under such circumstances, it took little supernatural foresight to sense danger.

The most spectacular achievements of modern prophets have a disturbing tendency to hinge on the undocumented say-so of a few individuals. These individuals tend to fall into one of three categories:

(a) the sponsors or collaborators of the prophet; (b) persons with a financial stake in the reputation of the prophet, i.e., authors of books or magazine articles about the oracle; and (c) individuals whose critical faculties are underdeveloped.

As I know from my reporting days, such individuals will stretch the truth to the point of disintegration. Some of the more credulous actually feel they are supporting a good cause. The cause is that of their miracle worker whose magic would produce untold good if only people could be persuaded to have faith. The reputation of almost all augurs and seers depends for the most part not on what they actually have said but on what people *think* they have said.

Yet, scattered at random among the "prophecies," there remain a few authenticated cases of precognition. "Precognition" may not be the correct term for some of these mystifying occurrences.

The outstanding example of this form of prophecy was Monsieur Bottineau, about whom we know very little except that he possessed the uncanny ability to forecast the approach of ships long before they came into sight. His prophetic talents extended no further than that, and he himself strenuously denied having any supernatural powers. But because his explanations were as baffling as were his predictions, he might be classed among the prophets.

The first and most exhaustive account of his activities was published in the March, 1834, edition of the highly respected British *Nautical Magazine*. In 1764, Bottineau (his first name is not recorded) was appointed beacon keeper on the Isle de France (today the island of Mauritius). He held this post until he returned to France almost 20 years later. For about 15 of those years the entire naval garrison of the colony, around 900 men, followed his feats—sometimes several times a week. On the island, Bottineau was regarded as a standard entertainment feature of the otherwise dull routine.

Bottineau would position himself on the beach, scan the empty horizon with his naked eye—he never used a telescope—and after a while announce: "Three vessels approaching—two from the south, one from southwest!" Officers would turn their glasses in the direction indicated but they never saw anything except water and clouds. Yet within one, four, sometimes seven days, the exact number of ships announced by Bottineau would become visible.

At first, the beacon keeper used his unique gift merely as a means of making extra money. The bored naval officers would wager considerable sums against his being right in the number or in the direction of the approaching craft. But he always was, and in due course the only bettors he could find were new arrivals who had not yet become aware of his forte.

Eventually the governor, Viscount de Souillac, began to keep an official record of the predictions, noting the time, date, and weather conditions when the forecasts were made, and the same data covering the actual sighting of the ships. After 18 months, Governor de Souillac sent a report to the Royal Ministry of Marine in Paris, informing that bureau that M. Bottineau had made "the surprising discovery of a new art, namely that of being able to observe the arrival of vessels 100, 150, and even 200 leagues distant." The report went on to state that Bottineau hardly ever made a mistake, and that when Bottineau's announced ships failed to arrive, it was always proved afterward that the craft in question had indeed been within two or three days' sail of the island but had proceeded to some other destination.

The Governor's report concluded:

> "However incredible this discovery may appear, myself and a great many officers, naval and military, must bear testimony to the announcements made by M. Bottineau. We cannot treat him as an imposter or a visionary. We have had ocular demonstrations for so many years, and in no instance has any vessel reached the island, the approach of which he has not predicted."

The Ministry must have been favorably impressed, for in May, 1782, it authorized the Governor to offer the beacon keeper a lump sum of 10,000 livres and a life pension of 1,200 livres annually if he would disclose the secret of his "new art." But M. Bottineau respectfully declined; he did not consider the remuneration sufficient. Instead, he himself set out for France, determined to make a more profitable deal with the government. He could not have gone at a more inopportune time.

Bottineau arrived home in 1784 when France was within an inch of bankruptcy and within five years of revolution. He first tried to approach the Minister of Marine, then a descending chain of underlings, only to find himself stalled, rebuffed, and spun around in ever-increasing bureaucratic circles. No one seemed to care a fig about his new art, on which he had bestowed the title "nauscopie"—one of the now forgotten words of the scientific dictionary.

Bottineau also handicapped himself by a mania for secrecy which prevented him from committing his thoughts to paper. He kept trying to verbally explain his discovery to people who either wouldn't listen or who couldn't understand him. The only written description he left was so vague as to be practically useless.

He appears to have found only one interested listener—Jean Paul Marat. But, although Marat became fascinated by nauscopie, he was then but an obscure physician with antiroyalist sentiments. A few years later, Marat emerged as one of the most radical and powerful figures of revolutionary France, but by then nauscopie, as well as its discoverer, had drifted into oblivion. For nauscopie died along with its inventor, leaving posterity the problem of deciding whether to class M. Bottineau as an unusually haphazard scientist or an unusually accurate augur.

No such decision is needed for our second example: prophecy in a pure, but far from simple, form. My first encounter with the pronouncements of Michel de Nôtredame — better known as Nostradamus — occurred at the age of 14 during a matinée at our local movie theater. It was wartime, and the movie short dealt with the rhymed predictions of the 16th-century Frenchman as they apparently applied to the outcome of World War II. The interpretations were delivered by a commentator and intoned against a series of newsreel shots showing marching armies, charging tanks, and gutted cities. The gist of it all was that this astounding Provencal had foreseen not only the war, but its end— the inevitable triumph of the Allies—roughly 400 years before that war came to pass. The movie must have been effective, because it left me with a vague but lasting conviction that, at least once, someone had been able to accurately forecast the future.

About 10 years later, I attended a session at a private film club at which were shown a selection of German war propaganda movies. And here, once again, was Nostradamus! Only the prophet had switched sides, and he was now working for Dr. Goebbels' UFA. The Nazi strip was almost identical to the Hollywood effort, but the commentary had undergone an amazing change. For now the oracular verses of Nostradamus predicted total victory for Adolf Hitler.

I was now determined to discover just what this Frenchman had *really* prophesied. And this, as it turned out, demanded considerable effort. First, I had to sort out all the false Nostradamuses. There were at least four of them, all of whom had adopted the style of the original savant as well as his pseudonym, and had kept on using both even after the real Nostradamus had died.

Nostradamus himself produced only 1,000 rhymed quatrains, none of them dated later than 1566. These four-lined stanzas were difficult to translate and even more difficult to unravel. Their author employed a Latinized French that was already archaic in his own time. The allusive symbolism of the verses is fuzzy. The text leans so heavily on anagrams and contemporary puns that a translator can shape many of the predictions to suit his own purposes. Neither the American nor the German propagandists actually falsified their film forecasts — they merely selected those quatrains that suited their needs.

The handy ambiguity of some of the rhymes is illustrated by the reference to a future warlord called "The Shaven One" who tries to subdue a vast realm "to the East," conquers a good slice of it, but is finally beaten and destroyed. Enthusiastic Nostradamians — there are thousands of them — maintain this is a clear prediction of Napoleon's defeat in Russia. But the prognostication could just as well have applied to Charles XII of Sweden who, likewise beardless, tried the same conquest a hundred years earlier and got as far as Poltava in the Ukraine before he was crushed by Peter the Great. Dr. Goebbels' experts claimed the verse referred to Winston Churchill, another "shaven one," and they capitalized on the fact that Germany lies east of Britain in order to prophesy that after initial successes, Churchill would come to grief.

In any case, most of the symbols used by Nostradamus to identify

MICHEL NOSTRADAMUS.
Médecin,
Né à St Remy, en Provence, le 14 Décemb. 1503.
Mort le 2 juillet 1566.

Paris chez Odieuvre Md d'Estampes, rue d'Anjou la dernière P. Cochero à gauche entrant par la rue Dauphine. C.P.R.

Babel invenit   et Sculpsit.

NOSTRADAMUS   A likeness by an 18th century French engraver of the cele-
brated physician and necromancer.

NOSTRADAMUS   *The frame of this etching of the famous prophet states that the doctor died at Salon on the 2nd of July, 1566, when he was more than 62 years old. The inscription on the base reads: "From verses more obscure than the Cabala/ I acquired the surname of prophet/But glory is very imperfect/When you are only the prophet of fools."*

certain nations can't be applied to the modern world. Today we assume the eagle symbolizes the United States. But over the past 400 years, the eagle has also stood for Prussia, Imperial Russia, Austria, Spain, Napoleon's France, Bismarck's as well as Hitler's Germany, Mussolini's Italy, Mexico, Albania, Poland, and Finland—depending on whether the huge bird was black, silver, golden or white—was double or single-headed—had wings spread or folded—and clutched what with which foot. The lion that crops up intermittently in Nostradamus might mean Britain, of course, but it could just as well be Holland, Bohemia, Sweden, or Persia—or it could even be the Lion of Judah, as featured by the emperors of Ethiopia. The bull, another recurring symbol, was the emblem of the Borgias, but the bull also served as emblem for at least eight other families of Europe's ruling nobility. With equal justification, the bull might have indicated any figure born under the zodiac sign of Taurus.

The verses included phrases in Hebrew, Greek, Italian, and Spanish, references inserted, it would seem, to render the sense even more obscure. And to further befog, Nostradamus would separate or run together certain words without regard to their spelling.

A number of the stanzas were probably not intended to be prophetic at all; they were political lampoons aimed at either Cardinal Mazarin, or at the German Emperor Charles V, or at various French nobles. The poetic code in which these stanzas were couched might have been reasonably clear at the time, but today, some lines are as lucid as the murky passages of the Cabala.

Nostradamus was a celebrated personality in his own time. Born Michel de Nôtredame at St. Remy, Provence, in 1503, he Latinized his name to Nostradamus after he set up practice as a physician, Latin being the language of medicine as well as theology. He practiced for a while in Marseilles, then moved to Salon, his reputation and clientele growing steadily. Contemporary descriptions of him say he had an exceptionally smooth bedside manner, coupled with considerable scholarship, and a knowledge of health diet, which was far in advance of his time.

However, he attracted royal attention not as a doctor, but as a

LES
PROPHETIES
DE M. MICHEL.
NOSTRADAMVS.

Reueuës & corrigées ſur la coppie Imprimée
à Lyon par Benoiſt, Rigaud. 1568.

M. DCV.

TITLE-PAGE OF ONE OF THE "CENTURIES"
This is the book on which the prophet's current fame is based.

necromancer. It was in this role that Catherine de Medici, the super-stitious queen of France's King Henry II, invited him to her court.

In 1555, he produced his first of three *Centuries*—the rhymed quatrains arranged in sets of a hundred—through which we know him today. Among them was one that caused Queen Catherine to hold him in awe for the rest of her life. The thirty-fifth quatrain of the first *Century* predicted the "cruel death" of her husband in a unique manner:

> *Le lyon jeune le vieux surmontera*
> *En champ bellique par singulier duelle:*
> *Dans cage d'or les yeux crevera,*
> *Deux classes une, puis mourir, mort cruelle.*

In other words, Nostradamus foretold that the king would suffer death through being blinded "in a golden cage" in the course of a duel—a prediction sufficiently specific and unusual to strike everyone concerned.

Four years later, in the summer of 1559, Henry II participated in a tournament, wearing a golden helmet with a barred visor to protect his face. While riding a course with a Welsh knight named Montgomery, the tip of the Welshman's lance smashed through the "golden cage" and penetrated the king's left eye, killing him instantly.

Nostradamus' quatrain thus stands out as clear prophecy. His reputation as an augur was made.

His final set of *Centuries* were not published until 1566, the year of his death. And here again, buried amid much Delphic and unintelligible verbiage there stands a verse capable of shaking any skeptic:

> *Le lys Dauffois portera dans Nanci,*
> *Jusques en Flandres electeur de l'Empire;*
> *Neufve obturée au grand Montmorency,*
> *Hors lieux prouvés delivré à clere peyne.*

Roughly translated, this means:

> *The Dauphin's lily will enter Nancy,*
> *Supporting the Imperial Elector as far as Flanders;*
> *For the great Montmorency, there will be a new prison,*
> *Where he shall be delivered to punishment in an unusual place.*

The verse, the 18th quatrain of the ninth *Century,* deals with two
unconnected events, both of which occurred after Nostradamus' death.
But they *did* occur, and under circumstances that mirrored the prediction so amazingly that the forecast and the event cannot be pooh-
poohed as mere coincidence. Chronologically, the two halves of the
verse are reversed, because the second prediction came true a year earlier than the first. But in every other detail, this quatrain is probably the
most astounding prophecy ever delivered in writing.

CENTVRIE IX.
L'ambaſſadeur non plaiſant fera ſciſme,
Ceux de Ribiere ſeront en la meſlée:
Et au grand goulphre deſnier ont l'entrée.
                    XVII.
Le tiers premier pis que ne fit Neron,
Vuidez vaillant que ſang humain reſpandre:
R édifier fera le forneron,
Siecle d'or, mort· nouueau Roy gräd eſclandr
                    XVIII.
Le lys Dauffois portera dans Nanſi,
Iuſques en Flandres Electeur de l'Empire:
Neufue obturée au grand Montmorency,
Hors lieux prouez deliure à clere peyne.
                    XIX.
Dans le milieu de la foreſt Mayenne,
Sol au Lyon la foudre tombera :
Le grand batard yſſu du grand du Maine,
Ce iour Fougeres pointe en ſang entrera.
                    XX.
De nuict viendra par la foreſt de Reines,
Deux pars voltorte Herne la pierre blanch
Le moine noir en gris dedans Varennes,
Eſleu cap. cauſe tempeſte, feu, ſang tranche.
                    XXI
Au temple hault de Bloys ſacre Salonne,
Nuict pont de Loyre, Prelat, Roy pernic
Cuiſeur victoire aux mareſts de la Lone,
D'où prelature de blancs abormeant.
                    XXII.

*PAGE FROM NOSTRA-
DAMUS'S "CENTURIES"
This volume, printed in 1605,
contains Quatrain XVIII, his
remarkable prediction of the
death of the "great Montmorency."*

In 1633, Louis XIII of France, who bore the title of Dauphin and carried the lily on his banner, occupied the walled city of Nancy. Later, the king took up the cause of the Imperial Elector against the Spaniards, and Louis advanced into Flanders in support.

In 1632, the Duke de Montmorency rebelled against King Louis and was captured. The Duke was locked up in the newly completed prison of Toulouse to await punishment. The punishment, beheading, was indeed carried out in an unusual place—the prison courtyard. Customarily, the execution would have been performed in the marketplace, but the Duke had many loyal supporters among the populace who might have staged a rescue attempt. The most remarkable detail, however, was the name of the executioner—a soldier called Clerepeyne. Nostradamus had used the term *clere peyne*—a term that also means "public punishment."

Here, then, are two genuine prophecies. These true auguries have been almost obliterated by the many cute readings made by those who have attempted to find all kinds of far-fetched meanings in the *Centuries*. But these few prophetic flashes remain—irrefutable proof of the existence of precognition—in some people—sometimes. We must call these pronouncements flashes. We cannot say—in fact there is evidence against our saying—that Nostradamus was a prophet who was always able to foretell the future. Such prophets have the gift at odd intervals (or once in a lifetime), and such powers are not capable of being induced by artificial means. There is no evidence of anyone ever succeeding in harnessing such powers according to definite rules, or in using such powers for a specifically practical purpose.

The Unknown 'Snowman'

The winding snake of heavily laden porters that was Lt. Colonel Howard-Bury's Mount Everest Expedition of 1921 labored over a ridge, some 16,000 feet up in the Himalayas. Suddenly, the Englishman felt his arm gripped by one of his Sherpa guides who pointed excitedly at something on the snowfield spreading way below him.

A figure, dark against the dazzling snow, was loping over the expanse, moving along rapidly with an upright gait that looked almost—but not quite—human.

"What's that, a man?" asked the officer.

The Sherpa shook his head. "No man, sahib. Kang-Mi!"

Howard-Bury gazed after the creature until it disappeared, straining into the glare that made it difficult to see more than a brownish blob. He had no idea what the guide meant. He would have been very astonished to learn that he had just experienced a historical event; he was the first white man to sight a yeti.

Five weeks later, Howard-Bury was back in India. He had failed to become the first conqueror of Everest. Among the incidents he related to interviewing journalists was the brief encounter on the mountain ridge.

A reporter for the *Calcutta Statesman* decided to follow up the story. He checked with several Sherpas and he discovered that the creature called Kang-Mi was quite familiar to them, but no description of the "thing" seemed to tally with any species mentioned in the zoology textbooks. Different Himalayan tribes called the unknown different names, Kang-Mi or Yeti or Shupka or Mi-go or Meti. It was said to roam

THE ROOF OF THE WORLD   The snow-clad Himalayas are believed by many explorers and scientists to be the home of the yeti. Fifteen hundred fifty miles long and 160 miles across, the Himalayas contain five of the world's highest peaks, all exceeding 27,500 feet: Mount Everest at 29,028 feet; K2 (or Godwin Austen), 28,250 feet; Kanchenjunga, 28,208 feet; Lhotse, 27,890; and Makalu, 27,790.

over the entire vast highlands stretching between India, Tibet, and Russia.

From these tidbits, the journalist concocted a dispatch which was promptly featured by half a hundred international newspapers, achieving global prominence for one of the most monstrous mistranslations ever. The newsman selected the Nepalese *Kang-Mi*, meaning roughly "Creature of High Places"; and somehow transmuted the term into "Abominable Snowman." The tag stuck, though no explanation was offered as to why and how the animal was abominable. "The Abomi-

nable Snowman" became a household word, even among folks who weren't quite sure whether the Himalayas were a tropical disease or a brand of breakfast food.

There had been various reports of such a creature before. Back in 1887, the mountaineering Colonel W. A. Waddell claimed to have found some remarkable footprints in the snow of Sikkim. The prints, he alleged, were 18 inches long, larger than those of any human foot. The marks resembled human tracks insofar as the toes were set close together; whatever creature made them had walked in long, regular

SHERPA VILLAGE   *Situated among the Nepal Himalayas, at an altitude of 13,000 feet, is the Sherpa village of Khumjung. The chief domesticated animal in these parts is the white, long-haired mountain goat. The sturdy stone houses are built with a slightly slanting roof so that the roof will hold enough heavy snow to act as insulation during the bitter winter. In the background are Mt. Kantesa and Mt. Taserku.*

strides. The big toe, however, was opposable, like a man's thumb. It was the trail of something who ranked somewhere between a tree-climber and a ground-walker.

Waddell's account met with the stoniest disbelief. Those Western scientists who bothered to comment at all alleged that the prints were either those of a Himalayan red bear or of a particularly big langur monkey. And that was that.

The scholars of the 19th century displayed an almost phobic reluctance to admit that there might be, somewhere, a type of animal they didn't know about, in spite of the fact that their earth still had immense patches marked "Unexplored." Until the 1830's, for instance, marine biologists insisted that the ancient Viking legend of the ship-sized "kraken" was based entirely on the scare image of some Norwegian sailors who had seen a biggish octopus. Then, the first giant squid was washed ashore on a Newfoundland beach; it weighed 29 tons, with a body 20 ft. long, with tentacles stretching to 35 feet.

The Phoenician navigator, Hanno, had left the description of a huge ape he called "gorilla," a beast which he alleged beat its chest with its fists when enraged. Darwin's colleagues had cleared that up to their own satisfaction. The beast Hanno meant was, of course, the chimpanzee—not exactly huge and definitely not given to breast-beating. It wasn't until August, 1856, that the Frenchman, du Chaillu, shot a gorilla in Equatorial Africa and set facts straight.

In 1900, the Englishman Harry Johnston, obsessed with the idea of capturing a unicorn, trudged through the almost impenetrable Ituri Forest of the Belgian Congo. He didn't find a unicorn. But he did come back with a creature that had feet like a zebra, ears like an ass, and the head of a giraffe. Zoologists had to find a name for it, and they accordingly christened it *"Okapi Johnstoni."* The okapi is still among the rarest of zoo inhabitants.

The list of "impossible" beasts is embarrassingly extensive: the Komodo dragon of Indonesia, the giant panda of China, the pigmy hippopotamus, the coelocanth of the Indian Ocean, supposedly extinct for an odd 50 million years but found alive and swimming in 1953. These discoveries have had a distinctly humbling effect on the scientists of our own age. Today, most scientists are willing to admit to the possibility of unknown animals existing in certain areas of the globe. The likeliest habitats would be the oceans, followed by some of the tremendously deep inland lakes, the rain forests of tropical South America, the mountain jungle of New Guinea, the interior of Tasmania, and the so-called "Roof of the World," the immense mountain region embracing Nepal, Sikkim, Bhutan, southern Tibet, and parts of Kashmir and Chinese Sinkiang.

Although politically dominated by India or China, these regions were forbidden territory to Westerners until just a few years ago. Up to 1955, fewer than 400 foreigners had ever visited the Kingdom of Nepal. Even today, a flight to its capital city, Katmandu, not over but *through* the Himalayan passes, can be a toe-curling experience. The "Roof of the World" is still a largely unmapped towering landmass.

Here is the alleged haunt of the "Abominable Snowman" who may be a mere legend, or may be a species of monkey, or may be a true humanoid—the long-sought missing link between ape and man. It is this last possibility that makes the yeti the greatest anthropological riddle of our time—more fascinating than the Java Man and the Peking Man because the yeti, if it exists at all, is alive.

For many years after the discovery of the first yeti footprints, the elusive creature remained a sort of by-product of unsuccessful Everest expeditions. Every party that returned after failing to climb the mountain brought back a batch of yeti stories.

Unfortunately, so much of these reports was hearsay. And a great many of these tales were based on nothing more substantial than local politeness. This maddening brand of courtesy—found among primitive peoples the world over—demands that the answer to an inquiry should not necessarily be the truth, but rather whatever the inquirer would *like* to hear.

A Western explorer would see a footprint and ask, "Yeti?" Whereupon the Sherpas would nod vigorously and agree that this was indeed a "Snowman" print, quite rightly assuming that this was what their boss would like it to be. Prodded for more information, they would trot out some second-hand, or tenth-hand report which might finally emerge

EXPEDITION LEADERS
Eric Shipton, Everest path-
finder, and Edmund Hil-
lary, the first man to reach
the top of Everest, are examining photographs of
the successful British Expedition of 1953. Ship-
ton was involved in ten
Himalayan expeditions,
five of them to Everest.
During his trail-blazing
1951expedition, he explored
the southern route to the
tallest mountain in the
world, preparing the way
for Hillary's successful assault in 1953.

as a personal encounter with the creature. The end result was often an inextricable tangle of fact and fairy tale.

For the "Snowman" is very much a figure of regional legendry, constantly used by the Himalayan mother to frighten her unruly off-spring. He is a half-human, half-ape monster of tremendous size that lives in mountain caves and carries off disobedient children. The ogre has feet like a man, but has his feet fixed backward, so that it can watch pursuers while running away.

Because the yeti is used as a bogeyman, educated compatriots treat the entire concept as a myth. Indian army officers would brush aside such talk as "old wives' tales." When the brother of the Tibetan Dalai Lama visited New York, he told interviewers that the beast existed only in the heads of illiterate mountain people.

SHERPA WOMEN   The young Sherpa girl and the woman carrying baskets wear typical garments. The wrap-around dress is covered with apron-like cloths, tied at the waist. The long hoe, carried by the girl, is used for clearing snow. The domestic life of a Sherpa family is exemplified by these simple activities of the Sherpinas. Spinning wool, weaving, and knitting are the normal activities of these mountain people who inhabit the villages of the Himalayas.   Using a hand loom, a woman weaves cloth from sheep wool.

TENZING AND HILLARY   The two climbers of Everest pause at the 27,000 foot level to assemble their gear. Below them at 16,500 feet, they can see the Thangboche Monastery. Stretching above is the final ridge to the summit. When they gained the peak, they stood for 15 minutes—literally—on top of the world.

The second World War put a temporary halt to Everest attempts and to the percolation of "Snowman" stories. But in 1948, two Norwegian uranium prospectors, Thornberg and Frostis, claimed to have actually fought some yetis. They were working in the Zemu Gap when they suddenly found themselves, face to face, with two large, vaguely ape-like figures, standing upright and covered with reddish-brown fur. The Norwegians tried to throw a rope over one, but the beast turned on Frostis and bit his arm. Thornberg then fired his rifle, and the two animals fled. The story tallied with Sherpa accounts of similar clashes, except that the Norwegians described the beasts as about man-sized, whereas the Sherpas usually had the yeti 10 feet tall.

What was still missing was concrete evidence. This was finally supplied by another Everest explorer, the Briton Eric Shipton. He and his party came across a set of fresh tracks on the Menlung Glacier; they followed them for miles, and took pictures of several of the impressions. The photos, which came out beautifully, showed a clear five-toed imprint, at least twice the size of a human foot. The footprints unquestionably indicated the trail of a biped, walking with a permanently erect posture, which ruled out both bears and every known species of ape or monkey, for while these animals will move upright for short stretches, they invariably will drop back on all fours when covering longer distances.

Then, in May 1953, came the conquest of Everest by the New Zealander, Sir Edmund Hillary, and the Sherpa, Tenzing Norgay. Both these men found yeti prints during the ascent march. To Tenzing, who grew up in a village on the Khumbu Glacier, they were old hat. Although he himself never claimed to have seen a live "Snowman," his father, "who was no teller of lies," had had a narrow escape from one. The beast, surprised while feeding, turned on Tenzing senior and chased him down a steep incline. The old man believed that the sloping ground saved his life, for while the yeti apparently moves fast while either climbing or running on level ground, its top-heavy build prevents it from moving downhill with speed.

The latest Everest epic injected an entirely new fillip into the "Snowman" conundrum. Hitherto, it had merely been an intriguing sideline, overshadowed by the lure of the unclimbed mountain. Now, for the first time, an expedition set out with the specific purpose of capturing, killing, or at least sighting a yeti. Financed by the *London Daily Mail* and headed by one of the paper's top journalists, Ralph Izzard, the party criss-crossed the high valleys of northern Nepal, the most prolific breeding ground of "Snowman" stories.

The results they brought back in 1954 were, to say the least, disappointing. They had neither seen nor heard a yeti, though they found and photographed numerous footprints, and they collected samples of what they believed was the creature's dung. The droppings contained both animal and vegetable matter, but absolutely no proof of their origin.

Izzard also brought back photographs of alleged yeti scalps which were preserved in the manner of religious relics at the monastery of Thangboche, the highest of the Sherpa villages. The Buddhist lamas showed Izzard one scalp which they claimed was more than 300 years old. It was conically shaped, about eight inches high, and had a base circumference of 26 inches, considerably bigger than any equivalent human measurements. But the thing was certainly no bear or monkey scalp because the bristly, coarse, reddish hair that covered it grew up from both sides, meeting at the top to form an inch-thick crest, a fearsome looking object, like a giant's wig—the kind of scalp we would imagine cavemen might have had if we did not know that our prehistoric forefathers were much smaller people than we are. Izzard was allowed to handle the scalp, and to pluck out a few hairs to substantiate his photographs. Subsequent analysis of the hairs proved inconclusive: they could not be identified as those of any known animal.

Three other safaris, all financed and led by the American magnates, Thomas Slick and F. Kirk Johnson, made for the Himalayas in 1957, in 1958, and in 1959. They were by far the best equipped parties ever to

HIMALAYAN EXPEDITIONS   From Katmandu, capital of Nepal, barefoot porters set out on their journey to the "Roof of the World." These Sherpa mountaineers leave the British Embassy (below) on their 21-day trek to the base camp of the 1957 expedition. Above, porters of the British-American Scientific and Mountaineering Expedition, led by Sir Edmund Hillary, begin their 1960 exploration which included a search for the "Snowman."

hunt the yeti. They carried an X-ray machine. More important, they carried special hypodermic rifles, air guns which could fire hypodermic bullets that would temporarily stun, but not kill, the prey.

But in spite of all this scientific gadgetry, and the tremendous drive, persistence, and enthusiasm of the groups, these expeditions came no closer to the elusive Kang-Mi than had their predecessors. All they succeeded in getting was additional evidence of the existence of the creature.

They met more than a dozen Nepalese who claimed to have had personal encounters with "Snowmen." Slick showed them pictures of gorillas, bears, and cavemen, and asked them to select the one that most closely resembled the Kang-Mi. They invariably chose the gorilla.

The Americans also learned that a number of natives from three particular villages had been killed by yetis—smashed against trees and torn by the animal's teeth. This seemed to indicate that while the "Snowman" resembled a gorilla, its method of attack was radically different. No gorilla has ever been known to hurl its opponent against a tree trunk. If it does attack—which happens very, very rarely—it uses a sideway swipe of its immensely powerful arm, a blow that would kill any human on the spot. While fighting each other—an equally rare event—they merely clutch and bite. The utilization of a tree trunk shows a rather more advanced technique of combat.

Slick and Johnson also returned with some excellent plaster casts of yeti tracks. They brought home scads of additional "Snowman" lore. The beast never came within sight of those ingenious hypo rifles, and refused to be caught in the snares staked out for it.

By this time, a disturbing note had crept into the great yeti hunt: the natives were beginning to capitalize on the Westerner's obsessive interest. The Sherpas, not all of whom were as financially innocent as the famous Tenzing Norgay, had latched on to the fact that the "Abominable" beast could be good business. Some of the sharper government officials in Katmandu led the way by imposing a quite unofficial "Yeti License" on foreign hunters, charging between $500 and $1,000 per animal. It took unmitigated gall to issue those elaborately stamped and embossed documents—like selling fishing permits for sea serpents. There was worse to come.

CONQUERORS OF EVEREST   Tenzing Norgay, 39-year-old Sherpa from the village of Thamey, and Edmund Hillary, later knighted for his triumphant feat, jubilant after their successful climb, the first men to scale the 29,028 foot mountain.

The main settlement of the Sherpa highland is Namche Bazar, which in good weather is a gruelling 12-day hike from Katmandu. The village lies 14,000 feet up, just below the edges of the glaciers that lick down from the chain of stupendous peaks. Mount Everest is the tallest of these mountains. Namche Bazar is the logical launching pad for a yeti safari; by the late 1950's this village was proceeding to cash in on its position.

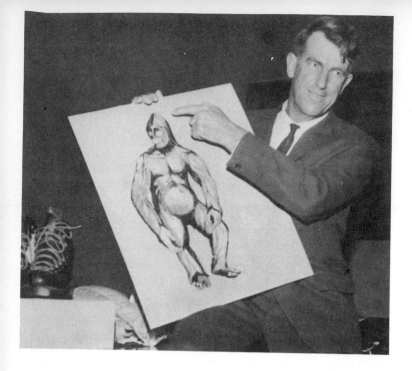

*"SNOWMAN" SKETCH   Hillary displays a drawing of a "snowman"
at the outset of his 1960-61 "Snowman" safari. The sketch is a composite,
based on accounts of alleged yeti sightings.*

*YETI FOOTPRINTS   The British Museum, in the Natural History Division, exhibits
a plaster cast of an alleged Snowman's footprint. Discovered initially by Eric Shipton, yeti
footprints were photographed during his 1951 exploration of the southern approach to
Everest. The prints measured 12 and one-half inches long and six inches wide, with a
stride of two feet six inches. With his simple statement of November 8, 1951, "We came
upon some strange tracks in the snow," Shipton reawakened world curiosity in the "Snowman."*

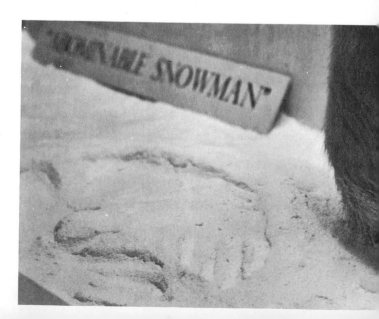

THANGBOCHE MONASTERY   Located in the Sherpa village of Namche Bazar, this world-famous monastery houses alleged yeti relics, typical of those preserved in similar monasteries throughout the Himalayas. Lamas guard these treasures zealously and are reluctant to part with what they regard as clear evidence of the existence of the "Snowman."

YETI FOOTPRINT   Photographed by Himalayan explorer Eric Shipton, the strange footprint constitutes much of the basis for the to-do about a yeti. The giant size of the print can be measured by the ice ax directly above the impression in the snow.

In the monasteries that dot the district and in some of the white shingled peasant huts, there was an astounding proliferation of Kang-Mi trophies—tufts of fur, teeth, dried droppings, even sexual organs. Most of these turned out to have belonged to yaks, langurs, or snow leopards. A Swiss paid about $25 for a "yeti jaw" which consisted of a human bone, studded with monkey molars. Other owners of relics did even better: they refused to sell their precious objects, but exacted a fee from every visitor who wanted to snap a picture of them.

Hunting parties were besieged by guides—mostly young boys—who virtually guaranteed to show them "Snowman" tracks. Incidentally, such "tracks" can be quite easily manufactured by wrapping bulky layers of rags around a man's feet, leaving only the toes free, and having him stalk across the snow toward a rock ledge where the prints, naturally, disappear.

Some of these Sherpa con men managed to give gullible explorers the thrill of their lives, by taking them out in gathering darkness, picking up fresh "droppings," then letting out a blood-curdling scream—from a "Snowman," of course—which rang through the gloom and froze the clients with terror.

The yeti relics of the lamas were no longer shown free to interested visitors; there was now a fee of ten rupees per peep per viewer. For a few additional coins some of the monks were willing to reveal the locations of "very gigantic" mummified "Snowman" bodies. The locations turned out to be other monasteries, deep inside Tibet which, as the monks well knew, was out of bounds for all foreigners since the Red Chinese takeover.

This rash of petty fakes did not necessarily detract from the weight of the real evidence gathered earlier, but the new wahoo made it damnably hard to sift fact from fiction. All the harder because the Sherpas, generally, have a fully deserved reputation for honesty, and very few Westerners are sufficiently cynical to suspect a genuine lama of fraud.

The "Snowman" mystery had developed into a sad parallel of that even more publicized creature that is supposed to inhabit one of the deepest lakes of the Scottish highlands—the Loch Ness Monster. Lake

SHERPA SIRDAR *Nima Lama, Nepalese Sherpa, is the headman of Tampathang, a mountain village north-east of Katmandu, situated between the capital and the Tibetan border. Originally from Tibet, the Sherpas settled mostly in northeast Nepal. Most of the mountain-climbing Sherpas come from the region of Solo Khumbu, over 15,000 feet high. They have participated in all the major Himalayan expeditions.*

Ness is a cold and calm ribbon of water, 24 miles long, about one mile broad, with a mean depth of 433 feet. During the summer of 1933, some road workers, a hotel proprietor, and an Automobile Association inspector, noticed odd stirrings and ripples in the slate-gray loch waters.

They then saw—or claimed to have seen—a fantastic marine animal with a long neck, several (as many as six) humps, and a reptilian head. Whatever it was they saw or didn't see, that find solved the economic problem of the area, bringing in streams of tourists from as far away as America, Japan, and South Africa. Almost at once, these visitors also began to see the beast, which apparently had the gift of changing its body structure with each sighting. One London couple even saw it "galloping across the road" in front of their motor car. It may or may not have carried a sheep in its mouth—they weren't certain.

YETI EXPEDITION LEADERS   Tom Slick, American oil magnate, (right), Peter Byrne, an Irish journalist, and A. R. Bachketti, an Indian zoologist, were the leaders of the 1957 expedition to the Himalayas. Slick financed three separate yeti expeditions, in 1957, in 1958, and in 1959. On the first expedition, he photographed and had plaster casts made of what he believed were yeti footprints.

KHUMJUNG SCALP   Sir Edmund Hillary displays an alleged yeti scalp which is a treasured relic of the village of Khumjung. On his 1960-61 "Snowman" expedition, Hillary persuaded the village elders to lend him the scalp for scientific study. With Hillary is Khumbo Chumbi, a Sherpa assigned as caretaker for the scalp. Some zoological experts concluded that the scalp was that of a serow, a goat antelope, native to eastern Asia. Mysterious parasites were found in the scalp. These were unfamiliar to science, which further confounded the mystery.

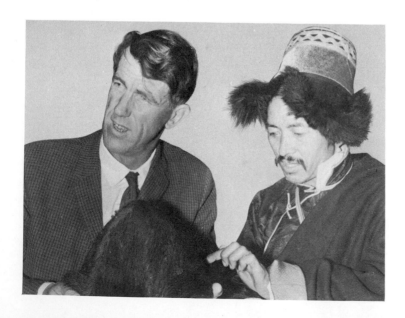

YETI DANCE   A Tibetan priest wearing a "Snowman" costume performs a dance during a native festival.

LEADER OF 1963 AMERICAN EVEREST EXPEDITION   Norman Dyhrenfurth rests with the Sherpa, Nowang Goma. During the Slick Safari of 1958, Dyhrenfurth discovered a cave with a bed of juniper branches, which was believed to be a yeti den. The branches had been pulled out of the ground, a feat no ordinary animal could accomplish. Like many Himalayan experts, Dyhrenfurth is of a mind "that the yetis are no mere figments of somebody's imagination."

Loch Ness became the most photographed patch of water on earth; every time a fish surfaced, a couple of dozen cameras clicked. Among the thousands of snaps, two or three did in fact reveal bulky shapes of unclassified origin. The most famous shot—widely denounced as a fake —showed the small head and long snake-like neck of the monster.

After the war, the loch region settled down into a regular "monster season" (from June to September) during which hotels were solidly booked, lake craft had to be hired in advance, and shops as far as Inverness did a heart-warming trade with monster buttons, monster post-cards, monster carvings, monster handkerchiefs, and monster bikinis, quite aside from such incidentals as spy glasses and film. In the chummy Scottish manner, the animal was christened Nessie or The Beastie—nothing abominable about *her*.

A body of scientists and interested amateurs formed the LOCH NESS PHENOMENA INVESTIGATION BUREAU LTD., which maintains a resident technician on the spot, as well as relays of observers during the summer. These loch-watchers are equipped with field glasses, log pads, and movie cameras with telephoto lenses. They also operate a powerful stereoscopic aerial camera. Whatever the cameras catch is sent to the British Air Ministry's reconnaissance center in London for expert interpretation. Expenses are met from membership fees. Anyone in the world can become a life member of the Bureau by paying a lump $300, or can become a subscribing member for $15 a year. The mark of membership is a dark blue tie, embroidered with monster emblems in silver.

Almost buried under the avalanche of ballyhoo is the likelihood that there *is* some kind of marine oddity in the lake.

Stories of such a creature date back to pre-medieval times; the beast was simply a big animal that lived in the lake.

There is reasonable scientific foundation for such belief. Geologists estimate that Loch Ness was an arm of the sea, a fjord, until about 5,000 years ago. It seems possible that some species of marine creature, now extinct in the oceans, has survived and continued to breed in that sheltered highland nook of water. Its nature is anyone's guess, though many scientists lean toward a gastropod—a huge form of sea slug.

To one unfamiliar with the lake, it may seem absurd that a large

LOCH NESS   In this Scottish highland lake, the Loch Ness monster is said to lurk. A 1961 photograph, examined by photo reconnaissance experts, showed what was "probably an animate object." It was estimated to be 92 feet in length, about six feet wide, and about five feet high.

and mobile object could escape positive detection for so long by an arsenal of instruments. But the term "mountain lake" conjures up a deceptive picture. Although Loch Ness is extremely narrow, it is also twice as deep as the North Sea, and is constantly fed by no less than five rivers and 45 mountain streams. Only six feet down, the water becomes

"SURGEON'S PHOTO"   *This famous picture, taken in 1934, shows what appears to be the head and neck of the Loch Ness monster.*

LOCH NESS HUMPS   *The often-reported series of humps is visible here. The ruined castle supplies a reference for estimating the size of the humps.*

LOCH NESS PHOTO   Taken in poor light, the
oft-reported configuration of an "overturned boat" is
very clear. At the right, there is a suggestion of a head.

EXPEDITION HEADQUARTERS   *Despite dedicated vigilance for five years on the part of its members, the Loch Ness Phenomena Investigation Bureau scored only one monster sighting for every 350 man-hours of watching. Extreme depth of the lake, which is twice that of the North Sea, and the murkiness of the water seem to be responsible for the disappointing total.*

impenetrably murky, the result of floating peat particles. This makes underwater exploration a hopeless task; lung divers grope around blindly. Neither helicopters nor planes can spot anything deeper than a few feet; boats, even less.

If, as it seems to be, the animal is a creature of the depths, there is no guarantee that it will ever be clearly photographed, much less caught. And sightings will remain a matter of luck, slightly improved by the summer-long vigilance of the Bureau watchers. Even their average is depressingly low: one sighting for every 350 man-hours of watching over five years.

But while the specialized observers have seen the beast very rarely, others claim to be seeing the monster constantly, particularly at the start of the summer season. Those "others" are mainly people with a stake in the tourist trade: hotel owners, boat renters, shopkeepers, excursion guides, and suchlike. Thanks to their gloriously technicolored descriptions, the monster has become a kaleidoscopic chimera between 10 and 100 feet long, with dragon scales, horse mane, fur, horned crests, forked tail, protruding fangs, and multitudinous humps. Sometimes, it utters foghorn ululations; occasionally, it devours sheep and cattle.

There is a sorry similarity between the developments in Scotland and the far Himalayas. In both places the profit motive has threatened to obliterate the few existing clues to the mystery beasts. At Loch Ness, it became quite impossible to determine who had seen or heard what. When? And where? The plethora of fake reports and doctored photographs may have discredited some genuine sightings. Not to mention the possibility of sincere mistakes caused by floating logs, overturned boats, schools of fish, and overdoses of whiskey. While the amount of cooked-up evidence concerning the yeti was minute in comparison, with the Loch Ness business there was enough of it to render every new find dubious.

But around the time of the second Slick-Johnson expedition an entirely new factor entered the search for the "Abominable Snowman." Now came the Russians.

The Soviets started on their yeti hunt with one great handicap and two big advantages. The big handicap lay in their Stalinist past, which insisted that everything—from architecture to zoology—be viewed through the perspective of "Socialist Realism." In this mental strait-jacket, folklore was automatically suspect as smacking of "illiterate peasant superstitions" which the Bolsheviks had struggled hard to eradicate among its people.

The "Snowman" was very much a legendary creature. Administrators and scholars had to ignore or suppress all rumors concerning such a being, unless they wished to risk being tagged "intellectual reactionaries." The Russians thus lost many clues that might have proved valuable later on.

One of their big advantages was geography: The Central Asian

hunting ground was well inside their frontiers. The Russians also had a pool of native scientists, hunters, and researchers who could talk to the locals in their own language. Since their efforts were government-sponsored, no one was likely to plant fake trails in their paths.

The second big advantage stemmed from their then close friendship with Communist China. Russian parties were able to probe through Tibet, Sinkiang, and Mongolia at a time when these areas were closed to Western expeditions. Moreover, once the Soviet authorities decided to delve into the matter, their explorers worked with virtually unlimited funds.

In January, 1958, Dr. Alexander Pronin, senior lecturer of the

RUSSIA'S YETI COUNTRY   A climber in Russia's Pamir Mountains, just north of the Hindu Kush, surveys an unusual snow formation. This range, of which Mt. Communism at 24,590 feet is the highest peak, is considered by the Russians to be the true home of the yeti. The stalagmite snow pattern is an effect of the sun.

Geographic Scientific Institute of Leningrad, published his account of a personal meeting with the "Snowman."

Apparently, it took Dr. Pronin quite a while to obtain official permission to publish the story; his encounter had taken place the previous August. A Western scientist would have rushed into print straight away.

The sighting occurred in the Pamir Mountains of the Tadzhik Soviet Republic, a wild, and partially unexplored, frontier province bordering on Afghanistan and China. Pronin had been sent there as head of a research team participating in the International Geo-physical Year. He was climbing up the densely wooded Baliand-Kijk Valley when he saw a curious figure standing on a high clifftop above him.

"At first glance," he wrote, "I took it to be a bear, but then I saw it more clearly, and realized that it was a man-like creature. It was walking on two feet, upright, but in a stooping fashion. It was quite naked

RUSSIAN SCIENTISTS   *Members of a Russian scientific expedition to the Pamir Mountains, the Russian "Top of the World," relax on the roof of their quarters. Their scientific station was built on the upper reaches of the Fedchenko Glacier, one of the largest glaciers outside the polar regions. The glacier and its surrounding area are claimed by the Russians to be yeti country. The scientific team remained atop this river of ice for two years. During their stay, both station and glacier moved down 400 feet.*

and its thick-set body was covered with reddish hair. The arms were over-long and swung slightly with each movement. I watched it for about 10 minutes before it disappeared, very swiftly, among the scrub and boulders."

Pravda, the official Government organ, quoted the report without comment, using the Russian word for the Snowman—*Galubyavanna*—to describe the creature. But the self-appointed guardians of "Socialist Realism" jumped Pronin at once.

"It seems strange that a visitor from Leningrad should meet something that no local citizen has hitherto noticed," sneered the *Tibilisi Daily* of Tiflis, Georgia. "Even more curious is the fact that none of the doctor's comrades on his team had such marvelous encounters, although they were wandering through the same area."

Komsomolskaya Pravda, the publication of the Communist Youth

Movement, was even more scathing. The paper's representatives interviewed other scientists in the same region and quoted them as saying flatly: "We do not believe one word of Dr. Pronin's report. It should have been double-checked before publication."

But despite the sniping of the diehards, the end of the Stalinist Ice Age also melted the ban on yeti stories. The next account followed a few weeks later; it was printed verbatim by many Soviet newspapers. The report came from the same Pamir region and stemmed from a Tadzhik officer of the frontier guards, Captain Astanaqull Olimi. He was leading a patrol of six soldiers over a plateau about 11,000 feet high when all of them—simultaneously—saw what they definitely took to be a *Galubyavanna*.

"We saw the creature clearly in the bright afternoon sunlight," the captain related. "It was perhaps 400 feet ahead of us, scrambling down a slope. The figure was man-sized and hairy, the hair being a dark brown. While descending downhill it stooped forward, but on two legs, the arms not touching the ground. The face was turned away from us, so we could not see its features. Before I could decide on pursuit, it had disappeared among the trees at the bottom of the incline."

By allowing a member of the Red Army to publicize this experience, the government had indicated official sanction. And from then on, a steady trickle of "Snowman" sightings enlivened the Soviet press.

Most of them, however, did not occur in the same area. The accounts related to happenings 1,500 miles to the northeast, in central Mongolia. These creatures could hardly be called "Snowmen," since they were reported as existing in the Gobi Desert, as well as the Khangai mountain ranges. The descriptions came from Mongolian zoologists, surveyors, and soldiers; the reports tallied sufficiently to give a fairly clear picture of the beasts. They were described as no taller than about five feet six, covered with reddish-dark hair, with very low foreheads, bushy eyebrows, and long arms dangling almost to their knees. Their walk was a curiously rapid, bent-knee shuffle; very much the gait of a creature that had only recently risen on its hind legs. But they were definite bipeds that—unlike all apes—never dropped on all fours when running.

And now, at long last, the Soviets resurrected some of the ancient Mongol stories concerning these beings, dating back to the time of Genghis Khan. The "hairy men" had, apparently, existed at least as long as the natives themselves. They were supposed to live in caves and rock crevices, where they slept during daylight, emerging only at dusk to feed. They ate virtually everything: plants, grubs, roots, berries, insects, lizards, and even carrion. They avoided men and scuttled into hiding as soon as a human being approached. In this fashion, they survived, remaining almost unknown. Which is quite possible when you consider that Mongolia sprawls over more than 600,000 square miles, and houses a population of fewer than a million.

Based on these accounts, the Russian Professor B. Porshnev formulated a theory according to which both the "Snowman" of the Himalayas and the creatures of the Mongolian wilderness were related species. They could represent a primitive race of ape-like, but humanoid, beings that might once have been scattered over most of Asia. With the spread of the weaker, but weapon-wielding homo sapiens, the beasts retreated farther and farther into the least accessible portions of the globe. They escaped extinction by remaining invisible.

Decidedly, these creatures might be "the missing link"—the bridge between ape and man—that anthropologists have been seeking for more than a century.

The opportunity of being the first to solve the evolutionary enigma spurred the Russians into concerted effort. They organized an exchange of information with Western scientists, which culminated in an international "Yeti Conference" held in Moscow in 1959. While the meeting broke no new ground, it did help to shift the "Snowman" from the realm of twilight legend into realistic perspective.

In the same year, the Soviet Academy of Sciences sponsored three lavishly equipped expeditions to scour the Pamir Mountains, Mongolia, and Tibet. A fourth probed into Chinese Sinkiang. None of these parties returned with anything more tangible than had their Western predecessors.

The areas to be searched were too huge and too rugged to yield their secrets to a few quick thrusts. As Professor Urianov of Kiev Uni-

*LOCH NESS OBSERVATION STATION   Here is a mobile
photographic unit with a 35 mm. camera.*

*MONSTER-SPOTTING EQUIPMENT   This huge camera is used
by the Loch Ness Phenomena Investigation Bureau, a private organization that maintains relays of observers on the spot during the summer
months. The camera is equipped with a 1,000 mm. telephoto lens.*

versity put it: "It may take as long as 10 years of constant effort to gain the scientific evidence we require to decide this question."

Unfortunately, Russia did not have 10 years. From 1963 on, her relations with Communist China deteriorated rapidly. Soviet explorers suffered the same ignominious exclusion from Chinese territory as had their capitalistic colleagues. Soon, the entire frontier facing China was placed on a defense footing. Further systematic searches became difficult, if not impossible. The great yeti hunt came to a halt, or something close to that.

The search still goes on—but in a desultory fashion. Much of the optimistic enthusiasm of the late 1950's has evaporated. Perhaps the solution of the "Snowman" riddle will have to wait until peace on earth extends to the "Roof of the World."

The Boy from Nowhere

The winding cobblestone streets of Nuremberg, Bavaria, lay almost deserted on the afternoon of May 26, 1828. It was Whitmonday, and the larger proportion of citizens had gone on that hallowed German holiday ritual: the "Ausflug."

There was hardly a soul in sight when an enigmatic creature came hobbling down the slight hill leading to Unschlitt Square. On normal days he would have attracted plenty of attention, for he was dressed like a scarecrow and moved with a curiously stiff-legged lurch, as if his feet had gone to sleep.

But the only other person in the vicinity was a local cobbler named Georg Weichmann. He saw the stranger, a well-built boy in his middle teens, and stopped to get a closer look at him. At this the boy approached him, mumbled a few words, and held out an envelope he was carrying. Weichmann saw that it was a letter, addressed to "The Captain of the 4th Squadron, 6th Cavalry Regiment, in Nuremberg."

The nearest military post was the New Gate guardroom, and Weichmann took the stranger there and handed him over to the sergeant in charge, still not sure whether the lurching, mumbling, ragged lad was drunk or sick. The sergeant, in turn, directed the boy to the house of the 4th Squadron captain whose name was Wessenig.

The officer was out, but his servants told the boy that he could wait with his letter until the "Herr Hauptmann" returned. When Wessenig arrived home, several hours later, he found his household buzzing with excitement.

The boy, it appeared, had tried to pick up the flame of a candle with his fingers, and had screamed with astonishment when he got burned. Offered some ham and a mug of beer, he reacted as if he had never before seen such victuals. Yet he greedily drank water, and wolfed black bread with every sign of a roaring appetite.

He had answered any question put to him either with incoherent mumbling or a constantly repeated "Weiss nicht." ("Don't know.") What's more, he was visibly frightened by the grandfather clock, which he seemed to regard as a living thing, and he gagged when the smell of cooking had drifted in from the kitchen.

THE MARKET PLACE IN NUREMBERG   *The city's central square as it looked during the lifetime of Kaspar Hauser, showing the famous "Frauen-kirche" (Women's church). The horseman in the foreground wears the uniform and crested helmet of the Royal Bavarian cavalry, the regiment Kaspar was so eager to join.*

After listening to the account of his servants, Wessenig opened the envelope addressed to him. It contained two notes, fastened together. The first one read:

"Honored Captain,

"I send you a lad who wishes to serve his king in the Army. He was brought to me on October 7th, 1812. I am but a poor laborer with children of my own to rear. His mother asked me to bring up the boy, and so I thought I would rear him as my own son. Since then, I have never let him go one step outside the house, so no one knows where he was reared. He, himself, does not know the name of the place or where it is.

"You may question him, Honored Captain, but he will not be able to tell you where I live. I brought him out at night. He cannot find his way back. He has not a penny, for I have nothing myself. If you will not keep him, you must strike him dead or hang him."

This curious missive, badly spelled and clumsily phrased, was neither dated nor signed. The second note, however, clearly dated "October 1812," ran:

"This child has been baptized. His name is Kaspar; you must give him his second name yourself. I ask you to take care of him. His father was a cavalry soldier. When he is seventeen, take him to Nuremberg, to the Sixth Cavalry Regiment; his father belonged to it. I beg you to keep him until he is seventeen. He was born on April 30th, 1812. I am a poor girl; I can't take care of him. His father is dead."

The subject of the two letters livened up considerably in the presence of the captain. He said several times quite clearly: "Want to be a soldier, like my father," and "Horse, horse." He also stroked the officer's saber, in its scabbard, with shouts of glee.

But Wessenig could make nothing of either the letters or the boy who, as he later put it, "appeared to be either a primitive savage or an imbecile." He therefore had the foundling taken to the police station.

The first thing the police did was to give the boy a pencil and paper and ask him to write down his name and address. He obediently and quite legibly scrawled the words KASPAR HAUSER, but nothing else. Further prodding produced merely the old refrain of "Don't know."

The next step was to strip and search the lad. This was done by a "Wachtmeister" (sergeant) named Wüst, to whom we owe the first— and probably the most accurate—description of this walking riddle.

According to the sergeant, Kaspar Hauser was a sturdy, broad-shouldered lad of around 17 years, with a healthy complexion, light brown hair, blue eyes, and very small hands and feet. Because of his clumsy gait, he was first thought to be crippled; but closer inspection showed there was nothing wrong with his legs. He merely had exceptionally tender soles which were badly blistered from unaccustomed walking.

The clothes he wore clearly didn't belong to him. The old hat and tattered shirt were too large; his boots were too tight; his shapeless trousers and jacket had been made for some adult of considerably greater girth. His pockets were found to contain a rosary, a couple of printed religious tracts, and a packet of salt. There was nothing on him that could have provided the faintest clue to his identity. Nothing, that is, except those two letters.

But it didn't take the police long to recognize them as fakes. They were written in different scripts; the first, in the stilted Gothic lettering taught only in German schools; the second, in the generally known Latin style. They had supposedly been penned by a man and a woman about 16 years apart. Yet both handwritings were quite similar, the type of paper was exactly the same, and the ink equally fresh on both of them.

The letters, then, had clearly been written very recently and by the same person, who obviously was trying to draw a red herring across the boy's background. Kaspar's own handwriting was promptly matched with the notes, but his scrawl was too childish to bear comparison.

Removed from the military stimulation of the captain, Kaspar became completely withdrawn again. He seemed almost grateful when his hosts locked him in a cell "for further observation."

The observing was done by a veteran turnkey named Hiltel who

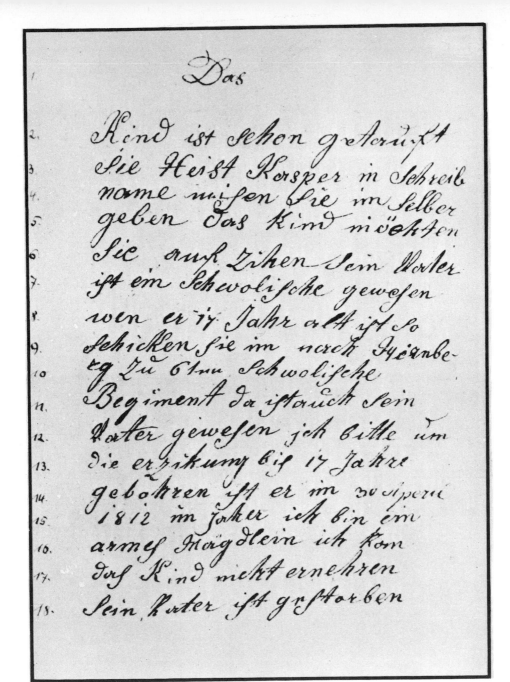

Das

Kind ist schon getaüft
Sie Heist Kasper in Schreib
name müsen Sie im Selber
geben das Kind möchten
Sie auch Zihen Sein Vater
ist ein Schwolische gewesen
wen er 17 Jahr alt ist So
Schicken sie im nach Nürnberg Zu 6ten Schwolische
Begiment da ist auch Sein
Vater gewesen ich bitte um
die erzikung bis 17 Jahre
gebohren ist er im 30 April
1812 im Jahr ich bin ein
armes Mägdlein ich kan
das Kind nicht ernehren
Sein Vater ist gestorben

HAUSER'S LETTER OF INTRODUCTION   This is the letter Kaspar
Hauser carried when he first appeared in Nuremberg in May, 1828. The communication purports to be from his mother who refers to herself as a "poor
maiden" unable to support her child.

An der Kärntner Gränz
Den ?ten ? ?
1828

Hochwohlgeborner ?. ?. ?. !

Ich schicke ihnen ... ... möchte seinem
König zu ... diesem verlangten ... dieser ...
ist mir gelegt worden, 1822 den ? October, und ich
selber ... armer Taglöhner, ich habe auch selber
... ... ich habe selber genug zu ... daß ich mich
forthringe, ... seine Mutter hat ... mir die ...
daß ... gelegt, aber ich habe seine Mutter nicht ...
fragen ... ... habe ich auch nichts gesagt, daß
... der ... gelegt ist worden, ... Landgericht
Ich habe mir gedacht ... ... für ... ...
haben, ich habe ihn ... ... erzogen, und haben ihn
seit 1812 ... ... weit aus ... Haus gelassen
daß kein Mensch nicht weiß davon, wohin auch gezogen
ist worden, ... er selber weiß nicht wie mein Haus
heißt und ... ... weiß er auch nicht, ... ihn
... fragen ... ... aber nicht sagen, daß lesen
und schreiben habe ich ihn ... gelassen ... ... auch
... ... schreiben wie ich schreibe, und wenn
wir ihn fragen was er würde so sagte er will auch
... ... werden weil sein Vater gewesen ist,

... ... hätte wir ... keine
... ... gelehrter ... worden ... ...
... ...,

Ich habe ... ... bis ... ...
... zu ... hingehen müssen ... habe zu
ihn gesagt wann er nie mal ein Soldat ist,
... ich gleich und ... ihn ... sonst hätte
ich mich ... mein ... gebracht

LETTER INTRODUCING HAUSER TO THE CAPTAIN *Kaspar's letter to the "High-wellborn Captain," allegedly written by a "poor laborer," ends with the admonition that the captain should either keep the boy or "strike him dead, or hang him."*

had watched legions of inmates and was struck by the boy's unusual reaction to confinement.

"He can sit for hours without moving a limb," he reported. "He does not pace the floor, nor does he try to sleep. He sits rigidly without growing in the least uncomfortable. Also, he prefers darkness to light, and can move about in it like a cat."

Kaspar Hauser.

KASPAR HAUSER Probably the best-known of the hundreds of Hauser pictures, this engraving shows the lad as he looked when he first turned up in Nuremberg in May, 1828. Like all of his portraits, it was probably drawn weeks, if not months, after his arrival. He is seen holding his letter of introduction.

Despite such intriguing observations, the police made no progress with their charge. At each interrogation, he repeated his desire to become a "Reiter (a cavalryman) like my father." Otherwise, he stuck to his know-nothing formula. As to his phoney letters, no one had the vaguest notion as to who might have written them or why.

But meanwhile, the people of Nuremberg had become interested in the odd newcomer. They arrived in droves to watch the "nature child" devour hunks of rye bread. He still refused to touch any other kind of food, and the smell of meat cooking made him physically ill. He would pen his only words, KASPAR HAUSER, on any piece of paper given to him.

His reactions to the most ordinary objects were those of a baby. He would spend hours listening to a ticking watch; he would grab a knife by the blade; he would gaze in wonder at the figures on playing cards; he would build houses with coins. What was even more amusing, he apparently didn't know the difference between the sexes, but used the same term "Junge" (boy) for both men and women.

Another of his all-embracing words was "horse," which he applied to all animals. Horses seemed to fascinate him, and he really came out of his shell when a visitor brought him a wooden one. He would adorn the toy with ribbons, conscientiously feed it every time he ate, and he would play with his wooden horse with great interest, exactly as a normal child might play with a toy steed.

Equally infantile was his ignorance concerning the passage of time. He didn't know the meaning of hours and minutes, days and nights. Finally—and this caused his visitors much delighted titillation—he had no sense of physical shame, but would perform his natural functions in front of a mixed audience.

By present standards, the idea of turning a cell occupant into a public freak show seems quite revolting. But 1828 was still the era of public executions, of guided tours through lunatic asylums, and of the public flogging of prostitutes and army deserters. Far from being perturbed by the crowds, Kaspar seemed to enjoy the attention lavished on him.

Now began the process that turned him from an oddity into a national figure.

He began to learn, with amazing rapidity, all the things most individuals acquire in the course of a decade or more. His vocabulary grew from a few words to fluent phraseology; his reading and writing prowess reached approximately fifth grade level; his ability to handle utensils like scissors, matches, quills, and lanterns increased to that of an ordinary adult.

All of which indicated that the boy, far from being mentally retarded, had somehow been *prevented* from learning the most elementary skills up to this stage of his life.

But prevented by whom? And why?

We do not know precisely how long after his arrival Kaspar Hauser had acquired speech sufficiently coherent for him to tell his own story. The first personal record was issued in the form of a bulletin, signed by Burgomaster Binder of Nuremberg and members of the Town Council, which was dated July 7th, just about six weeks after the boy's appearance. This first statement was later supplemented dozens of times by Kaspar himself. In effect, this is what the boy told:

For as long as he could remember, he had lived in a kind of cell, about seven feet long, four feet wide, and five feet high; the windows of the cell were boarded. The floor was bare earth with a bundle of straw on which he could lie back while sleeping. When awake, he would sit; there was no room for him to stand upright or to walk.

When he woke up, he always found a loaf of dark bread and a jug of water by his side. At certain intervals, the water would have a strange, bitter taste and send him into a deep sleep. On awakening, his clothes and straw would have been changed and his nails and hair were cut. The only other objects in his cell were three wooden toy horses.

He wasn't aware of being either unhappy or lonely. He simply didn't know any other form of existence. Nor had he known of the existence of any other beings. He accepted his food just as he accepted his toys—as something that just *was*—like sleep or hunger. He couldn't recall hearing any outside sounds, nor experiencing any change of temperature, nor change of lighting.

He had no way of telling how long he stayed in that cell, since he had no conception of time. But one day, a man entered the room and placed a board over his knees. Then he showed him how to hold a pencil, gave him a sheet of paper, and very slowly and patiently, taught him to write the name KASPAR HAUSER in block letters.

Over a period, the same man also made him repeat certain phrases and words, like "Want to be a soldier," "Horse," and "Don't know." These phrases were Kaspar's entire original vocabulary. The only painful incident of his early life occurred when he had been playing more noisily than usual with his horses, and the man stormed in and struck him on the arm with a stick.

Shortly afterwards, Kaspar awoke from one of his deep sleeps to find that his clothes had been changed, and that he was wearing boots. The man entered again, but this time led him out of his prison, upward, into the open air. The boy felt so dizzy and confused by the completely new experience that he only had the dimmest recollection of the journey that followed. They walked. His feet hurt badly. The man talked to him, promising him "a big, live horse after you become a soldier." Suddenly he was alone, trudging painfully through one of the gates of Nuremberg.

He couldn't remember being given the letters he carried, or any details about the road they took, or anything about the man's looks or build beyond the impression that he was "big and strong."

The story created a sensation. Nuremberg went haywire with excitement. Conversation over beer mugs and coffee cups dealt with hardly anything else. As the local wit Fridolin Leitner put it: "You would think that every woman in town had given birth to Kaspar Hauser, and that every man had fathered him."

Nuremberg had reason to make the most of its fantastic foundling. This was the age of the Biedermeier in Germany, the era of stifling pre-Victorian stuffiness that followed the prolonged turmoil of the Napoleonic wars. This was the time in which the nation was threatened to be smothered beneath an eiderdown of bourgeois respectability and political censorship.

In Nuremberg, sensations of any kind were few and far between. Architecturally, the town was a gem of medieval craftsmanship; and the town also, was thoroughly provincial. All the exciting scandals seemed to be happening in the much more glamorous Bavarian capital

of Munich. Nuremberg was a parched tinderbox of boredom, aching for
a spark to set it alight. Now the spark had fallen, and every Nurem-
berger set about busily fanning the blaze.

The Burgomaster and the Town Council led the way. By official
proclamation, Kaspar Hauser was made a ward of the municipality
which henceforth would pay for his upkeep. The town press turned out
thousands of handbills bearing his image, along with an appeal that anyone "possessing knowledge of his true identity or any intelligence pertaining to same" should come forward and inform the authorities and
collect a cash reward. Simultaneously, police agents were sent to scour
the Bavarian kingdom for his possible place of imprisonment.

The effort proved futile. Neither then, nor in the years to come, was
the reward claimed, nor was any trace of the boy's jail or his jailer
discovered.

Nuremberg, however, happily basked in the glory of its boy wonder. Within weeks, not merely Bavaria—but all of Germany, France,
Hungary, and even England—played the guessing game called "Who Is
Kaspar Hauser?" What made the game so intriguing was the obvious
supposition that none would have gone to such lengths to keep a lad
hidden unless that boy was a pretty important personage. To guess the
degree of importance—and thereby to implicate some high-ranking personality—was the exciting core of the pastime.

A regular pilgrimage to Nuremberg got under way. Dozens of major
and minor celebrities lines up for interviews with the foundling, some
of them traveling considerable distances for the privilege. Best-known
among them was the illustrious German jurist and criminologist, Anselm
Ritter von Feuerbach. This eminent lawyer questioned Kaspar many
times, and examined him physically as well. In the end, he accepted the
boy's account unreservedly; and he drew some pretty startling conclusions. However, he did not make these conclusions known until some five
years later—posthumously. In the meantime, he did nothing to counter
the ever-widening spate of rumors, according to which Kaspar was the
illegitimate offspring of virtually every high-born rake of the period,
kept out of sight by his noble parent for 16 years, and then finally turned
loose into the world when time had eliminated the danger of a scandal.

GEORG FRIEDRICH DAUMER
Hauser's first teacher was a Nuremberg
educationalist of considerable reputa-
tion. It was in his home that Hauser
suffered the first attack on his person.

Meanwhile, the city of Nuremberg got around to finding a suitable guardian for its famous ward. The man appointed to the task was one Professor Daumer, a local lecturer and scientist of sorts, whose chief interest lay in the field of "bodily magnetism," a subject which was then enjoying a tremendous vogue. Daumer conducted a series of magnetic experiments with his charge, the results of which are of no particular interest. But in the course of these tests, the professor discovered that Kaspar was ambidextrous, that he had a fantasically acute sense of smell, that he could see amazingly well in the dark, but very badly·in broad daylight·which continued to hurt his eyes.

In the professor's home Kaspar was no longer on general display. Here, he became a more exclusive figure. Accompanied by his guardian, he attended almost every event given by the town's social set; he was patted, lionized, quizzed and cooed over, and coddled the way only small town celebrities are.

His features were constantly scrutinized for possible resemblances with this or that count, duchess, or earl whose offspring he might be.

NUREMBERG   *Here are scenes of the city, drawn by contemporary artists in the time of Kaspar Hauser.*

And even those observers who couldn't discern a likeness to anyone in particular claimed to see "unmistakable nobility and high breeding" in his face. From the dozens of woodcuts, lithographs, and sketches we have of Kaspar Hauser, we know that his face was regular, fleshy, boyish, and perfectly ordinary. Which means that he probably did look like half a hundred young aristocrats—or just as many young grocery clerks—of the area and period.

Because he seemed to have responded to some Hungarian words spoken in his presence, a brand-new batch of rumors immediately linked him with a score of Magyar barons, whose morals, anyway, were worth raking over in detail.

Kaspar himself responded to the furore around his person in an all too human fashion. There was no doubt that he thoroughly enjoyed being the center of attention, and that he did his best to keep the interest alive. Thus, he was perpetually remembering further little details about his unique past; and although these minutiae really added nothing to his story, every new tidbit made effective party talk. In the end, it became quite impossible to sort out the bones of the original story from the meat added in Kaspar's series of afterthoughts.

The lad's rate of progress, though, was truly astonishing. In the summer of 1829—only 15 months after his illiterate arrival—he put his story in writing. It was published by the municipality. Ostensibly, the little volume was his own work; but we have no way of knowing how much assistance he received from Professor Daumer.

By then, however, the tale was too well known, had been printed and told too many times, to attract much attention. Public interest in the foundling seemed on the wane when suddenly an incident made the case of Kaspar Hauser flare up again with even greater intensity.

On the afternoon of October 7th, 1829, Kaspar was found unconscious on the floor of Daumer's cellar. He was bleeding from a gash in his forehead, and his shirt was torn to the waist. Taken to bed, he recovered after a short time and then gave an account of what had happened. He had, he related, been attacked by a man wearing dark clothes, leather gloves, and a silken mask. And here we come to one of the many inconsistencies that haunt the entire Hauser riddle. According to some contemporary accounts, he claimed that his assailant wielded a knife; other reports have it that it was a club. Whatever the weapon, the assailant struck Kaspar with it, knocking him out.

Almost immediately, persons came forward who claimed that they had seen such a man that same afternoon. The difficulty was that the assailant had been seen in a great many different places, and that he grew and shrank and changed his hair coloring and his walk almost as many times as there were witnesses. The police combed Nuremberg but discovered no one who fitted any description.

The city authorities were now truly convinced that their prize ward was in danger. They moved him from the professorial quarters into those of a certain Freiherr von Tucher, and the jurist von Feuerbach was appointed Kaspar's guardian. In addition, they assigned two police constables to be his personal bodyguards, both of whom slept in the room with him.

PAUL JOHANN ANSELM RIT-TER VON FEUERBACH A distinguished criminologist and legal expert (the "ritter" was a title meaning "knight"), Feuerbach examined Kaspar Hauser at great length, and his records serve as the best source of information about Hauser.

The public, however, had split into bitterly antagonistic camps. The majority insisted that the assault was the handiwork of the same highly-placed persons who had kept Kaspar locked away most of his life, and who now, for some unfathomable reason, were trying to do away with him altogether. But a tight little knot of skeptics declared just as noisily that there had been *no assault at all!* They said the whole business was only a stunt to attract attention. And they pointed out that it was, indeed, a curious kind of assailant who, alone with an unconscious victim, could inflict nothing more damaging than a cut on the forehead, a cut which Kaspar could just as easily have inflicted on himself.

The controversy was still crackling furiously when yet another odd character appeared on the scene. All the way from England, especially to meet Kaspar Hauser, came Lord Stanhope, one of the strangest eccentrics ever.

CHARLES STANHOPE   The English aristocrat who became one of Hauser's staunchest sponsors.

Stanhope had heard about the amazing Kaspar and wished to meet him in the flesh. To the Nurembergers, this visit confirmed the value of their star attraction, the prestige of wealthy English lords being then what it was.

After being removed from the home of Professor Daumer, further difficulties, never clearly explained, ensued. Once, for instance, a shot was heard from Hauser's room. When the two bodyguards rushed in, they found their charge quite safe but extremely upset. He had, he explained, lost his balance while leaning out of the window. Clutching at the wall for support, he had torn down a pistol hanging there, and had accidentally discharged it.

This episode had an unnerving effect on Kaspar's host. He indicated he would be rather glad to get him off the premises. This was followed by several changes in Kaspar's residence, with considerable bother for the authorities.

The town feud, too, showed no sign of abating, with a growing faction insisting that the boy was merely an impostor, milking the city for a soft livelihood and following up with a series of fabricated incidents to keep the con game going.

Stanhope met Hauser several times over lengthy intervals, interspersed with his usual jaunts to various European courts and principalities. Each time his interest in the boy appeared to grow, even to the point of trying to teach him English. And each time His Lordship returned to Nuremberg he found Kaspar more unsettled, the quarrels raging around him more acrimonious. A number of noble Bavarian families were threatening to sue the next person who publicly saddled them with Kaspar's paternity. At least one duel had been fought over the issue; several more threatened. So when Lord Stanhope, surprisingly offered to take over the boy's upkeep, the City Fathers clutched at the opportunity to rid themselves of the insinuation that they were squandering public funds on a fraud, and they accepted His Lordship's offer.

Kaspar remained in Nuremberg until May, 1833, when his guardian, von Feuerbach, died of a paralytic stroke. The old man was known to have been in the process of compiling a detailed legal report on his ward. The fact that he hadn't published it gave rise to a new crop of

KASPAR HAUSER   This portrait shows him in the last years of his life. The earlier woebegone expression has given way to a dandified head of curls and a somewhat smug smile. This was possibly the last picture made of Hauser during his lifetime.

rumors, one group claiming that he had been bribed not to, the other that he hadn't because he was ashamed of having been taken in by a hoax.

With the bickering rising to a shrill crescendo, the municipality grew weary of the living bone of contention. Lord Stanhope suggested removing Hauser, and the City Fathers agreed, though not without a proper display of reluctance.

This steady concern of the footloose Englishman for the German foundling seems decidedly strange, but no stranger than some of Stanhope's other quirks. Anyway, he took Kaspar to the nearby Bavarian

town of Ansbach, where he left him in the care of a local teacher, Dr.
Meyer, and under the special protection of a certain Captain Hickel,
a military officer temporarily working with the police. In those days of
"town soldiers" responsible for city security, the dividing line between
military and the municipal police was not too clearly drawn.

His Lordship departed for other fields. Gradually, things grew quiet
around Kaspar Hauser. Ansbach was a much smaller town than Nuremberg and correspondingly sleepier. The social whirl around the boy
thinned down to an occasional tea party. Nuremberg turned to other
subjects of discussion.

Then, on December 14, 1833, the Kaspar Hauser saga ended as
abruptly and bewilderingly as it had begun five and a half years before.
On the afternoon of that snowy Saturday, Kaspar came staggering
home. There was blood soaking through his coat on his right side, and
he gasped out what sounded like, "Man stabbed!—Knife!—Hofgarten!—
Gave purse!—Go look quickly!"

Meyer and his wife put him to bed and summoned a doctor. The
physician found that Kaspar had indeed been stabbed just below the
rib cage, though the wound didn't appear very serious. Meanwhile, Captain Hickel dashed to the Hofgarten, Ansbach's public park, to find the
assailant. The park was deserted and covered with snow. But Hickel
did find the purse, the silk moneybag Kaspar had mentioned.

Inside the purse, there was a note—another of those baffling epistles
that said nothing in a great many words. To make matters more compli-
cated, it was penned in "mirror writing." The piece ran:

> "Hauser will be able to tell you how I look, whence I came
> from, and who I am. To spare him that task, I will tell you
> myself. I am from...On the Bavarian border...On the River...
> My name is: 'M.L.O.'"

Contrary to the note's assertion, Kaspar couldn't tell anything much
about the man. Lying in bed, with an ever-growing throng of physicians, police officers, town dignitaries, and clergymen around him, he
had to repeat, over and over, the same brief account.

He had gone to the Hofgarten in order to meet a man who had

KASPAR HAUSER'S CLOTHES

This raiment—hat, coat, boots, vest, pants —was worn by Kaspar Hauser on the day he was stabbed. The clothing is now part of the exhibit in the Kaspar Hauser Museum in Nuremberg. The circle marks by the curator indicate the spot where the clothing was pierced when Hauser was wounded.

contacted him earlier by sending a message through a laborer. The man, described as "tall, with dark whiskers, wearing a black cloak," approached him with the question, "Are you Kaspar Hauser?" When Kaspar nodded, the man handed him the purse and then *he stabbed him*. The assailant then ran off. Kaspar dropped the purse in the snow and struggled home.

The entire town was mobilized. The search for the attacker extended far out into the surrounding countryside. Not a trace of him could be found. Instead, Captain Hickel revealed a very peculiar fact: in the area where he had picked up the purse, he saw only one set of footprints in the snow—only Kaspar's footprints. This evidence rendered the existence of the black-whiskered, black-cloaked stranger somewhat dubious.

The gathering around Kaspar's bedside began to take on the air of a courtroom. In between making him repeat his account, Dr. Meyer,

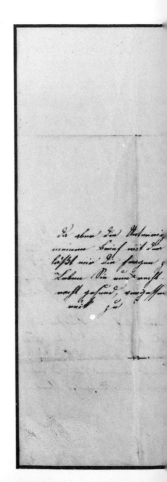

LETTER IN HAUSER'S HANDWRITING   This is the script he is supposed to have acquired during his belated education. This letter to the Bavarian baroness Alexandrina von Seckendorff was written after Hauser had been moved to Ansbach.

Hickel, and several others urged him to confess and unburden himself. Hauser clung to his story and reasserted his version of the previous assault. In a voice that was steadily growing weaker, he accused various people, including Lord Stanhope, of lacking faith in him. On the afternoon of December 17, he went into a coma; on the same evening, he died. His last audible and recorded words were: "I didn't do it myself."

The autopsy revealed that a sharp instrument, thrust upward, had cut through his diaphragm and penetrated the point of his heart. The postmortem was conducted by three physicians, one of whom gave the opinion that the wound could not have been self-inflicted. The other two were uncertain. However, both these doctors maintained that the blow had been struck by a left-handed person.

Hauser's death produced a din. Everyone jumped again into the arena. The air over Ansbach and Nuremberg was thick with charges and counter-charges. The printing presses spewed forth an avalanche of

Kaspar Hauser fecit. 1829

ART WORK BY KASPAR HAUSER   These pieces of art, alleged to have been drawn by the famous mystery figure, are now exhibited in the Kaspar Hauser Museum in Nuremberg. Each picture allegedly bears the signature of Hauser. Considering that according to the story Hauser was totally illiterate until age 17, these drawings seem much too sophisticated for credibility.

VIEW OF ANSBACH   This is how the town looked when Hauser was moved here by his protector, Lord Stanhope. Picture offers a view of the town's main churches, Gumpertuskirche and Johanniskirche, in the background.

pamphlets, books, and even poems about Kaspar and about everyone connected with him.

This tidal wave of paper continued to flow for years. When it had mercifully dried up in Germany, a few belated broadsides were fired in France and England. This literary torrent did nothing to clarify either Hauser's life or his death, but it almost succeeded in washing away the hard core of fact about this mysterious individual, burying the real evidence beneath soggy mud piles of spite, guesswork, and fabrication. According to some, Kaspar had been "teleported" to Nuremberg from another country. Some authors made him the creature of another planet. He was alleged to be the illegitimate son of virtually the entire Catholic Church hierarchy, from the Pope, down. He was supposed to have been the true heir to the throne of Bavaria, the bastard child of Lord Stanhope, the brother of the crown prince of Prussia, the outcast son of a Jewish girl by a gentile father.

The only contemporary volume to follow a logical pattern of in-

quiry was that compiled by Anselm von Feuerbach. Bearing the title
"Example of a Crime Against the Life of the Soul of a Man," the report
assumed that every word of Kaspar's story, as told by himself, was true.

Hauser, reasoned the old jurist, had to be a legitimate child, because no one would go to quite such lengths to hide an illegitimate
offspring.

Kaspar Hauser, insisted Feuerbach, had to be in line of succession
to a very high position, a position sufficiently exalted to induce the exertion of great power to effect his removal and confinement. Since, after a
certain period, his confinement was voluntarily brought to an end, it
follows that by then *someone else* then occupied the position formerly
usurped from Kaspar Hauser.

The only position, continued Feuerbach, sufficiently exalted to warrant such manipulations was a royal one. Ergo, Kaspar Hauser was of
royal blood.

Having reached this conclusion, Feuerbach cautiously refrained

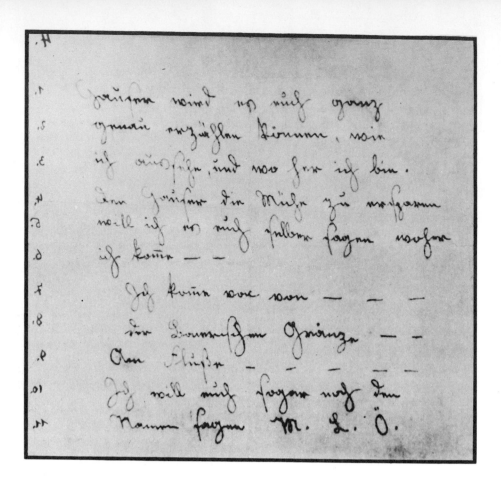

NOTE HAUSER RECEIVED FROM HIS ASSASSIN *For unfathomable reasons, the letter was penned in mirror writing. Even when deciphered, the letter yielded no clue to the motive of the attack. (The numbers on the side of the letter are museum marks, placed there by the curator to facilitate reference to any particular line.)*

from mentioning which particular crowned clan he had in mind. Libel of a crown was no laughing matter in 19th century courts.

But the sophisticated could fill in the gap without much difficulty. The only throne in question could be that occupied by the Grand Dukes of Baden. There all the heirs of the regular line had died in fairly rapid succession, some under highly suspicious circumstances. This left the road clear for the offspring of a morganatic marriage which the old Duke Karl Frederick, a widower, had contracted with an attractive 18-year-old commoner named Caroline Geyer. She, so the rumor went, had poisoned all the Duke's sons by his previous marriage, and by so doing had pushed her own progeny nearer to the throne. Kaspar Hauser, this delightfully gothic version went on, was a child of the regular line; he had been spared for sentimental reasons and merely had been tucked away in an underground cell until such time as he could be released without endangering the usurper. Then, when his appearance created more fuss than had been anticipated, the ducal clique had him eliminated by a hired assassin. This surmise had an added piquancy: Queen Caroline, consort of the reigning King Ludwig of Bavaria, was herself a former princess of the House of Baden, and she could thus be indirectly implicated in the mess.

The Grand Ducal administration reacted to the appearance of the book with monumental stupidity. They ordered the book banned in Baden, managed to have it suppressed in Bavaria, and pulled every string within reach to render the ban universal. Quite naturally, they failed; but they did succeed in giving the volume so much publicity that booksellers in the rest of Germany couldn't stock the title fast enough to meet the demand. In due course, Feuerbach's opus was translated into English, French, Italian and Hungarian. A concomitant result of the suppression was that the ducal clan of Baden was now widely accused of having poisoned old Feuerbach as well!

Amidst the general uproar, few contemporaries got around to casting a cool eye over Feuerbach's conclusions. Had they done so, they would have noticed that the entire structure of Feuerbach's thesis rested on very dubious premises. Those premises were the conflicts inherent in Kaspar Hauser's own accounts.

In compiling his records, Feuerbach, while carefully noting every word of Kaspar's story, had apparently ignored the testimony of the earliest witnesses of the affair. The cobbler Weichmann, for instance, related that after depositing the boy at the New Gate guardroom on his arrival in Nuremberg, he left him to find his own way to Captain Wessenig's house. Which, after being given verbal directions, Kaspar successfully did. But assuming that, according to his story, he had never been in a town before, and that his entire knowledge of language supposedly stemmed from a few phrases taught to him by his jailer, this feat seems, to say the least, improbable.

In the original description given of him by the policemen Wüst and Hiltel, he is said to have had a "gesunde Gesichtsfarbe," *a healthy complexion*. But anyone locked in a lightless room for 16 or so years would have the coloring of a corpse. Convicts become sickly pale within a couple of years, in spite of daily outdoor exercise as part of their routine.

The same police officials also noted that the soles of his feet were badly blistered and that he found walking both difficult and painful. If, however, he had been confined to a prone position since infancy, he would have found walking, not merely difficult, but impossible. And the crippling vitamin deficiency from living solely on bread and water would hardly have left him with enough strength to survive, let alone enough to ambulate.

Kaspar Hauser's original story, then, was open to rather more than considerable doubt. What about its aftermath?

We have Captain Hickel's testimony of seeing only Hauser's own footprints at the scene of his alleged attack. This leaves us with the question of whether Kaspar might have inflicted the death blow on himself, and why he should have done so.

Being ambidextrous, he would have found it easy to give himself a left-handed stab. But *why* is a more complex speculation.

MEMORIAL PILLAR   This monument marks the spot in the Hofgarten (the park adjoining Ansbach Castle) where Kaspar Hauser was fatally stabbed. The Latin inscription states: "On this place for mysterious reasons one mysterious figure was murdered by another mysterious figure."

HIC
OCCULTUS
OCCULTO
OCCISUS
EST
XIV DEC
MDCCCXXXII

KASPAR HAUSER'S GRAVE   *This highly sentimentalized poem is typical of the many writings which appeared throughout the German-speaking world commemorating, in one form or another, the life of the mysterious boy from nowhere. The theme of these verses is that a son was abandoned by his father and that the poor lad was the victim of a dastardly murder.*

Kaspar Hausers Grab
ZU ANSBACH.

r Höhe	Ihn hat — dem Tod verschworen	Doch nächtens ob der Klause
am Grab,	Nicht Weibesbrust gesäugt,	Da lucket sich das Moos,
d und Wehe	Keine Mutter ihn geboren,	Und von dem Bretterhause
...derstab?	Kein Vater ihn gezeugt.	Wird Band und Fuge los.
r Runde	Er fand am fremden Herde	Es weichen Brett und Riegel,
zen Raum	Verwaist das fremde Brod	Es hebet sich der Sand,
...wunde,	Und ach, auf fremder Erde	Und aus dem Grabeshügel
...enstraum!	Den unversöhnten Tod!	Huscht weißliches Gewand.
...hen Thurme	Die Hand, die ihn zum Hohne	Und um dieselbe Stunde
...yfer Ton?	Ins nackte Leben trug,	Steht vor dem Mörder schon
...t im Sturme	Weh, wenn sie selbst dem Sohne	Den Stahl in blutiger Wunde
...ohn!	Die Todeswunde schlug!	Der mordgefällne Sohn.
...Feste	Nun schwankt auf schwarzem Wagen	Und hebet auf die Falte
...es Thor,	Hinaus der schwarze Sarg,	Und lüftet das Gewand
...ze Gäste	Darein vor bangem Zagen	Und zeigt die Todesspalte
...ihm vor.	Der Gute sich verbarg.	Mit kalter Geisterhand.
...Erbe.	Es sinkt die finstre Truhe	Und schlingt die eisgen Glieder
...emdling, ein,	Hinab in tiefe Nacht,	Um ihn — der todte Gast:
...id, das herbe	Schlaf, Bester, schlaf in Ruhe,	„So kehr' ich nächtlich wieder,
...ngen seyn.	„Dein Gott, dein Rächer wacht!"	„Bis du gesühnet hast!"
...Schmerzen	Nun wechseln Tag und Stunden,	Und als das Bild verschwunden,
...blutge Mahl	Es rauschen Sturm und Wind,	Schließt sich des Grabes Schacht
...tillen Herzen	Und ruhig schläft da unten	Bis um die stillen Stunden
...Mordes Stahl.	Das elternlose Kind.	Der nächsten Mitternacht.

C. Scheuerlein

Nürnberg in der J. A. Endter'schen Kunsthandlung.

THE GRAVE OF KASPAR HAUSER   *Here is the final resting place of the boy from nowhere. The Latin inscription on the headstone in Ansbach Cemetery reads: "Hic jacet Casparus Hauser aenigma sui tempora ignota Nativitas occulta mors."*

Every person who knew him agreed that Kaspar thrived on attention and would produce some new and startling tidbit the moment the limelight threatened to veer in some other direction. After his move to Ansbach, he was decidedly out of the spotlight. Barring a fresh sensation, he had little hope of regaining the stage. A murderous assault on his person did create such a sensation. Was he himself the author of the attack?

In jabbing a knife into his side, Kaspar could have intended a reasonably slight wound. It was a cold day and his thrust had to pierce a thick overcoat, jacket, shirt, and undershirt; such a blow required considerable force. He was not wearing gloves, which meant his hands were cold, and therefore clumsy. He could easily have misgauged the power of that upward jerk.

But even if we accept this rationale, it leaves several points wide open. What, for instance, happened to the knife Kaspar used? No weapon of any sort was found in the park. Though a dagger was allegedly discovered after the snow had melted, there is no proof that it was the dagger which inflicted the wound.

Also, if Kaspar was really an impostor, he was surely the strangest ever recorded. He gained nothing from his fraud except a kind of livelihood and a great deal of notoriety. In return, he had to act a fantastically difficult role, year after year, observed by a partially hostile audience, and with nothing more enticing in view than the prospect of further years of playacting.

By now, the mystery of Kaspar Hauser has become merely an intellectual irritant, like an unsolved crossword puzzle in a newspaper which is slowly crumbling with age. But the inscription on the stone that marks his grave holds as true today as on the morning of his burial: "Here lies the Riddle of our Time. His Birth was Unknown; his Death, Mysterious."

The Eyeless Seers

There is a huge and qualitative difference between the astonishing and the inexplicable, between the marvelous and the miraculous. When Roger Bannister ran a mile in under four minutes—his remarkable athletic feat astounded the sports world; yet it is quite possible that in the far future some unborn athlete may sprint a mile in three minutes. Should this occur, it would be astonishing, though in no way inexplicable; the achievement would be based merely on the accentuation of known and normal human powers.

The matter becomes knottier when we deal with intellectual rather than physical faculties. Wolfgang Amadeus Mozart played the harpsichord at the age of three, wrote minuets at five, and composed a complete, technically valid symphony when he was eight. Still in his teens, he traveled to Rome to listen to the rendition of Gregorio Allegri's "Miserere" by the papal choir. This was a special piece of sacred music of which the only existing score lay in the vaults of the Vatican. The Pope had forbidden the performance of this particular composition anywhere except in Rome, and then only during Holy Week. Mozart heard the "Miserere" but once. Then he sat down and transcribed the entire lengthy and complex contrapuntal score from memory. The Pope was so staggered by this feat that he forgave the boy his breach of the ban, and presented the youngster with the Order of the Golden Spur. Now Mozart may have been the most remarkable genius in musical history, but his achievement stemmed entirely from faculties which—to a certain degree—are present in all of us. His powers, however astonishing, are comprehensible.

WOLFGANG AMADEUS MOZART   This engraving shows the musical genius at age seven.

The same estimate must be made of the Alabama Negro Tom Wiggins who, during the 1880s, toured America and Europe with a piano act that dumbfounded musicologists. Wiggins had been totally blind from birth, could neither read braille nor add the simplest sums, and had the vocabulary and expression range of a six-year-old. He had never seen a keyboard. Yet this prodigy was able to duplicate any given melody after hearing it once or, at the most, twice. This power not only applied to simple songs, but also to the most intricate fugues and concertos. Wiggins's skill went beyond the mere repetition of notes. After listening to the performance of a piano virtuoso, Wiggins could imitate that artist's personal style. He would follow subtle shades of expression, and he would exactly imitate the artist's manner of handling cadenzas. Wiggins, the son of a plantation slave girl, had never been given a piano lesson. He never expressed deep interest in music as such. He simply seemed capable of storing every note he heard in his brain, then finding those notes on an invisible keyboard, and then reproducing the music in the exact form in which he had heard it. Wiggins copied amateurish playing just as precisely as he duplicated excellence, and he gave no indication of being aware of any difference.

We have no name for this particular form of genius. The same fantastic auditory memory has more recently come to notice in a blind spastic English boy, one Jeffrey Janet, a resident of the London suburb of Ilford, who was born without eyesight, and without the use of his legs. Confined to a wheelchair, he spent most of his time listening to radio and television programs. Then, in 1960, he gave a series of memory demonstrations to newspaper men and medical boards that were barely credible. He could repeat—word by word and line by line—every feature that had been broadcast over the preceding three or four days. He included news bulletins, weather reports, documentaries, church sermons, full-length dramas, and comedy acts. He even reproduced the snatches of squeaky dialogue that accompanied the TV cartoons he couldn't see. He knew the exact hour each item had been on the air, its precise length in time, and the commercials, if any, that proceeded or followed each program.

Every generation seems to produce such a freak genius of one sort or another.

In 1934, the Polish government hired Dr. Salo Finkelstein to replace 40 trained men and 40 calculating machines in its treasury department. Finkelstein was able to perform like an electronic computer. Given a number like 3,108, he could—within seconds—reduce that number to the squares 52^2, 16^2, 12^2, and 2^2—a calculation that would take a mathematician at least four minutes to work out on paper.

Despite the wonder they aroused, no one credited the musical genius, nor the music mimic, nor the memory whiz, nor the prodigy mathematician with anything but natural powers. Among those of unusual talent, the person who achieved the greatest international fame undoubtedly was Erich Weiss of Appleton, Wisconsin, known all over the globe as Harry Houdini.

During a quarter of a century Houdini baffled millions of people and scores of scientists as well. He was billed as the "Wizard from Wisconsin," and America's home-grown Merlin was so far beyond the scope of a stage magician that a large segment of the population considered some of his feats to be supernatural. Protest as he would, some of the psychic glue stuck to his magician's cloak and could not be reasoned away; and occasional odd incidents increased its adhesive qualities.

SALO FINKELSTEIN   The Polish mathematical wizard is standing here in his suite in the Waldorf Astoria giving a demonstration. Here there is a column of 9 figures of 3 digits each which the lightning calculator added up in 13 seconds, beating the operator of the adding machine.

Before he reached world renown, Houdini went to London armed with a batch of certificates which had been signed by police chiefs of a number of American small towns, these documents attesting to his prowess as an escape artist. The magician presented these credentials to Dundas Slater, manager of the celebrated Alhambra Theatre, who remained noticeably unimpressed. After much palaver, Slater said to Houdini, "I'll make you a proposition. If you can get out of a pair of genuine Scotland Yard cuffs, I'll sign you." Houdini agreed. Together, they went to London's renowned police headquarters where Superintendent Melville listened to the request with much amusement. Without further ado, Melville produced a set of regular "darbies," pulled the American's arms around a pillar, snapped on the bracelets and sauntered to the door. "I'll be back for you in a couple of hours, old boy," he called over his shoulder.

"Wait a moment," said Houdini, "I'll come with you." There was a faint click, then a clatter, and Houdini stooped to pick up the steel bonds which had dropped to the floor. Then he gravely handed them back to the dumbfounded official, saying: "You forgot your handcuffs, sir."

Houdini had pulled the same trick dozens of times in the United States, only to have the stunt nullified to a large extent by the belief of an appreciable number of cynics and skeptics who alleged that the cops were in on it. But Scotland Yard, by Jove, was a different matter. The British would sooner have assumed Houdini to be in cahoots with the king than with the Yard. Every London newspaper ran the story, splashing Houdini's self-styled title, "The Handcuff King," under his picture. For months thereafter, Houdini packed the Alhambra. When he departed for Germany he left behind a city of fanatical fans. However, this was merely a start. Houdini's real triumphs began across the Channel. Paradoxically, the rigid controls imposed upon the German stage by a hawk-eyed and indefatigable *polizei* worked entirely in his favor. In the Kaiser's realm, the authorities made sure that all vaudeville performers lived up to their claims. Cannon balls were checked for weight, balancing utensils were checked for hidden wires, and ropes and chains were checked for strength. The German police regulations thus saved Houdini the trouble of having to prove the quality of his bonds.

The same type of pettifogging ordinances took good care of his publicity, too. The American had worked out a new stunt for the occasion. He was to be handcuffed and pushed into a river or lake. He declared that he would free himself under water and then come to the surface waving the discarded chains. Excellent—except that in every German city it was strictly forbidden to push anyone into any water, handcuffed or otherwise. The ban didn't stop the performance, but it insured that in each town he visited, Houdini was holding it before a magistrate, solemnly fined one mark, and subsequently featured in the local press, which otherwise might have ignored his stunt. The same drama was enacted in 11 different towns, Houdini forking out one mark in each case, and raking in a thousand times that amount in free advertising. The sole variation occurred in Dresden where the fine was doubled, one mark for being pushed into a pond, another for having stepped on the surrounding lawn. Meanwhile, Houdini's stage performances left his audiences gasping. And this, in spite of the fact that he had not yet developed the really spectacular feats of his later career. His success was largely due to the absolute faith of the Germans in their efficiency and in the efficiency of their restraining equipment, and their profound shock at seeing these iron bonds and chains treated as if they were bits of parcel string.

In Essen, engineers of the Krupp works devised a special set of chains for his benefit. Equipped with a brand-new triple lock, the two inventors, in person, fastened the chains on Houdini's wrists. All Germans were agreed that no man who ever lived could break these all-powerful bonds. But only three and one-half minutes later—timed by a stop watch—the American handed the open cuffs back to their inventors with a polite *danke schoen.*

In Cologne, the American's performance was so astounding that it seemed utterly beyond belief, so much so that a member of the local constabulary named Werner Graff was minded to insert a notice in the local press branding Houdini as a charlatan, and his entire act as "unmitigated and brazen fraud." The magician brought suit against the police officer for libel, and joined in the action the entire Cologne police force for good measure. When the American appeared before the lower court, he informed the judge that he was prepared to substantiate on the spot any and every claim made on his publicity posters. Accordingly, the judge invited the defendants to do their damndest, and the police force went at things with a vengeance. They loaded Houdini with chains, around his wrists, his elbows, his ankles, and even around his neck—fired by the quite erroneous belief that the more metal the magician was weighed with, the harder would be his getaway. If the jurors had expected a dramatic struggle, they were destined to be disappointed. All they saw were a few twists of Houdini's body, a jerking of his arms and legs, too fast to be followed. They saw nary a lock open, but merely heard clicks, followed by the rattling of chains dropping on the polished courtroom floor. The entire procedure took less than two minutes. Houdini stood up free, and the verdict was but a formality.

Graff and company appealed the case to the higher court. Before that tribunal, the defendants produced a contraption especially made for the occasion. It was a lock, they explained, which could not even be opened with its own key once the lock had been snapped shut. Houdini asked permission to retire to a prisoner's cell in the basement. A few minutes later he emerged with the open lock dangling jauntily from his index fingers. Again, the verdict went to the American. But the Cologne police, nothing if not persevering, felt they hadn't yet made big enough fools of themselves. They dragged the case into the Prussian Supreme Court. This time, they introduced a new test. Houdini, their

HOUDINI BEFORE A GERMAN COURT   *The caption on this artist's drawing of Houdini's trial in Germany in 1902, states in part: "The Imperial Police of Cologne slanderously libeled* HARRY HOUDINI, *stating his advertised tricks were swindles!* HOUDINI *answered them by sueing for 'An Honorary Public Apology.' The Police lost the case in the three highest Courts, as they were unable to fetter or chain* HOUDINI *in an unescapable manner. . . . Having lost the case in all three trials the Police were ultimately compelled to publicly advertise 'An Honorary Apology' and pay all costs of the trials."*

plea now ran, had claimed to be able to open safes as well as locks; yet he hadn't opened a single safe in Germany. Ergo, he had not substantiated his claims. The red-robed, white-bearded judge gravely considered this defense. Then he announced: "I think we can test this matter immediately. I happen to have a very powerful strongbox in my chambers, so if Herr Houdini would oblige us . . ." Though the defendants didn't realize it, at that moment they had the plaintiff very worried indeed. Houdini could handle any American safe, but he had never had experience with a German safe. Yet there was no backing out for him now. He could merely ask permission to be left alone with the strongbox, hoping to discover its secret. The judge led him into his chambers and withdrew. Houdini stood facing a massive steel cube whose workings, he knew, were quite different from the trans-Atlantic breed. Tentatively, he tried the handle—whereupon the door swung open. The judge had forgotten to lock it!

Just for drama, he waited a few minutes before strolling back into court ostentatiously wiping his fingers with his handkerchief. There was no appeal from this final verdict, which forced the Cologne police to eat humble pie on the front pages of 41 German dailies, an act of mastication that echoed far beyond the borders of the Fatherland. The following day, Houdini was the most famous and popular performer on the European stage. From an average income of $75 a week, his salary skyrocketed to ten-fold that amount. When he returned to the United States, the great Houdini legend was beginning to take shape.

The alleged endowment of occult powers later became the bane of his life. An artist of outsized vanity, Houdini took inordinate pride in his physical skill and courage, and seethed with rage whenever his achievements were attributed to anything else, for he only claimed to be a magnificent trickster.

Nevertheless, some of his stunts seemed quite miraculous. His most famous *tour de force* was performed under the title of "The Man who Walks through Walls." For this act, a wall was erected on stage—was actually built in front of the audience with brick and mortar by volunteer bricklayers from a local union. The wall rose sideways to the auditorium, so that the audience could always see both sides of the wall. Built on top

HOUDINI IN RUSSIA   In 1903, Houdini was challenged to escape from a steel-lined Siberian prison van. His successful negotiation of this feat became an international sensation. In this artist's drawing, Houdini is about to be incarcerated in the van by Russian officials. The caption reads: "Chief of the Secret Russian Police LEBEDOEFF has HARRY HOUDINI stripped stark naked and searched, then locked up in the Siberian Transport Cell or Carette, May 10, 1903 in Moscow and in 28 minutes HOUDINI had made his escape to the unspeakable astonishment of the Russian Police."

of a carpet, the construction was inspected by a committee of prominent citizens. The solid carpet which covered the floor ruled out the use of a trapdoor. The end of the wall stood flush against, and at right angles to, a solid metal sheet which was likewise inspected by the committee. The arrangements were all made in full sight of the audience.

After the wall was built, the committee positioned itself on one side of the wall. Houdini stood on the other side. Folding screens were then put up, shielding the magician and the wall from observation. Houdini,

HOUDINI IN CHAINS   *A typical set of fetters, locks, and chains with which Houdini was bound by police officials. Note the iron collar around his neck fastened to a rubber tire, which in turn is fastened to another rubber tire to hold his feet rigid.*

obviously standing near one of the walls, and obviously within the screens, waved his hands above one of the screens, calling out to the audience, "Here I am!" Then his hands disappeared, as his voice rang out, "Here I go!" A moment later, his hands appeared again. But now they were above the screen on *the other side* of the wall. The screens were removed, and there was Houdini. Apparently, he had passed through the wall. Again, the committee examined the wall, the carpet, and the metal sheet. All were intact. How did he do it?

Among the multitudes who found this trick convincing proof of Houdini's paranormal capabilities was Sir Arthur Conan Doyle. For while the creator of Sherlock Holmes was an inspired novelist, he was quite gullible when it came to psychic matters. Sir Arthur drove the magician frantic by proclaiming in print that Houdini dematerialized himself and that the magician was wafted through the bricks in ghost-like fashion. Spiritualist publications throughout the world enthusiastically embraced this theory and never tired of citing Houdini as a living example of disembodiment.

Poor Houdini! He couldn't afford to reveal the secret of his top act, so a secret it remained until his death when his notebooks revealed the ruse. There was a large trapdoor underneath the carpet. The moment the screens were put up, this trapdoor was swung open. When the trapdoor opened, the carpet under the wall sagged ever so slightly—so slightly that even a child couldn't have squirmed through the resultant space. But Houdini could! When he had wriggled through, the trapdoor swung shut, leaving the carpet as solid-looking and as taut as it had been before.

Another stage classic of the master was even more difficult and certainly more dangerous. The "Water Torture Cell" consisted of a glass cage filled to the top with water. The magician's feet were locked in an iron grill. He was then lowered—head down—into the water, and the grill was then locked to the top of the glass cage. A screen was then placed in front of the tank and remained there for perhaps 30 seconds. Presumably, Houdini had been incarcerated in a watery cage—feet up—head down and unable to move. But when the screen was removed, the audience saw Houdini standing beside the cage, dripping wet but smiling. *The water was still in the tank, and the grill was fastened to the frame as tightly as before!*

In performing this trick, Houdini always took the risk of drowning. The framework of the tank was constructed of thin iron bars, and a crosspiece vise of iron inside the tank was visible at the top of the frame. To this piece, Houdini's legs had been locked. The incredible man used this bar to lever himself upward. While bent double, he sprung the padlock on the grill and thus released his feet. Then he hoisted himself out of the tank, snapped the lock back into place, and then jumped down. It was a feat of fantastic dexterity, which no one in his day could fathom.

Houdini's power over locks certainly seemed magical, but behind that skill lay 20 years spent in studying, designing, and making locks. His fingertip sensitivity enabled him to manipulate locks in utter darkness. He had also invented a tiny pick that he could secret in his mouth, or in his rectum, or between his fingers.

During a career of 25 years, Houdini would regale the citizens of America's larger cities with what became a standard performance. He would announce that handcuffed, shackled, and bound, he was going to jump off the local bridge into a lake or river. Townfolks would gather at river banks or seashores to watch Houdini being nailed into a barrel, or into a coffin, or into a packing case. The box was then hurled into the water. The outcome never varied. Within a minute after the container had sunk to the bottom, Houdini bobbed up at the surface. The container would be fished out, and found to be absolutely intact, the nails still firmly in the wood. All the shackles—sometimes half a dozen of them—would be lying inside the box. The vital point in performing this stunt—a point the public never realized—was the elaborate nailing-down procedure of the lid. Houdini's assistants used many more nails than were necessary. The time involved to do all this nailing gave Houdini,

THE WORLD FAMOUS SELF-LIBERATOR

HOUDINI,

Presenting the Greatest Performance of his Strenuous Career, liberating himself after being Locked in a

WATER TORTURE CELL

(Houdini's own Invention) whilst Standing on his Head, his Ankles Clamped and Locked above in the centre of the Massive Cover.

A FEAT WHICH BORDERS ON THE SUPERNATURAL

$1,000

HOUDINI offers this sum to any one proving that it is possible to obtain air in the upside-down position in which he releases himself from this

Water   Filled   Torture   Cell.

HOUDINI POSTER   The master magician publicizes his "Water Torture Cell" stunt by offering $1,000 to anyone who can prove that it is possible to obtain air in the water-filled compartment in which he will be locked.

DUMPED OVERBOARD   *Houdini is being submerged in a securely*
nailed box.

inside the box, ample time to get loose of his bonds. When the case hit
the water, he was already free.

Every container that Houdini used was built with a trick panel or
barrel stave which pivoted inward when pressed a certain way. Houdini
would wriggle out of the small aperture, then slam the panel back into
position, and strike for the surface. At the subsequent inspection, public
attention was always focused on the lid of the box, which of course,
remained firmly in place.

Though performed again and again, his water stunts were extremely
dangerous. In case of a hitch—and hitches did occur—nothing could save
him but his extraordinarily coolheadedness. He never panicked. As he
once put it:

> *Everything depends on preserving an absolute serenity of
> spirit; fear is fatal. The public have no conception of the tor-
> tuous preliminary self-training that was necessary to conquer
> fear.*

One of his aquatic exploits led to the somewhat premature announcement of his demise. In December 1906, he undertook to be pushed

handcuffed from the parapet of Belle Isle Bridge into the frozen Detroit River. A large hole was hacked into the ice. With no packing case to shield his body, and the temperature of the water about 36 degrees, this loomed as a nonpareil exhibition, and the public thronged to see the daredevil perform.

At 11 a.m., the bridge was jammed with Detroiters who watched shivering while the wizard stripped to his bathing trunks. A police officer fastened the regulation bracelets on Houdini, who standing almost naked in the wintry gale, gave the reporters a blue-lipped grin. Then one of his assistants shoved him off the rail. He landed in the hole, and disappeared into the black water.

Three minutes—four minutes—five minutes passed. No Houdini! The crowd had fallen silent. His assistants, clearly worried, looked at each other. When six minutes had ticked by, the reporters raced off, each trying to beat the other to their newspapers with the story of Houdini's death.

Two minutes later—a head suddenly appeared in the hole. A tremendous cheer burst from the crowd on the bridge. Houdini minus the handcuffs, was helped ashore; but he was manifestly in the last stages of exhaustion. He had been under the ice for eight minutes!

After his ordeal, he was made to lie down and rest. In the meantime, Mrs. Houdini suffered the worst shock of her life. For in the street outside her hotel window, newsboys were bawling: "Special bulletin! Houdini drowned in river! Extree! Houdini dead!" By the time she had sent someone out to buy a paper, her husband arrived back home with the story of his narrow escape. Only his wife and a few close friends learned what had actually happened during that awful experience.

Houdini had not reckoned with the strong current underneath the ice. In the few seconds it took him to slip out of the manacles, he had been swept a considerable distance away from the hole; and so, when after releasing himself from his handcuffs he swam to the surface of the river, he found a solid sheet of ice above his head.

This was a moment when panic would have meant death. Houdini swam a few strokes further, found no sign of an opening, and did some fast thinking. He calculated that there might be a little air space just

HOUDINI IN NEW YORK HARBOR　　*In 1914, the magician is about to*
be submerged in a tightly nailed box.

under the surface of the ice. So instead of bumping the ice with his head,
he cautiously held up his nose to the ice. His surmise turned out to be
right: there was perhaps half an inch of air beneath the ice sheet. Floating on his back and inhaling very slowly and carefully, he filled his lungs.

HOUDINI POSTER   *This English poster is typical of the publicity material used to advertise Houdini appearances.*

Then he set about to locate the hole. It took him close to eight minutes under the ice to find it.

It was Houdini's fantastic breath control which had saved his life. He had practiced his exercise in breath control in a cold bath, timing himself with a stop watch, adding a few seconds at a time. His public record was four minutes, 16 seconds under water, but he insisted that he had privately achieved four and a half minutes.

After the Detroit episode, nothing Houdini could say would convince people that he was a normal man with an ordinary pair of lungs. Even the highly intelligent Sarah Bernhardt fell for the persistent fable. She met Houdini during her 1917 tour of the United States, shortly after she had lost one of her legs. The "Divine Sarah" seized hold of the magician's hands and, with tears welling in her beautiful eyes, pleaded: "You will use your powers to restore my limb to me, won't you, monsieur?"

In his autobiography, Houdini related that details of his fanatical self-training in body control. One of his earliest exercises, performed at the age of nine in the family woodshed, was to pick pins off the floor with his eyelashes, while hanging upside down by his knees. By the time he reached his late teens, he could slacken or tighten parts of his skin at will, thread needles and shuffle cards with his toes, slip his arms and legs out of joint, and snap them back into place as if they were puppets on a string. He could use his fingers like monkey-wrenches, his teeth like can openers, and his sphincter like a vise. He could flex every muscle of his body more or less like other men flex their biceps; his strength was great enough to literally bend iron bars, burst oaken planks, tear heavy canvas, and pry two-inch screws out of wood. His tactile sensibility was fantastic; he could, while blindfolded, tell the exact number of toothpicks he was kneeling on, and he could count the strands of a tightly twisted rope with his toes.

To execute his handcuff escapes, Houdini had his special picklock hidden on his person, sometimes fastened to the sole of his foot with surgeon's cement, sometimes inserted rectally, sometimes clamped between his fingers as he held his arms extended while being searched. Before all his exploits, he was always searched; frequently, by highly practiced police officers; occasionally, by medical men; but no one ever discovered the gadget. The real wonder, however, lay in his ability to use this pick while fastened with as many as six sets of manacles. This was something he never revealed, not even in his private notes. He merely indicated that he was able to use his toes as fingers and, in a pinch, could spring a lock with his teeth. Most of his escapes were performed in darkness or behind some sort of covering. When he worked directly in front of an audience, he twisted his body in such a way so as to cover the particular lock he was working on.

He could manage his straitjacket escapes without the use of tools, and he left a detailed description of his method for anyone who might

HOUDINI STUNT   Harry Houdini is encased by policemen in a strait-jacket and hauled up on a scaffold, head down. A few minutes later, in full view of the policemen, he will wriggle himself free.

care to try it. But the feat requires a physical dexterity far beyond the capacity of most athletes. Some of his exploits may well be inimitable, but since he has explained his procedures, these exploits are comprehensible—at least to anyone except the psychically brainwashed. Houdini baffled, but he himself does not constitute a bafflement.

✧   ✧   ✧

In January 1960, NBC ran a television program entitled *People Are Funny*. On one occasion, the program starred an engaging little teenager from Virginia named Margaret Foos. Miss Foos's claim to fame was that she could see while tightly blindfolded.

At the beginning of her performance, two thick wads of cotton-wool were placed over Margaret's eyes and held in place by yards of bandages. Then she read, haltingly, a passage from a book. Warming up and becoming more fluent as she went on, she proceeded to read snatches from magazines and newspapers picked at random by members of the audience. She identified the colors of various posters held several feet away from her, and she described gestures made by people at a distance. Finally, she played a game of checkers.

Her father, who was her business manager, insisted that his daughter's extraordinary gift was something akin to a special athletic knack which he had carefully nurtured and sharpened until it developed into a sixth sense.

The professional magicians who watched the performance said that Miss Foos's repertoire was nothing but an ancient music hall act, usually dubbed "The Lady With X-ray Eyes." The young girl's skill lay only in her ability to peer down her nose where the blindfold did not fit snugly. Miss Foos's talent lay in her being able to do this without a noticeable lowering of her head.

Yet there may be cases of authentic eyeless sight—or at least cases for which no plausible explanation has been offered. The first reasonably authenticated instance of this kind was reported from Graz, Austria, in 1872. One Alois Burgel, son of a local coppersmith, blinded during a fire in his father's workshop at the age of nine, was alleged to have developed such a sixth sense. His blindness seems to have derived from hysterical rather than physical causes, for 11 years later, the young man recovered his sight as suddenly as he had lost it. During his years of darkness, Alois had become an expert basket weaver.

Alois was taken to a Dr. Grohweiler for a check-up. Several days after the lad had regained his sight, Dr. Grohweiler, while testing him, found that his patient could "see" or perceive nearby objects while blindfolded. There was no question of making Alois read anything, since the young man had never learned to read or write. But with his eyes bandaged, Alois could call out the number of fingers the doctor held out, name the colors of various ribbons, and describe the pictures on a deck of cards, though he could not identify the cards by their names. The knack was curiously inconsistent. To quote Grohweiler:

> Sometimes the patient had no difficulty discerning and describing a vase of flowers placed at the opposite end of the room. At other times I had to let him touch a picture with his fingertips before he was able to make out its subject.
>
> I experimented with various blindfolds; trying in turn surgical bandages, velvet cloth and folded silken handkerchiefs, but found that this made no difference to his ability. The deciding factor seemed to be his power to concentrate. On days when his concentration was weakened, his 'vision' dimmed.
>
> In spite of my constant questions, he was not able to tell me by what means he saw through the blindfold; being a simple man, he lacked range of expression. I could not, for instance, discover why he occasionally had to touch objects while yet being able to recognize others at considerable distance. Throughout the experiments we were handicapped by his limited vocabulary. There were also hazy spots in his memory. He appeared to have no recollection of the fire that had caused his blindness . . . .

Dr. Grohweiler wrote an account of his experiments for a Viennese medical journal, but the article did not attract much attention. In December 1872, he demonstrated his remarkable patient to a private gathering of colleagues in Graz. Quizzed by the doctors, Burgel offered the same witless and frustrating explanation he had repeated all along: "I see it before my eyes."

The following year, Burgel fell sick with consumption and died. Very little is known about Dr. Grohweiler's qualifications either as a physician or as an observer, and his tests appear to have been somewhat haphazard.

The next report came from one of the then celebrated Italian physicians, Cesare Lombroso, who flourished in the later part of the 19th century. Lombroso also dealt with a case of hysterical blindness, but his particular patient remained blind. Although her eyes failed to react to flashing lights and other irritants, she could read a book if it was held at a certain angle in front of her face. In order to rule out trickery, Lombroso bandaged the eyes of the blind girl, and then held up objects at various angles and asked her to identify them. She correctly named colors, described pictures, and read a letter. According to Lombroso, the girl saw with her *nose*. It says a lot for the doctor's courage that he included this case in one of his books. He made no attempt, however, to explain how his patient operated, nor did he detail the exact nature of the blindfold he had used.

CESARE LOMBROSO Italian physician who made notable observations on hysterical blindness.

Lombroso had achieved eminence in abnormal psychology through the publication of a tome entitled *The Criminal,* a work which wielded enormous influence over the police procedures of his time, but has no standing today. According to the learned doctor, criminals of every ilk form a distinct anthropological type, recognizable, with the aid of a pair of calipers, by the shape of their skulls and the dimensions of their jawbones. Other distinguishing marks of inherent villainy are: a receding forehead, over-developed frontal sinuses, prominent eyebrows, large quantities of body hair, and what Lombroso chose to call "a wild look." All these characteristics undoubtedly fitted some criminals; they also happened to fit Michelangelo and Abraham Lincoln. The Lombrosian system of equating certain physical patterns with anti-social tendencies was so patently absurd that most of the doctor's other observations were thrown overboard along with it. This may have been a loss to science, for in many respects Lombroso proved himself to be a remarkably astute analyst. But his report about eyeless sight attracted scant attention.

Much the same fate befell two other doctors who also claimed to have discovered a sixth sense in their patients. In 1923, the Frenchman Jules Romains published a book under the title of *Eyeless Sight* in which he related a series of tests, stretching over several years, conducted with both physically blind and artificially blindfolded men and women. Although none of his subjects were able to read while blindfolded, he found that a number of them were able to distinguish forms, colors, and movements while demonstrably incapable of using their eyes. He came to the conclusion that microscopic rudimentary organs of vision are present everywhere on the body in cells of the skin, and that some people have the ability of actually seeing with these cells, a theory which the medical profession did not accept then, and does not accept now.

In the 1930s, Dr. Manuel Chaves of Sao Paulo, Brazil, arrived at an almost identical conclusion. After testing some 400 patients, all of them blind, Dr. Chaves concluded that about a dozen of his subjects, either children or teenagers, appeared to have the gift of "skin vision." Of these, only three were able to distinguish actual color shadings, though others could tell whether something was light or dark. Chaves made no attempt to train and possibly strengthen this "other sight," as he called it. Had he

JULES ROMAINS   French author and scientist whose experiments with eyeless sight, though dismissed as "hopelessly unscientific" by most of the medical profession, found a measure of acceptance among some intellectuals of the day, including Anatole France.

done so, there is no telling what some of his more gifted subjects might have accomplished. But even so, his findings were startling. Youngsters who did not have the use of their eyes could distinguish red from green, and even name horizontal bands of pastel shades. The pupils of the eyes of these subjects did not change size when exposed to a concentrated light—a condition no one can fake. The conclusion of the Brazilian was the same as that of the Frenchman: his patients saw with other parts of their body.

Both Romains and Chaves found the performance of their subjects maddeningly erratic. The same teenager who one afternoon could fluently call out an entire color chart would fail to distinguish black from white the next morning. Cold, heat, noise or any slight illness might reduce vision to the vanishing point. None of the girls were capable of seeing during her menstrual period. All performed badly in the presence of strangers. On the few occasions that Chaves demonstrated his charges to other physicians, his patients fell lamentably short of their best, even though the doctors remained quietly in the background. The sum total of their alleged sight was unimpressive.

Neither Romains nor Chaves believed in clairvoyance; both were convinced that their patients saw by purely physical means. But neither could lucidly explain to the satisfaction of the medical world just how such sight was accomplished.

Today, the greatest living exponent of eyeless sight is the Pakistani Kuda Bux, who becomes hopelessly vague when trying to account for his accomplishment. "All I know is that it depends entirely on an inner faculty of the mind," he says. "I see with the mind's eye—with my intense concentrative powers."

Kuda Bux who was born in Kashmir, is now 62 years old, and still gives occasional demonstrations in the United States. However, his most spectacular triumphs took place in the pre-TV era.

In London, in 1934, he gave a display of his powers to one of the most distinguished medical panels ever assembled for such a purpose. The group included the superintendent of the Bethlehem Royal Hospital, and Edward Andrade, professor of physics at London University. The first task of the group was to devise a blindfold impenetrable enough to satisfy them as to perfect opacity. They began by placing lumps of dough over his eyes, and then followed with metal foil. Then came a wool bandage, and finally, multiple layers of gauze.

Professor Andrade was about to place a book before Kuda Bùx, when one of his colleagues stopped him. "Just a moment," he said. "Let's eliminate the possibility of telepathy in this case. I suggest we select books that none of us have read." So they sent to a bookstore for some titles none of them had read.

The books were put on a table in front of Kuda Bux. The Muslim held his hands over one of the volumes—rather like bestowing a blessing on the print—and then started to read aloud. He read fluently, with a slight sing-song accent, until he was halfway down the page. Then Professor Andrade switched the books, opening another at random. The interruption hardly broke the bandaged man's stride. He kept on reading in the same melodious voice that had the flavor of a prayer recital, page after page, regardless of how often the panel members exchanged the books.

Mr. Bux asserts that some years back, in Hull, England, he permitted a physician to drop atropine into his eyes. The effect of this drug is to temporarily blur one's vision. He claims he was tested while under the influence of the drug, and that he was able to read small print at that time while heavily blindfolded. Any peeking would be of inconsequen-

BLINDFOLDING KUDA BUX   *This photograph taken in 1936 in Manchester, England, shows a local doctor placing heavy wads of dough and cotton wool over the eyes of the "Eyeless Seer," prior to affixing the complete bandage.*

tial service while the eyes were under the influence of atropine. Upon another occasion, a doctor insisted on putting a film of collodion over his eyes to make sure that he could not see. This treatment, too, did not inhibit his ability, he says, to peer, so to speak through a blindfold.

The fact is that Kuda Bux has undergone innumerable tests throughout a long career. A typical report is that to be found in the Montreal
Daily Star of February 14, 1938:

> *The doctors who presided at the examination were not sat-*
> *isfied with ordinary bandages. They decided to apply a paste of*
> *flour to his eyes. One of the doctors mixed the dough and*
> *applied a large lump to each eye. On top of this, a large pad of*
> *cotton wool was added and forced down tight around the nos-*
> *trils. Tape was applied to stick the pad tight around the eyes,*
> *and further, doubly assure that all eyesight was obstructed.*
> *Then cotton gauze—26 feet of it—was wound mummy-fashion*
> *around the head. Over the bandages, dough, and cotton pad, a*
> *further thick cotton pad was added. Then one of the reporters*
> *present produced a scarf and wound it around and around. Fi-*
> *nally, half a dozen napkins were wound around and around the*
> *Mohammedan's head. Kuda was then led into another room*
> *quite alone. The most distinguished medico present introduced*
> *an envelope. Kuda read it without trouble. A reporter flashed*
> *a reporter's pass, and Bux quickly read out the words, 'Lesser-*
> *Passer.'*

If Kuda Bux impressed the scientists, he most certainly stunned the
public. Among his many talents was a flair for publicity that would have
done credit to a Madison Avenue exec. On the afternoon of his first show
in Manchester, accompanied by several newspaper reporters, he strode
into a local hospital and asked one of the doctors to blindfold him, "But
please, as thoroughly as you can, sir." While the reporters watched, the
doctor obliged, beginning with dough plasters, over which were placed
thick pads of cotton-wool. Then the physician used *three* rolls of bandages to wrap up, not merely the man's eyes, but his entire head—carefully pinning down the ends.

"Are you sure he can't see?" asked one of the reporters.

"Absolutely!" said the doctor. "I guarantee you that he can't see a
thing."

Kuda Bux bowed politely. "Thank you very much, doctor. I am most obliged to you."

Whereupon the Pakistani left the room and walked with unfaltering steps down the hospital corridor, mounted a bicycle and pedalled away, weaving carefully through the afternoon traffic, giving all the obligatory hand signals laid down by the British Highway Code. On his bike were two signs which read:

KUDA BUX, THE MAN WHO SEES WITHOUT EYES

TONIGHT, SEVEN-THIRTY, AT THE HIPPODROME

That afternoon, Kuda Bux pedalled through the Manchester traffic without accident, steering as effectively as if he could see everything in front of him.

On September 11, 1937, the Pakistani gave a hair-raising demonstration in Liverpool, England. Atop a building some 200 feet high, Mr. Bux, fully blindfolded, walked along a very narrow ledge on the edge of the roof, a perilous perambulation which would have made almost any man quail, even if he had the full use of his eyes. Any slight misstep could have meant a plunge to death.

In 1938, Bux came to the United States upon the invitation of Robert Ripley of *Believe-It-or-Not* fame, who invited the Pakistani to give an exhibition of firewalking. A huge pit of burning charcoal was constructed in Rockefeller Plaza. The newspaper reporters estimated that the heat was 1,400 degrees. Bux walked only half-way across the pit before he quit, but he had been exposed to the searing heat long enough to have been fatally burned. Before his ordeal, he had been examined by doctors who confirmed that no application of protective chemicals protected his feet. A subsequent examination revealed that save for a few small blisters, no damage had been suffered.

When asked about his firewalking exploit, Bux says, "Courage and faith, that's all it is. Faith within yourself. There are no chemicals, no trickery. You can't create trickery with fire. Firewalking has been done in Ceylon, in Burma, and in some of the Polynesian islands. There they walk across heated hearthstones; I walk across burning charcoal," thus

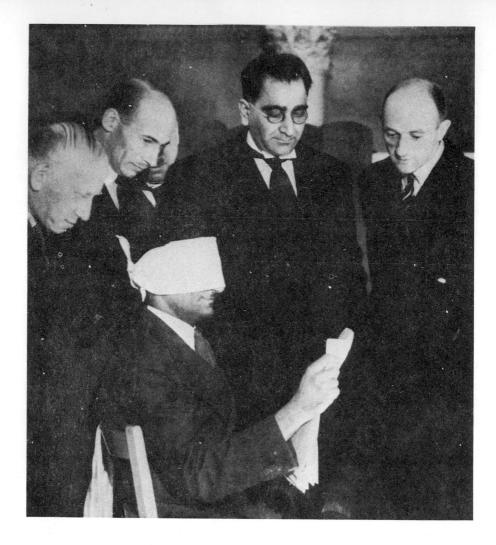

A DEMONSTRATION OF EYELESS SIGHT   *Here is Kuda Bux in a department store in Manchester. His audience includes a number of medical men.*

implying that his exploit had exposed him to greater danger than other
firewalkers.

Kuda Bux claims that his art is self-taught, and that it took him 11
years to master it. Moreover, he alleges that "anybody can develop it."
After a spell with an Indian magician, he worked for a while as a bit-

player in a traveling theater group. During this period of his career, he met a guru in Hardawar who agreed to instruct him in mental concentration. He learned how to concentrate on one thing and one thing only. Bux claims he can empty his mind of all thoughts, until nothing exists except the one object he is concentrating on. This is a staggeringly difficult task, since random ideas and images pass through the mind in uninterrupted flow. Controlling the stream of consciousness, stopping it at one specific item for even a few seconds, is beyond the powers of most people. To do so for a full minute is a feat learnt only through mental drill. Kuda Bux chose the face of his brother as his focus. He says that after two and a half years of practice he could hold that image completely for a full minute—timed by stop watch. This was but a preliminary discipline for his later powers of concentration, for according to him, eyeless sight is entirely a matter of concentration, requiring the exercise of supreme will to visualize what the eye cannot actually see.

After receiving basic instruction from the Hardawar guru, Kuda Bux worked on concentration by himself. He performed conjuring tricks for a living, but he practiced concentration at night.

Kuda Bux relates that he had heard of the ability of some yogis to see objects with their eyes closed. He set out to acquire that power. Each night, after visualizing his brother's face, he would impress certain items of his room in his mind, then blindfold himself and try to retain the vision. In due course, he established a link between his mind and whatever objects stood before him—a link unconnected with his eyesight. He could, in other words, make out things he was physically unable to see. He practiced with furniture, with pictures, with maps, with flowers, finally, with printed words. After more than ten years of blindfold practice, he says that he became capable of reading books.

He rejects the term X-ray vision, which is a phrase which he privately confides he uses only to dramatize his ability. "X-ray vision would imply that I can see *through* my blindfold. But I cannot see through anything; I see with something else than my eyes. I see with the mind's eye."

Some skeptics hold to the opinion that Kuda Bux has perfected some unique method whereby he alone can penetrate even a blindfold fitted by skilled medical hands. These cynical observers point to a long tradition of trickery in this field. They recall that many an Indian street magician would claim that he could see through a black velvet sack. Any member of the audience could pull the sack over his own head and convince himself that the sack was absolutely opaque and couldn't be seen through. Then the magician would take the same sack, put it over his own head, and distinguish anything held up before him. For the sack contained a thick inner lining which was only partially sewn to the outer cloth. When a spectator tried the sack, he naturally pulled it straight over his head. When the magician handled the sack, he inserted his face between the two layers of cloth and saw through the quite transparent velvet. One would think that such a ludicrously primitive piece of chicanery would have been easily discovered. But the fact is that this trick was accounted as one of India's supreme mysteries for a couple of centuries, and that it fooled European researchers and police officers as neatly as it baffled the crowds in the bazaar.

Skeptics point out that the feats of Kuda Bux may trick us in some such manner. They insist that neither slabs of dough nor yards of bandages can prevent a really dextrous performer from peeping. This type of blindfold works, they assert, on the curiously inverse principle that the more bandages that are applied, the easier the cheating. Dough plasters alone would be much more effective than the whole rigamarole of dough, tinfoil, and bandages. For dough will adhere to fabric stronger than it will to skin. While the performer is being blindfolded, he presses his fingers against his eyes, causing the dough to stick to the elastic cloth. When he takes his hands away, the dough pads are lifted from his eye sockets. Then he adjusts the bandages ever so slightly where they encircle his nostrils, a gesture that appears to be natural, as if the fabric wound over his face has hampered his breathing and made him a wee bit uncomfortable. In reality, he has shifted the inner layer of bandages from his eyes, and pushed these bandages and the dough clinging to them just high enough to peer out underneath the coverings. To all purposes, he is seemingly as securely blindfolded as before, but the outer layers of gauze act as a screen for what has happened underneath. It is fairly easy to peer through three or even four layers of surgical gauze, which is all that is likely to be in front of a small portion of his eyes. The rest of

KUDA BUX IN NEW YORK   In 1945, the Pakistani rode a bicycle through the heavy traffic of Times Square while blindfolded, and of course, attracted hordes of onlookers.

the swaddling merely covers his face and this looks as impressive as it is ineffectual.

In refutation of this theory, it should be pointed out that peeking is always done by peering *downward*. If the performer is peeking in this manner, it can be easily disguised if the magician sits in a stationary manner or is walking very slowly, but if the performer is running or is riding a bicycle, peeking by peering downward would be quite difficult, if not impossible. To peek at such an acute angle would alert the spectators who would notice that the magician was holding his head in an unnatural manner. Kuda Bux, for one thing , keeps his head level while pedaling along, and he even lowers his head in a fashion typical of cyclists.

KUDA BUX TODAY   This is a portrait of Kuda Bux, the "Eyeless Seer," at age 62.

In further refutation, it should be stated that Kuda Bux has performed his feats of eyeless sight even when he has been bandaged by just a single heavy cloth. Witnesses standing close to him could easily see whether there was any perceptible shifting of the blindfold. These simple blindfolds, such as a wool scarf, were completely opaque—at least completely opaque to the eyes of the witnesses themselves.

Mr. Bux asserts: "If my powers were achieved through trickery, how is it, then, that no magician throughout the world has been able to copy this trick." The thrust of this argument is somewhat blunted when it is recalled that no magician could duplicate the feats of Harry Houdini during his lifetime. Houdini simply baffled everyone, professional and tyro alike. But Houdini made no claim to extra-sensory powers, and roundly declared that his feats were mere illusions. Yet no one alive could solve some of Houdini's mysteries.

Now it could be that Kuda Bux is able to outwit not only the medical profession but the magicians as well. If this is so, the secret is his alone. As far as our knowledge goes, and until his trick—if trick it be—is discovered, when Kuda Bux performs his feats of eyeless sight he is technically blind. This would make him the only living example of a sensory talent for which science so far offers no explanation.

Index